T0252396

Internet of Things in Business Transformation

Scrivener Publishing
100 Cummings Center, Suite 541J
Beverly, MA 01915-6106

Publishers at Scrivener
Martin Scrivener (martin@scrivenerpublishing.com)
Phillip Carmical (pcarmical@scrivenerpublishing.com)

Internet of Things in Business Transformation

Developing an Engineering and Business Strategy for Industry 5.0

Edited by

**Parul Gandhi, Surbhi Bhatia,
Abhishek Kumar, Mohammad Alojail
and Pramod Singh Rathore**

Scrivener
Publishing

WILEY

Library of Congress Cataloging-in-Publication Data

ISBN 978-1-119-71112-4

Cover image: Pixabay.com
Cover design by Russell Richardson

Set in size of 11pt and Minion Pro by Manila Typesetting Company, Makati, Philippines

Contents

4 Transformational Technology for Business Transformation in the New Era

Md Shamsul Haque Ansari and Monica Mehrotra

Preface

The Internet of Things (IoT) has seen phenomenal growth over the last few years. Not only is this emerging IoT paradigm enhancing lives, it also has the potential to impact economic growth. And because IoT enables new insights into the business world, it continues to be very helpful in transforming business strategies and operations. However, before its full potential can be realized, it is necessary to confront several challenges by addressing the issues posed by the IoT and provide technological solutions to them. To help in this mission, many of the powerful features of the IOT and how they can be used to build strategies for a successful business are discussed in this book; and, in order to generate insights into various domains, IOT tools and techniques are also discussed in detail.

This book is written based on many years of teaching and research experience. Our goal is to provide researchers and students a complete package covering the fundamentals of the IOT and how it helps in various domains, its common practice in business and industry as well as all research aspects of IoT applications. Therefore, when choosing a format for a book that would be accessible to both researchers and university students, an attempt was made to simplify the content and emphasize real-life examples to make the information more easily understood.

After reading the entire book, the reader will come away with a thorough understanding of the rapid development of IoT-based systems and their impact on several scientific and engineering domains, including healthcare, smart homes, agriculture, robotics, industries, integration of leak detection in pipeline custody transfer of hydrocarbon products, and many others. Current trends and different architecture domains are explained systematically to motivate those in academia and industry to become familiar with the power of IoT. Also included are the heterogeneous used to enhance IoT security and an explanation of the framework of intelligent spaces needed for IoT-based optimized and secure ecosystem for the energy internet, handled by pervasive computing environment. The chapters thoroughly explain the transformation of business and ways of addressing its current needs, including how machine learning approaches play a greater role in achieving business intelligence in large commercial organizations, the role of big data analytics with the concept of automation, a roadmap for businesses to leverage big data analytics for creating business value implementing smartness in a smart environment where people are living and making an effort to develop it. Also, an analysis is conducted to examine how human and artificial intelligence might evolve together in future years and how it will impact humans with the help of business intelligence. Finally, this book portrays the difficulties experienced in business development consisting of a self-governing autonomous group setup with resources from both the IT and business advancement side of the organization.

On behalf of the entire editorial board, our heartfelt appreciation goes out to all the authors for considering us to publish their valuable work. Their overwhelming response has been a real factor in keeping us motivated and moving forward with this book, and therefore merits our sincere acknowledgement. The quality and diversity of their contributions have made the book more impactful, and their trust, patience and kind cooperation throughout the various stages of production played a vital role in its success. We also wish to thank the people at Scrivener Publishing for their guidance and support in bringing this edited collection to completion.

The Editors
November 2020

Applications of IIoT-Based Systems in Detection Leakage in Pipeline Custody Transfer of Hydrocarbon Products

Pragyadiya Das

National Institute of Technology, Trichy, India

Abstract

Custody transfer via pipelines has always been prone to losses due to leakages. Moreover, due to the large lengths of pipelines, leak detection is a tedious task. There are various methods that employ mechanical, mathematical and signal processing based approaches to detect leaks and their location. With the advent of Industrial Internet of Things and Machine Learning, the method of leak detection of pipelines using various machine learning methods have been analyzed and implemented in this chapter.

Keywords: Custody transfer, pipelines, leak detection, industrial Internet of Things, machine learning, ensemble learning

1.1 Introduction

The world of Oil and Gas has been moving at an alarming rate. The world is getting energy hungry [1] and the need for oil (or natural gas) is not going to go down anytime soon [2].

With this increased need for fuel, there is a constant need for the fuel (gasoline etc.) to be transported from one place to another. This gives rise to a need for a medium of transfer that would effectively transport the fuel in a secure and accountable manner.

Email: daspragyaditya@gmail.com

Parul Gandhi, Surbhi Bhatia, Abhishek Kumar, Mohammad Alojail and Pramod Singh Rathore (eds.) *Internet of Things in Business Transformation: Developing an Engineering and Business Strategy for Industry 5.0*, (1–14) © 2021 Scrivener Publishing LLC

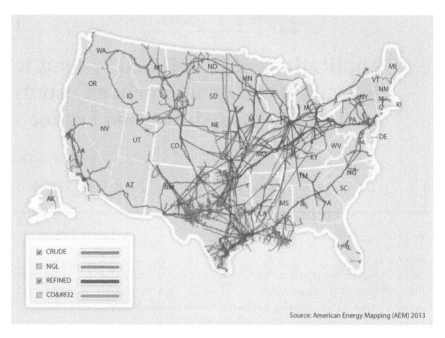

Figure 1.1 Pipeline mapping—US.

As per data released in India's official website (https://community.data. gov.in/), the total length of Natural Gas pipelines went from 10,246 to 17,753 km in the period of 31st March 2010 to 31st March 2017. That is a growth of 57% [3]. This is a significant growth and shows the need and increasing utility of pipeline in the energy scenario of an energy hungry nation like India [4].

Similarly, USA has a motor gasoline consumption of about 8,682 thousand barrels per day [4], and has a very significant crude and product pipeline, Figure 1.1 [5] explains this fact.

Looking at pipelines a major method of custody transfer of Gasoline, Diesel and other energy related fuels, it is important that there is proper monitoring of these structures to prevent any kind of adulteration, or more importantly, leakage causing financial losses.

With the advent of Wireless Sensor Networks (WSN) and Internet of Things (IoT), the monitoring of long distance pipelines have now become a task that can be achieved.

1.2   Industrial Internet of Things

The concept of "Internet of Things" has its core concepts set out as the interconnection of devices that have the capability to talk to themselves and "act" or take "decisions" based on each other's statuses.

Usage of Industrial grade sensors to monitor industrial processes in real time and later achieving their interconnection is called Industrial Internet of Things.

Modern day refineries and pipelines consist of numerous numbers of sensors. The data that is generated is huge. This poses as a great opportunity to drive data analytics and Industrial Internet of things in this sector [6].

IIoT is the utilization of smart sensors (or actuators) to enhance man-ufacturing and industrial processes. The idea behind IIoT is intelligent machines are made better humans at capturing and analyzing data in real time, in addition they are also made better at prompting information that can be used to make decisions in lesser time and more effectively [7].

1.3   Pipeline Leaks

Pipelines are undoubtedly the most safe and reliable mode of custody transfer of fuel. Major reasons contributing to pipeline failure are depicted in Figure 1.2 [8].

The below detail explains the varied kind of reasons that are faced while analyzing pipeline leaks.

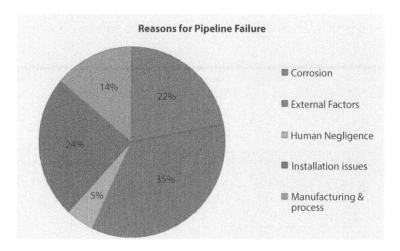

Figure 1.2 Percentage break-up of reasons causing pipeline leaks.

1.3.1 Various Techniques used to Detect Pipeline Leak

The methods that are usually used are divided into two classes,

1. Hardware techniques.
2. Software techniques.

We shall discuss in brief about three of the most common non-analytic and hardware-based technique used in pipeline leak detection. They are as follows:

a) Vapor Sampling Method:
   This is the most common method used for detection of pipeline leaks. This is an augmented system that has gas detection and gas ppm measurement systems in it. In this method, a gas detection/measurement unit runs along the line of the pipeline. A representation of the same is below in Figure 1.3.

b) Acoustic Signal Processing [9]:
   In this method, the occurrence of the leak is treated as a fault in the wall of the pipe. The pressure difference profile inside a pipeline is usually from a higher-pressure potential to lower-pressure potential, this can be treated as an incident beam of light traveling from one end to the other end of the pipeline. A leak on the pipeline causes a disturbance in the pressure profile that can be seen a translucent substance in the path of the incident beam. Now, based on the time needed for the reflected beam to reach the pumping station,

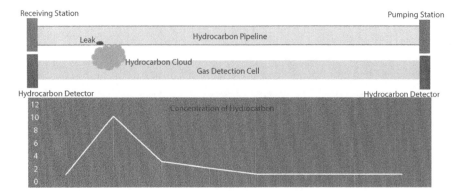

Figure 1.3 Vapor Sampling method of pipeline leak detection.

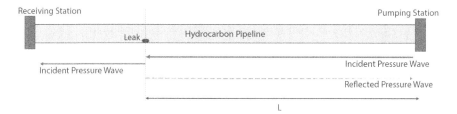

Figure 1.4 Acoustic method of leak detection.

the exact position of leak is determined. A representation of the same is given in Figure 1.4.

Since, the speed of sound wave propagation is in a single-phase, rigid pipe is found using the application of law of conservation of mass and comes as,

$$v = \sqrt{\dfrac{1}{\rho\left[\dfrac{1}{K} + \dfrac{D}{E_e}\phi\right]}}$$

Here, v is the wave propagation speed in m/s, ρ is the density of fluid in kg/m³, E_e is the Young's modulus of the piping material in N/m², K is the bulk modulus of the liquid and ϕ is a factor of restraint based on the Poisson ratio.

c) Fiber Optic Method [10]:

In this method, a helical strain of fibre optic cables runs along the length of the pipeline. The leak that is generated on the pipeline is seen as spikes in the strain profile of the fiber optic cable that is running along the pipeline. This strain profile is calculated using Brillouin Optical Time-Domain Analysis (BOTDA) [11]. BOTDA can be calculated using traditional mathematics and data analysis methods [12].

We shall discuss in brief about three of the most common analytic and software-based technique used in pipeline leak detection. They are as follows:

a) Negative Pressure Wave method [13]:

In this method, the drop in line pressure and speed profile is used to detect the leak, however, in this case, the process is heavily dependent on software techniques rather than hardware. The pressure wave is captured using sensors positioned in the upstream and downstream of the pipeline. The captured wave is then put through the extended Kalman Filters (EKF), used for non-linear systems to estimate the number of states required to model the pipeline system [14]. Extended Kalman filtering technique is used to estimate the state vectors that contain information about the segment of the pipeline, this combined with the virtual leakage rate gives an expression [15] that accurately derives the point of leak on the pipeline, provided that the initial conditions of the virtual leakage rate and that of the pipeline are same [16]. In addition, techniques like Haar Cascading are also done to do waveguide transformation/decomposition and analysis for detection of leakages [17].

b) Digital Signal Processing:

This method uses process data such as pressure profile, flow profile, strain, entropy in flow, etc. to identify and analysis various features which help in identification and detection of leaks in pipeline systems.

Features such as energy of the signal, entropy of the signal, zero crossings cut and energy distribution in decomposed wavelet is analyzed [18].

Of these, zero crossings cut is the most significant, as it identifies the events where a high value (defined as 1.5 times the mean of the signal amplitude (positives only)) occurs immediately after a 0 or negative value). These features show us spikes in the flow data and which are then run through a Fast Fourier transform (FFT) for signal decomposition and transformation. This transformed signal wavelet or flow data is then run through a Neural Network, that classifies suitable data as leakages.

A representation of the process is given in Figure 1.5.

c) Dynamic Modeling Approach:

This is a method that is gaining popularity with the advancement of our understanding of the usage of classical and modern statistical techniques. We have already discussed the used of states of the fluid flow in the method that used EKF for feature extraction. Using the concepts of Fluid mechanics, the flow can be modelled in terms of partial differential equations, which in turn can be transformed into state space equations, these state space equations are used to determine

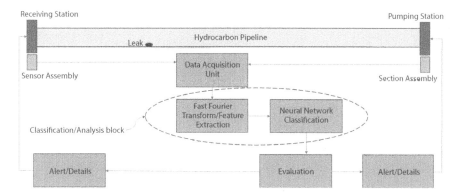

Figure 1.5 Digital signal processing based pipeline leakage detection.

the behavior (wave profile, pressure profile, flow profile etc.) of fluid and any disturbance can then be analyzed to detect leakages. In addition, computational fluid dynamics (CFD) is being used to model and detect leakages in pipes.

1.3.2 Use of IIoT to Detect Pipeline Leak

Use of IIoT is gaining popularity with the advent of usage of more connected devices being used in industries day in and day out.

A typical IIoT based unit shall have all devices interconnected with each other. These devices are again connected to a network that terminates at a gateway. The gateway has a two way terminal connecting the analytics block with itself. The analytics block again has a two way terminal connecting it to the rules and controls unit.

In our case the pipeline is the system that has its upstream and downstream connected to each other. The sensors at the upstream, downstream and along the length of the pipeline are interconnected among each other and are also in turn connected to an edge gateway. This gateway connects the system to analytics and transform unit that is used to generate leads for the process. This connection is through an access network, which is typically a network that can handle high volume of uploads and downloads. After this the leads are sent to control unit which based on the leads generate controls or rules for the system, this is again through a network called the service network and has to be able to handle high volume of uploads and downloads.

A representation figure describing the usage of IIoT architecture in detection of leakage in pipeline custody transfer, is given in Figure 1.6,

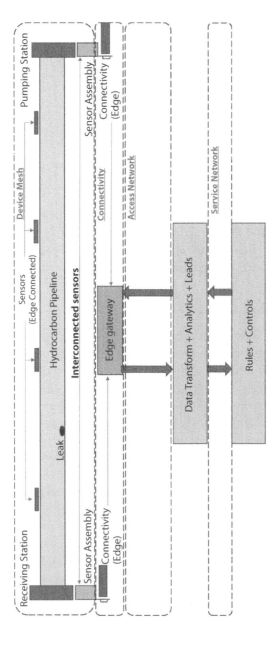

Figure 1.6 Industrial Internet of Things-based architecture for pipeline leak detection.

1.3.3   Use of Machine Learning Algorithms to Detect Pipeline Leak

Machine Learning and Data science has gained a lot of popularity in the last decade. In the earlier sections of the chapter, we demonstrated the usage of Neural Networks for detection of leaks in a pipeline, that itself was a pre cursor of introduction of machine learning in the field of leakage detection of pipeline transfer of hydrocarbon.

Several machine learning algorithms have started being used for detection of leaks. Advanced techniques such as Neural Networks [19] and Support Vector Machines [20, 21] have already been used and proved to have given excellent results. In addition, more advanced methods employing deep learning and convolutional neural networks [22] are also being explored, in fact application of Variational Autoencoders have already been tested and used.

We shall now discuss the technique of implementation of each of these methods (Neural Network and Support vector machine based) in brief, in addition, we shall also try to implement a novel strategy to use ensemble learning algorithms to detect leakages in pipelines [23].

a) Neural Networks-Based Strategy for Detection of Pipeline Leak Detection
   The overall architecture of the system is already designed in the section where leakage detection using digital signal processing is explained, in the section a representative system architecture. Here, we only analyze the details of the neural network from a very computational point of view. In the paper 3-layer neural network is used with a sigmoid activation function. In the method, the error is decreased by backpropagation.

b) Support Vector Machines-Based Strategy for Detection of Pipeline Leak Detection
   We have already seen the use of negative pressure wave method for leak detection in earlier section. We see that in negative pressure wave method, various computational methods are used to detect the leakage from the huge dataset that contains the leakage information as well as the noise from the pipeline, pipe fittings and environment. Use of these computational methods makes the model very expensive from a computational point of view. Therefore the use of Support vector machines in conjunction with negative pressure wave architecture proposed.

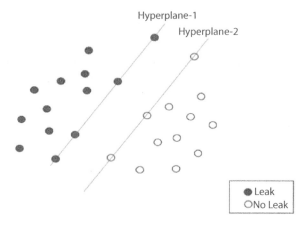

Figure 1.7 Use of support vector machine for pipeline leak detection.

A support is used to detect extreme cases—for our case the extreme cases are Leak or No Leak case. This is depicted in Figure 1.7.

The data class is separated by hyper planes that divide both the classes clearly. The hyper planes are also called support vectors.

Negative pressure wave method has pressure information from two different scenarios, one is when there is no leak and the pressure profile is usual and the other is when there is a leakage and the pressure profile has disturbances, support vector machines are used for correctly classifying these data and generating leads for detection of leak.

A representative figure for showing the usage of Support Vector machines for negative pressure wave method is as follows,

1.3.4 Design and Analysis of Ensemble Learning-Based Approach for Pipeline Leak Detection

Ensemble learning is basically the method of taking advantage of more than one model to get the combined prowess of the models to achieve better accuracy of analysis. Due to the complexity of the data that we aggregate from a pipeline system, we may require the usage of multiple classification models to come to the conclusion. While there are various ensemble learning models, we choose random forest classifiers. Random forest classifier is one where we break the actual dataset into various bootstrapped samples

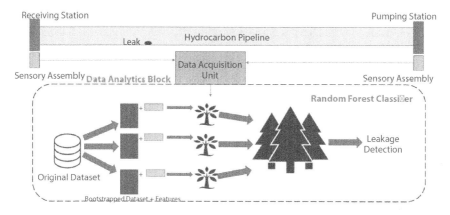

Figure 1.8 Evaluation of random forest classifier for leakage detection.

and bind them with particular features that we want to classify them on. Then we fit these datasets into trees considering selected features only. Then the result that we get from these trees is averaged to get the final result. A representative figure to explain is given in Figure 1.8.

1.4   Conclusion

It is seen from the literature and analysis given in the chapter that there is a lot of work that is being done in the field of combining connected devices with the power of analytics and machine intelligence to make a system that has minimal to zero human interference.

Implementing algorithms to get desired output is a requirement is something that can only be explored through continuous experimentation and testing.

This chapter aims at making the foundation strong for a beginner in the field of Pipeline engineering, Industrial Internet of Things and Machine learning.

References

1. "In an energy-hungry world, natural gas gaining the most", Amy Harder. Axio.com, June 2019.
2. Pydata 2018 Video (Youtube), Hot Water Leak Detection Using Variational Autoencoder Model—Jay Kim.

3. Na, L. and Yanyan, Z., Application of Wavelet Packet and Support Vector Machine to Leak Detection in Pipeline. *2008 ISECS International Colloquium on Computing, Communication, Control, and Management*, 2008.

4. Ibitoye, Olakunle & Shafiq, Omair & Matrawy, Ashraf. (2019). A Convolutional Neural Network Based Solution for Pipeline Leak Detection.

5. Pipeline Stats in India, https://community.data.gov.in/length-of-natural-gas-pipelines-in-india-from-2010-to-2017/.

6. Pipeline—data as per plot, https://www.indexmundi.com/energy/?product=gasoline&graph=consumption&display=rank.

7. Where are pipelines located?, https://pipeline101.org/Where-Are-Pipelines-Located.

8. Lim, K., Wong, L., Chiu, W.K., Kodikara, J., Distributed fiber optic sensors for monitoring pressure and stiffness changes in out-of-round pipes. *Struct. Control Hlth.*, 23, 2, 303–314, 2015.

9. Gamboa-Medina, M.M., Ribeiro Reis, L.F., Capobianco Guido, R., Feature extraction in pressure signals for leak detection in water networks. *Procedia Eng.*, 70, 688–697, 2014.

10. US Oil and Gas Pipeline Stats, https://www.bts.gov/content/us-oil-and-gas-pipeline-mileage.

11. Definition of IIoT, https://internetofthingsagenda.techtarget.com/definition/Industrial-Internet-of-Things-IIoT.

12. Bolotina, I., Borikov, V., Ivanova, V., Mertins, K., Uchaikin, S., Application of phased antenna arrays for pipeline leak detection. *J. Petrol. Sci. Eng.*, 161, 497–505, 2018.

13. Adnan, N.F. *et al.*, Leak detection in gas pipeline by acoustic and signal processing—A review. *IOP Conf. Ser.: Mater. Sci. Eng.*, 100, 012013, 2015.

14. Wang, L., Guo, N., Jin, C., Yu, C., Tam, H., Lu, C., BOTDA system using artificial neural network. *2017 Opto-Electronics and Communications Conference (OECC) and Photonics Global Conference (PGC)*, Singapore, pp. 1–1, 2017.

15. Shibata, A., Konishi, M., Abe, Y., Hasegawa, R., Watanabe, M., Kamijo, H., Neuro based classification of gas leakage sounds in pipeline. *2009 International Conference on Networking, Sensing and Control*, 2009.

16. Feng, W.-Q., Yin, J.-H., Borana, L., Qin, J.-Q., Wu, P.-C., Yang, J.-L., A network theory for BOTDA measurement of deformations of geotechnical structures and error analysis. *Measurement*, 146, 618–627, 2019.

17. Three reasons why Oil will continue to run the world, https://www.forbes.com/sites/judeclemente/2015/04/19/three-reasons-oil-will-continue-to-run-the-world/.

18. Chen, Y., Kuo, T., Kao, W., Tsai, J., Chen, W., Fan, K., An improved method of soil-gas sampling for pipeline leak detection: Flow model analysis and laboratory test. *J. Nat. Gas Sci. Eng.*, 42, 226–231, 2017.

19. Chen, H., Ye, H., Chen, L.V., Su, H., Application of support vector machine learning to leak detection and location in pipelines. *Proceedings of the 21st*

IEEE Instrumentation and Measurement Technology Conference (IEEE Cat. No.04CH37510), Como, Vol. 3, pp. 2273–2277, 2004.

20. Thorley, A.R.D., *Fluid Transients in Pipeline Systems*, D&L George Limited, pp. 126–129, 1991.

21. Tian, C.H., Yan, J.C., Huang, J., Wang, Y., Kim, D.-S., Yi, T., Negative pressure wave based pipeline Leak Detection: Challenges and algorithms. *Proceedings of 2012 IEEE International Conference on Service Operations and Logistics, and Informatics*, 2012.

22. Hou, Q. and Zhu, W., An EKF-Based Method and Experimental Study for Small Leakage Detection and Location in Natural Gas Pipelines. *Appl. Sci.*, 9, 15, 3193, 2019.

23. Peng, Z., Wang, J., Han, X., A study of negative pressure wave method based on Haar wavelet transform in ship piping leakage detection system. *2011 IEEE 2nd International Conference on Computing, Control and Industrial Engineering, Wuhan*, pp. 111–113, 2011.

2

Heart Rate Monitoring System

**Ramapriya Ranganath*, Parag Jain†, Akarsh Kolekar‡,
Sneha Baliga§, A. Srinivas¶ and M. Rajasekar****

Microsoft, Intel, Delloite, PESU, Dayand Sagar, PESU, India

Abstract

Internet of Things (IoT) is a new and evolving concept that provides connectivity to the Internet via sensing devices and embedded systems to achieve intelligent identification and management in a heterogeneous connectivity environment without human–human or human–computer interactions. Current medical developments have essentially moved the patient monitoring devices typically found in a critical care room such as ECG, pulse oximeter, blood pressure, temperature, etc., into a discharged patient's home, with the nurse's station being a computing device connected to a broadband communication link. The primary limiting factor is the cost of this collection of devices. Mobile Healthcare, or mHealth, is defined as "mobile computing, medical sensor, and communications technologies for health care". Our aim is to design a prototype of a wearable comprising of medical sensors, in this case, a pulse sensor, which transmits data to LinkIt One, a proto-typing board for IoT devices, which then sends real time data to a database, from where data is retrieved and used to plot a dynamic graph on an app (Android and iOS). mHealth is required to prevent medication errors from occurring and to increase efficiency and accuracy of existing medical health systems.

Keywords: Internet of Things, LinkIT One, mobile computing, medical sensor, Mobile Healthcare

**Corresponding author*: ramapriya288@gmail.com
†*Corresponding author*: coolparag2@gmail.com
‡*Corresponding author*: akarshkolekarr@gmail.com
§*Corresponding author*: sbikr@gmail.com
¶*Corresponding author*: srinivas2@gmail.com
***Corresponding author*: rajaseka2@gmail.com

Parul Gandhi, Surbhi Bhatia, Abhishek Kumar, Mohammad Alojail and Pramod Singh Rathore (eds.) *Internet of Things in Business Transformation: Developing an Engineering and Business Strategy for Industry 5.0*, (15–26) © 2021 Scrivener Publishing LLC

2.1   Introduction

Internet of Things (IoT) is the inter-communication of various sensors and embedded systems, without human to human interaction and human to sensor interaction, via the internet and its ability to transfer data over a network, which all work together in order to provide a feasible and much desired output. IoT is autonomous and independent of human interaction. It is the need of the hour. IoT in healthcare, is not only desired but is very necessary. Internet of things makes it possible to capture and analyze data sensed from the human body. IoT makes it possible to reach people anywhere and at any time. Using IoT, we can look out for people who stay in remote locations and provide them with high class medical treatment and constant monitoring [1].

A major problem nowadays is the monitoring of patients. This includes both the discharged patients as well as admitted patients in a hospital. The elderly discharged patients are dependent on others. Some patients do not return to medical facilities for post-discharge testing, assessment and evaluation due to non-availability of their dependents. The proposed system intends to make communication of the patient with doctors and other family members much quicker and simpler. The patient can be monitored and prioritized by the doctor based on how critical their condition is. In the golden hour, each second matters. It is a life or death situation and the most critical patient is prioritized. Even for patients admitted, within the hospital there is prioritization. Using such IoT devices, data can be collected, processed and developed for a large sector of people which include the elderly and those with cardiovascular issues. A doctor can make the required administrations with full knowledge of the patient's medical history and with continuous flow of real time data regarding the patient's present condition.

Implementation of IoT in healthcare is used to process one's data effectively and diagnose the patient's condition. The data is presented to the doctor in a clear setup. The patient registers on the app via Google authentication. Post-login, the doctor will be able to view the profiles of his subscribed patients through MQTT protocol. New patients have to register [2].

The doctor gets a notification once his subscribed patient data reaches below or beyond medical thresholds. This is useful as the doctor in the current scenario treats the patients in a round robin scenario, there is no priority process established yet. The patient admitted in a particular hospital would want the best doctor to treat them, but this is really hard as the doctor can treat only a small set of patients on a daily basis. Using our mechanism we show the doctor to treat the patient on a priority cycle [3]. As we collect data from a patient dynamically, we can update the list with the highest priority patient. This will ensure that the patient with the most requirements is treated first as during the golden hour they need to be given higher priority. The transmission of the data from the board to the database is done by running node on the board. The chunked data is continuously transmitted to the server and retrieved in the form of a graph on the doctor's app. On the app, a dynamic plot of the person's pulse is obtained. There are many advantages to using the LinkIt One development kit. It has an in-built Li-Ion battery. So, constant power supply to the board is not an issue. This does allow the user to move around freely, as other boards would not allow this. It also has an in-built Wi-Fi module. The person can thus, move about freely [4].

Signals sent from the sensor to the LinkIt One are used to calculate the Inter Beat Interval (IBI), which is in turn used to calculate the Beats Per Minute (BPM) of the patient. The system supports the continuous flow of data from the patient, processed by the LinkIT ONE to be accessed by the doctor who is given accessibility to the patient's information. If the data, crosses a given threshold (upper and lower) the doctor is alerted and immediate attention is given to secure the patient. Here, data is processed and displayed in highly efficient manner which is doctor-friendly and patient-friendly.

Distinct advantages of the proposed system are cost-effectiveness and personalization for chronic patients. Doctors can monitor the health of their patients on their smartphones after the patient gets discharged from the hospital.

A solution involving the Internet of Things has been provided. It includes designing a wearable which would transmit crucial medical sensor data such as pulse, etc. to a remote server, from which data could be accessed by authorized medical professionals on the app, and appointments could be made accordingly between the medical professional and the patient [5].

2.2   Project Objectives

The following are the objectives of the project:

- Configure existing devices/sensors to transmit data in a wireless manner to a server.
- Create a database to maintain the signal data.
- Design a cross platform app which can display critical medical parameters received from devices/sensors with minimum latency.
- Set up a pulse monitor on the app to display pulse.

- Implement emergency SMS service, when critical parameter threshold of patient is crossed.

Patient parameter list for critical care is as follows:

1. Pulse
2. Temperature
3. Blood Pressure
4. Respiratory Rate
5. Oxygen Saturation

Pulse sensor was chosen as it measured the most important parameters from the human body and thus ideal to be used in a wearable. The system is now modularized to incorporate new sensors [5].

2.3   System Architecture

Hardware Components:
The main hardware components used are:

- Pulse Sensor—Pulse Sensor heart rate sensor for Arduino and Arduino compatible boards. It adds amplification and

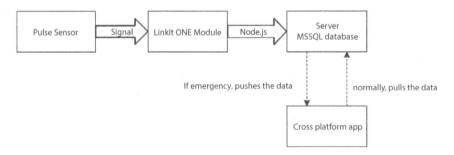

Figure 2.1 Hardware components.

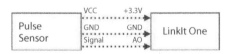

Figure 2.2 Pulse sensor connection.

noise cancellation circuitry to the hardware. It's noticeably faster and easier to get reliable pulse readings. Pulse Sensor works with either a 3 V or 5 V Arduino. A Color-Coded Cable, with a standard male header connector. As we know that the ear lobe and the thumb are the most sensitive areas in the human body, we attach the sensor using the ear clip to the ear lope or using the Velcro we attach it to the thumb of the user. There is a small camera placed in the sensor along with an infrared sensor. Infrared sensors work on the principle of reflected light waves. Infrared light reflected from objects. The reflected light is detected and then the BPM (Beats per Minute) is calculated [6].

- LinkIt One—It is a high performance-development board. It provides similar pin-out features to Arduino boards, making it easy to connect various sensors, peripherals, and Arduino shields. LinkIt One is an all-in-one prototyping board for IoT/wearable devices. The advantage of using this board is that it has inbuilt GSM, GPRS, Wi-Fi, GPS, Bluetooth features. It also has a Lithium ION battery which will ensure the board can be used without being connected to a socket always. This is a very important feature for us as this will not restrict the user's movement. The users are free to move around with this board unlike other boards (Figure 2.3).

Proposed System: The proposed automatic, IoT system is used to monitor the patient's heart rate. It is also used to display the same in the form of an ECG (electrocardiogram). The system has the parts:

1. Sensing Sub-System
2. Data Transfer Sub-System
3. Data Display Sub-System

1. Sensing Sub-System

This comprises of the pulse sensor and the LinkIT One. The Pulse sensor is worn on the tip of the thumb or on the tip of the ear lobe (using and ear clip) as these are sensitive parts. It sends pulse signals to the LinkIt One. The LinkIt One performs the programmed operations on the signal and calculates the Inter-Beat Interval (IBI) and hence the beats per minute (BPM). The connections for the Sensing sub-stem are (Figure 2.2): the pulse sensor, ear clip and Velcro (Figure 2.4).

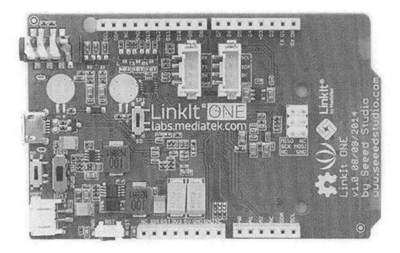

Figure 2.3 The LinkIt One Board.

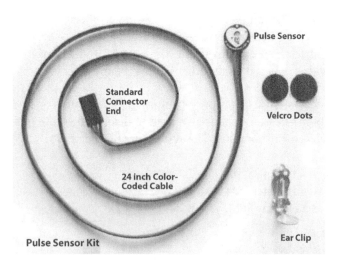

Figure 2.4 Pulse sensor kit.

2. Data Transfer Sub-System

In this sub-system, using the Wi-Fi module, provided on the LinkIt One, NodeJS runs on the LinkIt One. As the data is collected from the users, this encrypted data is chunked and transmitted to the server. The data is obtained via a periodic fetch. The LinkIT One uses the high performance Wi-Fi MT5931 which is said to provide the most convenient connectivity functions. It is of small size and low power consumption and the quality of the data transmission is very good. We use a MSSQL database to store the data. The advantage of the above is that it can be used in areas with weak Wi-Fi [7].

3. Data Display Sub-System

This sub-system consists of a cross platform app (Android and iOS) which is used to present the data to the doctor. The data is stored on the database which is retrieved onto the app and the data is plotted onto a dynamic plot and is represented as a graph in the doctor phone. If the patient's parameters go below or beyond the medical parameters then an immediate message is transferred to the doctor, ambulance and patients relatives. We wanted this to be user friendly and hence we designed a cross platform app. Here to secure the data of a particular patient we use MQTT protocol. MQTT is a connectivity protocol. It is an extremely lightweight publish/subscribe messaging transport. It is useful for connections with remote locations where a small code footprint is required and/or network bandwidth is at a premium. Here, it has been used in sensors communicating to a server, request connections with healthcare providers. It is also ideal for mobile applications because of its small size, low power usage, minimized data packets, and efficient distribution of information to one or many receivers.

In the app we have implemented Google OAuth. The confidentiality of each patient is maintained and only the doctor treating the given patient can access his/her details. The app has a framework as follows (Figure 2.5).

The basic flow is as follows (Figure 2.6).

The doctor can sign-in using their Gmail account as depicted (Figures 2.7 and 2.8).

The doctor can view and access his available options (Figure 2.9).

Post login there is a patient-list view page. Here, all the patients the doctor treat are given and can be easily accessed. The list will be provided as follows (Figure 2.10).

The doctor can also input the patient's ID in a 'Search ID' search bar for quicker access of the data. He can also upload a patient's data the same

Figure 2.5 Sign-up flowchart.

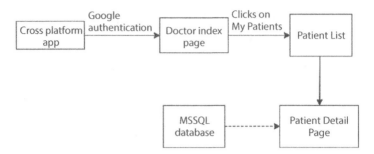

Figure 2.6 Basic flow.

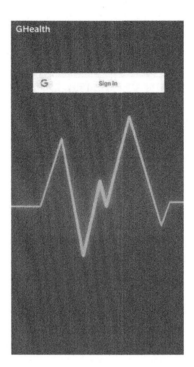

Figure 2.7 Sign-in page.

way. He can select 'View Details' to view the details of the given patient as follows (Figure 2.11).

The data is pulled from the database to the app and is displayed in the form of an electrocardiogram (ECG). We interface the GSM Module with the LinkIT One, so that upon a threshold being crossed (if the heart-rate is above 100 beats per minute or if it is lower than 60 beats per minute), an emergency SMS is sent to those who matter to the patient, like doctors and

Figure 2.8 Choose an account.

Figure 2.9 Options.

Figure 2.10 List of patients.

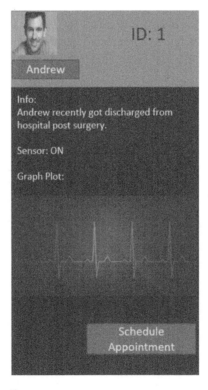

Figure 2.11 Patient details page.

close relatives. The SMS indicates the ward number of the patient if he/she is in the hospital, else it provides the patient's house address. If the threshold is crossed the graph turns red indicating danger.

2.4   Conclusion

A prototype of a system was designed and constructed which takes in signals from a medical sensor, such as a pulse sensor, performs operations on it, calculates the beats per minute, and data is transmitted to a database, from which data is retrieved and displayed on a dedicated website for medical professionals. A cross platform app is also created for the same.

We believe that this is a step forward in the field of remote patient monitoring, as patient data, i.e., critical medical parameters such as pulse, blood pressure, oxygen saturation, etc. can be monitored by medical professionals from the convenience of their offices, or even homes, and post-hospitalization care will become more accessible and efficient. Patients who live far away from medical care centers need not travel large distances, just to undergo check-up. This is a cost effective and efficient solution.

References

1. Hu, F., Xie, D., Shen, S., On the Application of the Internet of Things in the Field of Medical and Health Care. *2013 IEEE International Conference on Green Computing and Communications and IEEE*, 2013.
2. Jimenez, F. and Torres, R., Building an IoT-aware healthcare monitoring system. *2015 34th International Conference of the Chilean Computer Science Society (SCCC)*, 2015.
3. Chiuchisan, I., Costin, H.-N., Geman, O., Adopting the Internet of Things Technologies in Health Care Systems. *2014 International Conference and Exposition on Electrical and Power Engineering (EPE 2014)*, Iasi, Romania, 16–18 October, 2014.
4. Luo, J., Tang, K., Chen, Y., Luo, J., Remote Monitoring Information System and Its Applications Based on the Internet of Things. *2009 International Conference on Future BioMedical Information Engineering*, 2009.
5. Istepanian, R.S.H., Sungoor, A., Faisal, A., Philip, N., *Internet of M-Health Things, m-IOT*. Imperial College London ... Taccini, 2005.
6. Amendola, S., Lodato, R., Manzari, S., Occhiuzzi, C., Marrocco, G., RFID Technology for IoT-Based Personal Healthcare in Smart Spaces. *IEEE Internet Things J.*, 1, 2, 144–152, 2014.

7. Stankovic, Q., Cao, Doan, T., Fang, L., He, Z., Kiran, R., Lin, S., Son, S., Stoleru, R., Wood, A., Wireless Sensor Networks for In-Home Healthcare: Potential and Challenges. *2015 34th International Conference of the Chilean Computer Science Society (SCCC).*

3

An Efficient Clustering Technique for Wireless Body Area Networks Based on Dragonfly Optimization

Bilal Mehmood and Farhan Aadil*

Computer Science Department, COMSATS University Islamabad, Attock Campus, Attock, Pakistan

Abstract

Wireless body area network (WBAN) is a network of tiny health monitoring sensors, implanted or placed on the human body to collect and communicate human physiological data. WBAN used to have a connection with Medical-Server to monitor patient's health. It is capable to protect critical patient's lives, due to its ability to continuous remote monitoring. Inter-WBAN system provides a dynamic environment for patients to move around freely. While moving, some of the WBANs (patients) may or may not be in the range of Remoter Base Station (RBS). Here we need an efficient approach for inter-WBAN communication. In the proposed clustered-based routing technique network overhead is reduced and cluster lifetime is increased. The cluster head act as a gateway in between cluster members and external network. Moreover, for the selection of optimized cluster heads, we used evolutionary algorithms to select the most optimized solution, within the set of solutions. In the clustering approach, network efficiency is dependent on the cluster's lifetime. The proposed technique forms efficient clusters with an increased lifetime along with remarkable network and energy efficiency.

Keywords: Wireless body area network (WBAN), energy-efficient clustering, inter-WBAN routing

*Corresponding author: farhan.aadil@cuiatk.edu.pk

Parul Gandhi, Surbhi Bhatia, Abhishek Kumar, Mohammad Alojail and Pramod Singh Rathore (eds.) *Internet of Things in Business Transformation: Developing an Engineering and Business Strategy for Industry 5.0*, (27–42) © 2021 Scrivener Publishing LLC

3.1   Introduction

WBANs are a network of small size, lightweight, low power, wearable/ implantable sensors. These sensors monitor human's physiological activities like Patient's Heartbeat, blood pressure, Electrocardiogram (ECG), EMG, etc. WBANs allow connectivity in between heterogeneous body sensor to a portable hub devise that provide a connection to the external internet. There are a variety of applications of the WBANs. Military can use it to monitor the physical location, physical condition, and vital signs of a field person. In the medical perspective, we can keep track patient's physiological condition, to provide medical facilities [1]. On a single body, multiple sensors can be placed and these nodes used to form a single WBAN. Each WBAN has a centralized entity called Personal Server (PS). It gathers data from other sensors and acts as a gateway. PS has a connection to RBS directly or with multiple hops. Communication of two types, intra-WBAN and inter-WBAN occurs in the WBANs. Intra-WBAN is a communication within the sensors of a single WBAN. On the other hand, Inter-WBAN is communication among multiple WBANs. Information collected by the sensors is transmitted to the remote Medical-Server, which is situated in the hospital. Inter-WBAN communication provides dynamic access when patients are doing their normal routine work (during movement in home, office, market or playground). In this case, sensor residing on the human body may or may not be in the range of RBS. So cooperation of multiple WBANs is required for hop-to-hop communion, to reach the RBS. RBS is responsible for further transmission to Medical-Server via the internet. WBANs are capable of protecting human lives by detecting patient's critical conditions at its early stages. Many human lives are dependent on the performance of the WBAN. Routing strategy is the key to network efficiency. There are different routing mechanisms of inter-BAN and intra-BAN communication. Each WBAN needs to be connected to the external network with the help of a gateway.

This gateway can be a Cellular device, a computer system, or a router which is capable of establishing a connection between inter-WBAN nodes and external internet. The problem arrives when WBAN do not have access to gateway device due to some reason. It is a common experience in a crowded area, like in stadium of international games or any kind of international event, where a huge amount of people access the same network and share their photos and videos. Due to congestion, degradation in the performance of network occurs. Although nowadays cellular networks provide a highly efficient network, it is not enough in some cases, that's why a

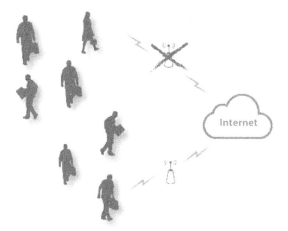

Huge number of people

Figure 3.1 Base station is not in access of some WBANs.

separate public safety radio system is used by police, firefighters and emergency medical technicians. It operates in separate portions of the 800 MHz band, which consists of a spectrum at 806–824 MHz paired with spectrum at 851–869 MHz. Another scenario is the battlefield where there is no Access Point available in the vicinity of every soldier as shown in Figure 3.1.

Inter-WBAN communication can be useful in both of the cases. As WBAN consists of low power energy nodes, we required an efficient energy consumption routing technique. Clustering is one of the best solutions for efficient routing, where a cluster head is responsible for the transmission of data of multiple WBANs. Network efficiency is dependent on the cluster's lifetime. In this paper, we proposed an optimization technique of clusters formation using Evolutionary Algorithms. Each cluster head (CH) is a gateway in between cluster members (PSs) of multiple WBANs and the external network. CHs are selected on the bases of fitness.

3.2   Literature Review

As the patient's lives are dependent on the data traveling from both inter and intra-BANs network, it needs to be secured. Researchers proposed different techniques, some techniques form clusters among the sensors nodes on a single body, the reason to make these clusters is to efficiently utilize the energy of the nodes in tier 1 transmission. On the other hand, cluster formation in inter-BAN nodes of different WBANs is for efficient hop-to-hop routing for tier 2 transmission. A multi- hop routing protocol is proposed by Sriyanijnana *et al.*, it performs well in the perspective of energy consumption, Packet Delivery Ratio (PDR) and network lifetime [2]. A number of fixed nodes are deployed in the network. A cost function is calculated for or the purpose of selection of Forwarding-node. The defined cost function is based on distance from the coordinator nodes, transmission range, residual energy, and on velocity vector of receiver. With clusters a dual sink approach used by DSCB [3], this clustering mechanism use two sinks. They also used the cost function for the purpose of selection of forwarding nodes. Forwarder node is selected by measuring distance of nodes from sink, its residual energy and transmission power. This clustering mechanism provides better performance in the prospective of network scalability, energy and an end to end delay.

A Balanced Energy Consumption (BEC) protocol is designed by [4]. In this protocol the relay node is selected with cost function which is based on distance of node form sink. To distribute load uniformly each relay node is selected for a specific round. Nodes nearer to the sink can transmit data immediately to the sink, otherwise data is passed to closest relay node. A threshold value of residual energy is also fixed on meeting the threshold value node only send critical data to sink. A simulation study has shown the better performance in term of network lifetime. Another attempt to achieve better throughput in terms of energy-consumption is achieved in heterogeneous WBAN [5]. It also works on the same principal. Residual energy, data rate and distance from sink, is the basic selection criteria for selection of relay node. Key requirement of any WBAN is minimum delay and energy efficiency. To improve the clustering in WBAN a load balancing and position adaptive technique is proposed by [6]. For the selection of cluster head the author used probability distribution method. A centralized clustering method is proposed by [7] to optimize the consumption of energy in WBAN. The cluster tree based structure is designed for the formation of uniform clusters.

An adaptive routing protocol is deployed by the author in [8]. The channel/ link information is used for the purpose of selection of best relay nods for reduction of energy consumption per bit. Sender node only sends the data to sink, by relies on nodes only when the link quality is up to the predefined level of threshold. Otherwise it transmits information to the sink, directly. Omar Smail *et al.*, proposed an energy efficient routing protocol for WBANs [9]. They use residual energy to increase network lifetime. This method used to select energy efficient stable links. In [10] a fuzzy adoptive routing protocol is proposed. It uses clustering mechanism for direct communication with sink node. In decision of forwarding it takes in account the criticality and location. Another routing protocol is proposed by [11] in which routing is managed by mobile-sink, it discovers the shortest route among numerous unequal clusters. This makes sure to avoid the energy hole problem in the network. Results have shown that this clustering technique performed well. A secure cluster base strategy for both inter-WBAN and intra-BAN is purposed by [12]. For intra-WBAN they used to generate a pairwise (PV) key. The best thing about PV is the keys generation on both sending and receiving end is the same. In the result of the highly dynamic nature of the human body, generated PV is time-variant. In inter-BAN communication, clusters are formed on the bases of two parameters (residual energy and distance). The node which has more energy is more likely to form clusters, in the same way, the node that is more closer to the RBS will have a high probability of becoming the cluster head. Some other authors also used genetic algorithms in WBAN [13–16]. A concept of a virtual cluster is given by [17], they form clusters only among intra-BAN nodes. Although nodes in intra-BAN are fairly close to each other, but due to energy limitation in sensors nodes, this technique gave remarkable results.

3.3   Clustering Technique

By creation of the long-lasting clusters, frequent path search is reduced. We are considering the scenario where multiple WBANs are present. Instead of having a connection of each WBAN with RBS, we considered some of the WBANs are not in the range of RBS. Each WBAN consist of one Personal Server (PS) and multiple sensor nodes. The sensor nodes pass their collected data to the PS and this PS is responsible for further transmission. In our purposed technique PS of different WBANs form clusters. Each cluster contains a cluster head and cluster members (CM) in its vicinity. CH is a selected PS of a WBAN within the WBANs of a cluster. Now all other WBANs will be connected to the CH, multiple CHs of different WBANs can have hop-to-hop communication, and this way data is passed to the nearest AP.

Our communication can be classified into following hierarchal groups.

- Sensor node to PS
- PS(CM) to CH
- CH to RBS

Figure 3.2 is describing the actual working of the clustering technique. WBANs of cluster "A" and its CH are not in the range of RBS. But cluster

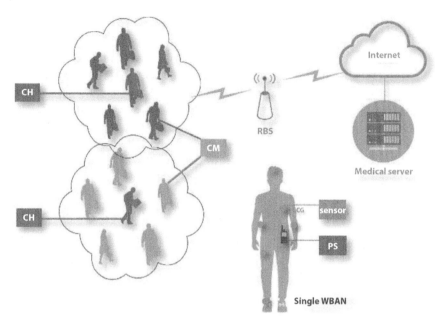

Figure 3.2 Inter-WBAN clustering.

"B" is in the vicinity of RBS, so cluster "B" is capable of communication with RBS. In this case, cluster "A" required the help of cluster "B". Members of cluster "A" have a direct link with A's cluster head, further CH-A can establish a connection with CH-B. It is a simple mechanism of clusters communication.

3.3.1   Evolutionary Algorithms

For cluster formation in our purpose methodology we are using Evolutionary algorithms. These nature inspired algorithms form multiple solutions the most efficient and the optimized solution is selected among all solutions. For NP-hard problem there is no known polynomial algorithm so time for finding solution grows exponentially with the size of problem. For solving these problems, we define the desired criterion where our algorithm should terminate. Our defined problem (Clustering in inter-WBAN) is also an NP-hard, as we need to find optimum clusters with multiple nodes and multiple parameters. Most real word problems may have to achieve multi-objective, these objectives may be different in nature. Multi-objectives problems required simultaneous optimization. Each objective is achieved with its specific objective function. These objective functions are measured in different units, and usually, they are conflicting and competing. Suppose we want to buy a railway ticket with low cost and less time to reach the destination. It is a fact that with cheap ticket, railway service will be compromised, and will stop on every station and cost more time. On the other hand, an expansive ticket train may cost less time to reach the destination. Multi-objective functions with conflicting objectives raise the set of optimal solutions, as no single solution can be considered to be best, with respect to all objectives. These solutions can be classified on as dominated and no-dominated sets Figure 3.3.

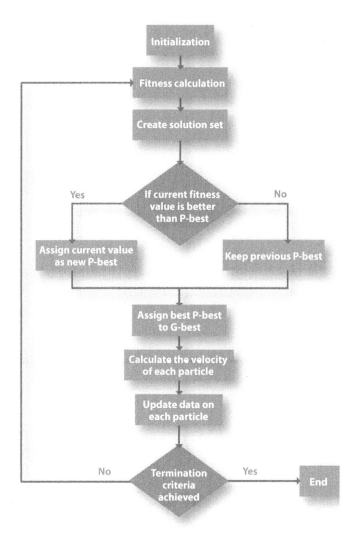

Figure 3.3 Flow chart of proposed scheme.

a) Fitness Calculation

Evolutionary algorithms are used to find a different solution. Every solution generally signified as a string of binary numbers (Chromosome). To come up with the best solution it is required to test all these solutions. For this purpose, we need to identify the score of each solution to find how closely it meets the overall specified desired result. This score is generated by the application of fitness function.

b) Local Best/Global Best

We calculate two values local best and global best, the local best value of everyone, if the current value of velocity of an individual is better than older value, the local best value will be replaced with the new one, otherwise, remain the same. The same goes for the global best value. Global best value is the best value among all the solution sets till now.

3.4   Implementation Steps

Our algorithm consists of two parts. The first part is network creation part, where we specify the basic parameters. Our network is a grid of 1 km × 1 km in size. We specified the transmission ranges from 2, 4, 6, 8, 10 and alternatively we run it with number of nodes from 50, 100, 200, 250, and 300. Network creation part randomly deploys the nodes on the grid. Once the network is created, Evolutionary algorithms start to find optimum clusters. In our experimentation, we used three algorithms,

- Comprehensive Learning Particle Swarm Optimization (CLPSO)
- Dragonfly Algorithm (DA)
- Multi-objective particle swarm optimization (MOPSO).

The best cluster head is one who increases network efficiency and network lifetime. Selection can be performed based on defined parameters. To find the optimum solution we consider, the current fitness value of each node in comparison with the new fitness value, if the current value is better than the previous one, the old value is replaced by a new one, otherwise stays same. Figure 3.4 is presenting the flow of proposed scheme. Table 3.1 is describing defined simulation parameters.

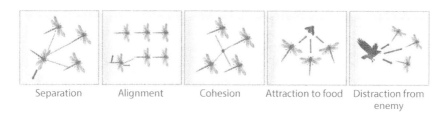

Separation   Alignment   Cohesion   Attraction to food   Distraction from enemy

Figure 3.4 Primitive corrective patterns between dragonfly.

Table 3.1 Simulation parameters.

Parameters	Values
Population size	100
Maximum iterations	150
Lower bound (lb)	0
Upper bound (ub)	100
Dimensions	2
Transmission range (m)	2, 4, 6, 8, 10
Nodes	50, 100, 150, 200, 250, 300
Mobility model	Freely mobility model
W1	0.5
W2	0.5

3.4.1   Dragonfly Algorithm

The main objective of the dragonfly is the survival. So they need to be attracted towards the food and distracted form the enemies [18]. Five main factors for position updating are shown in the Figure 3.4. Alignment formula is shown in Equation (3.1) [18].

$$X_+ - X \tag{3.1}$$

Table 3.2: Proposed Technique. Here Vj is the velocity of the j-th neighbor. Cohesion calculation formula [18].

Table 3.2 Dragonfly Algorithm.

1) Initialization of WBAN's randomly in the network
2) Random direction of WBAN's is defined
3) Speed and velocity of each WBAN is initialized
4) Mesh topology creation among nodes
5) For all Dragonflies same radius is initialized
6) Calculation of distance among all WBANs, normalizing and associating the distance values with corresponding nodes
7) For (iteration = 1) 1 to 10
   8) Available nodes for cluster formation = All Node
      a) WHILE (Nodes Available for clustering! = empty)
      b) End while
   9) FOR Drag-fly(i) = form 1 to Total population
      a) Source (Food/enemy) = empty, Food Source Cost = infinity, and Enemy Source cost = -infinity
      b) Objective Values calculation, of Dragonflies
      c) Update the radius
      d) Update sources (food and enemy)
      e) Update weights
   10) END FOR
   11) FOR Drag-fly(i) = From 1 to Total population
      a) FOR Drag-fly(i) = 1 to Total population
         i) Update neighboring radius
      b) ENDFOR
      c) Calculate Separation, Alignment, Cohesion, Enemy and Food weights
   12) IF neighbor! =0
      a) Velocity Update
      b) Position Update
   13) Else
      a) Levy flight
   14) END IF
   15) END FOR
   16) Best cost == Food fitness
17) END FOR
18) IF not clustered nodes>20%
   a) Goto line #1
19) Else
   a) Output
20) End IF

$$Ci = - X \qquad (3.2)$$

Attrition for food calculated as [18]:

$$= X^+ - X \qquad (3.3)$$

Here X+ is position of food source. And X is current position of an individual.

Distraction away from an enemy [18]:

$$= X^- - X \qquad (3.4)$$

X—is position of an enemy.

3.5   Result and Simulations

The experimentation is being performed on the grid size of 1 km × 1 km. The transmission range of each node is varying from 2m, 4m, 6m, 8m, and 10m. To find the number of clusters we kept the number of nodes static against each transmission range. Number of nodes varies from 50, 100, 150, 200, 250, and 300. The proposed algorithm finds an optimized solution against each transmission range, which is presented in graphs below. One thing is commonly observed in all solutions less transmission range produce high number of clusters, it is because, with low transmission range, nodes have less coverage area, only a few other nodes are in the vicinity. So, with less transmission range number or clusters is increased, with a low number of CMs. In the comparison of CLPSO, DA, and MOPSO, we see that Figure 3.5A is describing the cluster formation for the number of nodes 50. On minimum transmission range 2, no clusters are formed by all three algorithms. But with an increase in transmission range, cluster formation tends to start. In Figure 3.5A, on transmission range 4 CLPSO is giving the worst result with a maximum number of cluster heads. On transmission range 6 MOPSO is worst and on Transmission range 8 again CLPSO is forming the maximum number of clusters. The variation between CLPSO and MOPSO can be seen in Figure 3.5A. DA is giving the best results with a minimum number of cluster heads in all Transmission ranges. By looking at all graphs (A,B,C,D) of Figure 3.5 it can be seen DA is giving the best results with a minimum number of cluster heads. There is a slight variation between the results of CLPSO and MOPSO.

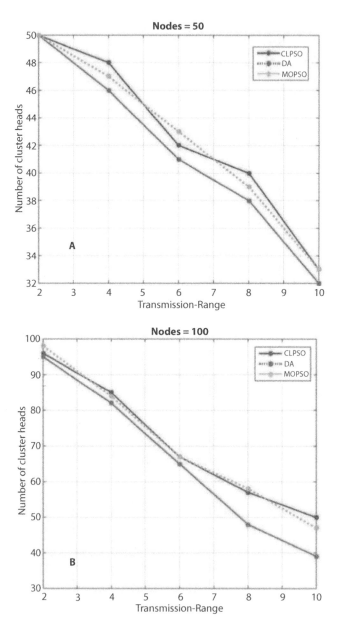

Figure 3.5 Transmission range versus Cluster Heads for Nodes 50–200.   (*Continued*)

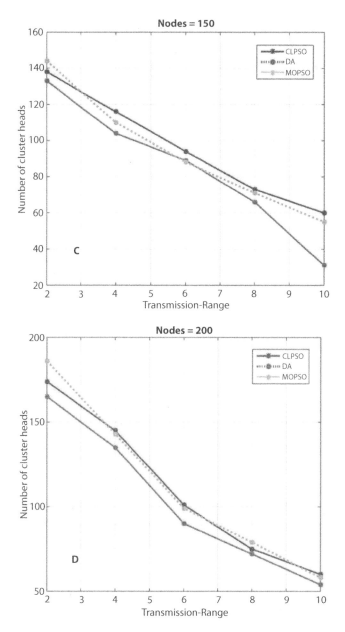

Figure 3.5 (Continued) Transmission range versus Cluster Heads for Nodes 50–200.

Figure 3.6 is showing the results for nodes 250 and 300. In both Figure labels A and B it can be seen that DA with a higher number of nodes is giving remarkable efficient results. On starting transmission ranges of 2, 4, and 6 DA's performance is extremely different than CLPSO and MPSO.

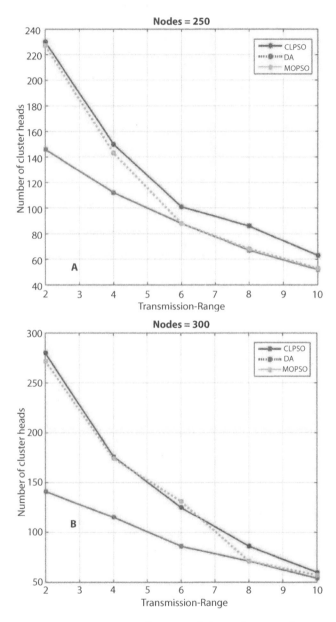

Figure 3.6 Transmission range versus Cluster Heads for Nodes 250 and 300.

As transmission range increases to 8 and 10 MPSO is also trying to meet DA. But if we analyze overall results DA stands alone as the best participant. That formed a smaller number of clusters in almost all number of nodes and transmission ranges.

3.6 Conclusion

Wireless Body Area Network (WBAN) protects the patient's life by its continuous monitoring and data transmission mechanism. For load balancing the most important method in WBAN is clustering which provides practical approach for energy optimization of senor nodes. We designed a cluster formation technique using Evolutionary algorithms. Optimized clustering is grouping the nodes of the network in the most efficient way. We also need a minimum number of possible clusters, long-lasting in the network. We analyzed the performance difference in Comprehensive Learning Particle Swarm Optimization (CLPSO), Dragonfly Algorithm (DA), and Multi-objective particle swarm optimization (MOPSO). Our experimentation has shown that the overall performance of DA is the most efficient among all three algorithms, as it forms fewest optimized long lasting clusters.

References

1. Adhikary, S., Choudhury, S., Chattopadhyay, S., A new routing protocol for WBAN to enhance energy consumption and network lifetime, in: *Proceedings of the 17th International Conference on Distributed Computing and Networking*, ACM, 2016.
2. Ali, A. and Khan, F.A., Energy-efficient cluster- based security mechanism for intra-WBAN and inter-WBAN communications for healthcare applications. *EURASIP J. Wirel. Comm.*, 2013, 1, 216, 2013.
3. Chang, J.-Y. and Ju, P.-H., An energy-saving routing architecture with a uniform clustering algorithm for wireless body sensor networks. *Future Gener. Comput. Syst.*, 35, 128–140, 2014. *Intelligence in Data Mining*, pp. 793–801, Springer, Saudi Arabia, 2017.
4. Kachroo, R. and Bajaj, D.R., A novel technique for optimized routing in wireless body area network using genetic algorithm. *J. Netw. Commun. Emerg. Technol. (JNCET)*, 2, 2, www.jncet.org, 591–628, 2015.
5. Kim, T.-Y. *et al.*, Multi-hop WBAN construction for healthcare IoT systems, in: *2015 International Conference on Platform Technology and Service*, IEEE, 2015.
6. Kumar, P. and Sharma, A., Data Security Using Genetic Algorithm in Wireless Body Area Network. *Int. J. Adv. Stud. Sci. Res.*, 3, 9, 675–699, 2018.

7. Maskooki, A. *et al.*, Adaptive routing for dynamic on-body wireless sensor networks. *IEEE J. Biomed. Health*, 19, 2, 549–558, 2014.

8. Mirjalili, S., Dragonfly algorithm: A new meta-heuristic optimization technique for solving single-objective, discrete, and multi-objective problems. *Neural Comput. Appl.*, 27, 4, 1053–1073, 2016.

9. Movassaghi, S. *et al.*, Wireless body area networks: A survey. *IEEE Commun. Surv. Tutor.*, 16, 3, 1658–1686, 2014.

10. Nayak, S.P., Rai, S., Pradhan, S., A multi-clustering approach to achieve energy efficiency using mobile sink in WSN, in: *Computational*.

11. Sahndhu, M.M. *et al.*, BEC: A novel routing protocol for balanced energy consumption in Wireless Body Area Networks, in: *2015 International Wireless Communications and Mobile Computing Conference (IWCMC)*, IEEE, 2015.

12. Singh, K. and Singh, R.K., An energy efficient fuzzy based adaptive routing protocol for wireless body area network, in: *2015 IEEE UP Section Conference on Electrical Computer and Electronics (UPCON)*, IEEE, 2015.

13. Singh, S. *et al.*, Modified new-attempt routing protocol for wireless body area network, in: *2016 2nd International Conference on Advances in Computing, Communication, & Automation (ICACCA) (Fall)*, IEEE, 2016.

14. Smail, O. *et al.*, ESR: Energy aware and Stable Routing protocol for WBAN networks, in: *2016 International Wireless Communications and Mobile Computing Conference (IWCMC)*, IEEE, 2016.

15. Suriya, M. and Sumithra, M., Efficient Evolutionary Techniques for Wireless Body Area Using Cognitive Radio Networks, in: *Computational Intelligence and Sustainable Systems*, pp. 61–70, Springer, Switzerland, 2019.

16. Ullah, Z. *et al.*, DSCB: Dual sink approach using clustering in body area network. *Peer Peer Netw. Appl.*, 12, 2, 357–370, 2019.

17. Umare, A. and Ghare, P., Optimization of Routing Algorithm for WBAN Using Genetic Approach, in: *2018 9th International Conference on Computing, Communication and Networking Technologies (ICCCNT)*, IEEE, 2018.

18. Yadav, D. and Tripathi, A., Load balancing and position based adaptive clustering scheme for effective data communication in WBAN healthcare monitoring systems, in: *2017 11th International Conference on Intelligent Systems and Control (ISCO)*, IEEE, 2017.

4

Transformational Technology for Business Transformation in the New Era

Md Shamsul Haque Ansari[1]* and Monica Mehrotra[2]

[1]Research Lab, Department of Computer Science, JMI, New Delhi, India
[2]Department of Computer Science, JMI, New Delhi, India

Abstract

In terms of management, business transformation takes place with the fundamental changes in the way the business takes place to cope up with the shift in market environment day by day. Urbanization also has a major role in the environment of market shift as the large number of populations is being shifted from rural areas to urban areas. Hence, we require inventive and innovative technologies which may sense urban dynamics automatically and give essential information to improve the sustainability of smart cities. To make the life easier, do work efficiently and generate more revenues according to the limited time, the technology plays an important role. The recent trend of business transformation requires huge transformation in technologies as we are moving towards the concept of smart city. Apart from the various benefits of using recent technologies, some challenges are also there which we must handle in different fields like energy conservation, security system especially related to banking transactions, etc.

Keywords: IoT, smart city, digital transformation, business transformation

4.1 Introduction

In the current scenario, if we talk about the business organizations whether it is small size organization or large organization, they are adopting business transformation with the fundamental changes in the way the business takes place to cope up with the shift in the market

---

Corresponding author: shamsshamsul@gmail.com

Parul Gandhi, Surbhi Bhatia, Abhishek Kumar, Mohammad Alojail and Pramod Singh Rathore (eds.) *Internet of Things in Business Transformation: Developing an Engineering and Business Strategy for Industry 5.0*, (43–60) © 2021 Scrivener Publishing LLC

environment day by day. Urbanization is one of the major components for business transformation in the shift of market environment as the large number of populations is being shifted from rural areas to urban areas and the majority of the population are getting more aware about the market, products and services.Hence, we require inventive and innovative technologies which may sense urban dynamics automatically and give essential information to improve the business processes which must maintain and increase the revenue of the business organization and hence the sustainability of the organization too. Business transformation is the biggest challenge for every organization towards their sustainability in the market. To make the life easier, do work efficiently and generate more revenues according to the limited time, the technology plays an important role [1].

Technology is a term which makes the organization capable to move forward with their competitor in the competitive environment of the market. There are multiple objectives of business transformation including market share, customer satisfaction and cost-cutting. If we talk about the customer satisfaction, it is one of the major dimensions of business on which any organization must focus regularly. In the last decades, we were using the traditional business system where competition was also less and nowadays the scenario is just contrary [2].

In almost every sector we are getting the support of recent technologies like Internet of Things, Artificial Intelligence, Blockchain, etc. For example: - if we talk about the Healthcare System, we can monitor our patient remotely where communication plays an important role in terms of Wi-Fi Connectivity, Zigbee, etc. Such communication medium is also being used for the tracking of assets, remote workers, and shipping with the help of GPS. In the recent trends, we are using RFID tags for the identification or monitoring of devices, patients, pets, tracking of trucks and all which makes our work more convenient. In the education system, the processes have become modernized which makes the learning easier in terms of e-learning resources, in terms of smart classes, use of various teaching and learning aids like audio-visual aids, etc. [3]. A variety of businesses whether they are dealing in manufacturing of several audio-visual aids or dealing with providing various services plays an important role in the education system. It increases the productivity of the education process [4]. Apart from this, we are also having the technological support for the research and development. If we talk about the automotive, there are various options for the crash avoidance, fleet management, establishment of smart factories, smart homes, etc. There are a lot of options for the media/entertainment in terms of set-top boxes, smartphones, smart televisions, self-service, smart home gateway, etc. Companies like IBM, CISCO are spending huge amount for incubating technologies which helps in the implementation of smart city concept as well [5, 6].

4.1.1   Business Transformation

The term transformation has become a buzzword today which is used in various ways to run the organization smoothly which makes the process easier and productive. Corporate Renewing Centre organized a conference at INSEAD where the term business-transformation was defined as "A fundamental change in organizational logic, which resulted in or was caused by a fundamental shift in behaviors" [7]. While defining transformation in detail, following four constructs were given:

- Re-engineering: It is a technique to improve organizational efficiency by redesigning the business processes so that the organization may get self-aligned for future and raise its market share and profit margins.
- Restructuring: It is required whenever a business model of the organization gets changed due to any reason or factor for the survival of the organization and ultimately for the growth of the organization. It reduces the cost, emphasizes on main items, adopting recent technologies, proper utilization of resources available, etc. Merging with other companies can also take place.
- Renewing: It's a continuous and knowledge oriented process because there are various changes which are faced by the organization on a regular basis and some of them have the potential for major strategic change in organization's operations which add the stability factor for the organization. For example, when a new technology is in the market, strategy has to be reviewed to find out that organization would get benefited by adopting it or not?
- Regeneration: It is a technique which reproduces the organization so that they become capable of incorporating the new employees while organizations are losing the old and experienced employees and at the same time an introduction of new employee's capabilities, attitude and goals takes place. In today's world almost all the organizations are getting changed and hence facing with regeneration. Regeneration improves the current business processes and primarily revising the ways and other opportunities available [7, 8].

As we observe from the current scenario where people prefer online shopping just to save the time and also they are getting good quality products or services at their doorstep in the competitive environment of the organizations, hence lots of businesses are taking the initiatives for adopting the business transformation from traditional system. In the next section, we are going to discuss digital transformation, various technologies which support digital transformation and its challenges. In INDIA we are moving towards the implementation of smart city concepts as well, so we need smart environment where automation of the processes in majority may take place [9, 10].

4.2 Digital Transformation and its Big Trend

4.2.1 Digital Transformation

The term "Digital transformation" has become the first choice of the market leaders who are adopting recent technologies for adding more values to their valued customers, employees, and other stakeholders. Digital transformation reforms various businesses processes, IT operations and corporate culture of the organization [11]. It uses digital technologies available in the market for the designing and implementation of a process to make it more productive or valuable for the organization. The motive behind this is to use recent technologies not only for the sake of repeating existing services digitally, but also to apply technology for the transformation of those services into something considerably more better as improved alternative. In digital transformation, several recent technologies can be considered like cloud computing, Internet of Things (IoT), blockchain, big-data, data analytics, and artificial intelligence. Many projects based on digital transformation have major contribution in the competitive environment for the large organizations to compete with quicker and purely digital competitors. Other types of small business organizations are also moving in the same direction hence the use of recent technologies has been increased nowadays [12].

4.2.2 How Important is Digital Transformation?

According to the survey done by IDC (International Data Corporation), the worldwide investment on various technologies which are required for the implementation of digital transformation including hardware, software, and services has reached to $1.3 trillion by the year 2017. Companies dealing with the technology research expect costing to almost double as compared to now and by the year 2021 the overall investment for digitalization will exceed $2.1

trillion globally. A survey has been conducted by IT analyst Gartner regarding business issues of the business leaders as well as some technological aspects. Around 460 business leaders including CEO and senior executives has participated in the survey. Figure 4.1 shows the CEO top business priorities for the year 2018 and 2019. 62% of the executives said that the initiative was taken by the management or the management had a transformation program to transform their business more digitally. More than half (approximately 54%) of the executives said that the objective of their respective digital business is totally transformational, whereas 46% of the executives said that the motive behind the initiative taken by the management is optimization [13]. Above data can be represented and easily analysed with Table 4.1. Approximately half of the executives were agreed for the objective as optimization.

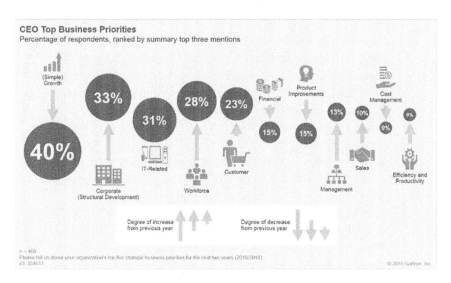

Figure 4.1 CEO Top Business Priorities for 2018 and 2019 Source: Gartner.

Table 4.1 Various objectives of organizations for transformation given by 460 executives.

S. No.	Percentage of executives answered	No. of executives answered	Objective
1	62	285 (Approx)	Make their business more digital
2	54	248 (Approx)	Business objective is transformational
3	46	212 (Approx)	Optimization

4.2.3   Digital Transformation Examples

As the customer expectations are growing, and every business is trying hard to keep up with them. Today it is far easier than ever before for consumers to explore alternatives to meet their needs. That is why each company has to make extra efforts to ensure that their customers stay with them. It will be possible only if the company digitally transforms itself to cater to its customer expectations. Every industry needs to adopt this new digital world by moving towards a digital transformation. There are few examples of big companies that successfully underwent a digital transformation.

1. Domino's: It is a very common and best example of user-centered process design which utilizes the power of operations. Technology running for pizza tracker system lets the customers to get into the operational process of the company. It allows users to know exactly which stage in the operation process the pizza is. Company ensures customers a guarantee of 30-minute deliveries and an app to track if the order is being placed, in queue, pizza is being made or in route to the user which helps in increasing user satisfaction. Other examples are:

2. Walmart: They have to reinvent the approach to the customer. They did it so successfully, that Harvard Business Review named the company 'the digital winner'.

3. Disney: They went fully digital when they introduced RFID technology used in the parks covering various stages/processes like identifying all the guest's tickets or passes which is further shared with the connected wireless system to make the visit more convenient for the visitors.

4. McDermott International: Oil and gas industry requires heavy machinery and hence, transformation is taking place in the industry. Company is creating computerized model for the facilities of oil and gas which are made available for the clients. This model is also known as a digital-twin. The company predicts a hike of 15% in operational margins with the use of digital-twin approach for major fields such as predictive maintenance. Digital-twin refers to a digital replica of potential and actual physical assets, processes, people, places, systems and devices which can be used for different purposes. As per the belief of Gartner, near about 50% of the organizations will adopt the digital-twin approach by the year 2021.

5. Rolls Royce's R² Data Labs: They are using the concepts like data analytics, artificial intelligence, and machine learning for creating variety of innovative services. The team of R² Data Labs, including various data architects, managers, engineers and scientists has helped the firm to deliver around £250 million through the activities of engine-health monitoring in 12 months [14].

6. Logistics: The Company dealing with logistics like "United Parcel Service (UPS)" is using data analytics and keeping an eye on major business operations. Company is utilizing the strength of data analytics and artificial intelligence on real time data to assist their employees for making improved decisions. UPS has just introduced their Chatbot which uses artificial intelligence for helping their customers to find charges and tracking details.

7. Blood and Transplant: In a public sector like National Health Service (NHS) is attempting for the implementation of digital transformation from last two years. Various trials has been completed which also includes the utilization of predictive analysis and managing the waiting time for an organ. Making the organs available for the patient is the major concern for the healthcare [15].

8. General Electric: It's a reality that not all the strategies related to digital transformation are similar according to its success rate. The company made strong efforts for the integration of the traditional system with the new system designed on software basis. If we talk about the digital transformation, company released the product behind the schedule and lacking in features as required by the customers. There were various problems like poor decisions of investments, major changes in the leadership. Some people blamed the company's failure just because it was not enough capable to focus key area of improvement. Currently, General Electric is making good effort and is focusing on redesigning their digital strategy [16].

9. Banking: Banking industry has transformed its services massively in the last decades. Banks ATM has replaced the banking tellers (cashier) for cash deposits, withdrawals or cheque deposits. With the excessive use of smart phones in our society, most of the banking transactions taking place through mobile apps rather than visiting to a bank. Money can be transferred in various secured ways available like NEFT, IMPS, etc. All of this became possible because

banking industry has taken initiative for adopting digital transformation.

10. Insurance: Most of the insurance related work can be done through self-service portals or mobile apps. Users can compare and customize their insurance plans available in the market and without taking any help from the insurance agent. Insurance may be related to automotive, life, health, business or home. User can have the various alternatives on a single portal like policybazar.com and all.

4.2.4   Importance of Digital Transformation

Digitalization supports the business leaders and entrepreneurs in changing the existing economy of the company which reflects everywhere. Amazon has a great impact on retailing whereas Facebook has affected publishing by providing services to their customers instantly. As a result, traditional companies are facing challenges by various digitally aware competitors. However nearly three-fourth of business leaders are alert and attentive that their organization is under threat from distraction, therefore various business leaders are not interested to adopt the change [17].

4.2.5   Digital Transformation vs Business Transformation

The process of business transformation is going faster as it is running with the assistance of various digital technologies available in the market. Implementing digital transformation into a business doesn't mean that to apply technology which does the process digital, but it is more than that which includes the way that the employee works with different tools available and work with teams. Hence digitalization is an approach to assist in the business transformation. "There is not an IT or a business strategy; instead, there's a single digital business strategy," validates Lisa Heneghan, who is the global head of KPMG's Chief information officer advisory board.

4.2.6   What Does Digital Transformation Look Like?

Recent technologies whether it is IoT (Internet of Things), Artificial Intelligence, Big Data, or Cloud computing are providing assistance to various business leaders for developing new models for the existing business which changes the traditional method of running business operations. Such technologies are not just the recent buzzwords for the current scenario but the "Tangible value coming from these technologies in terms of improving product optimization, increasing production output, and directing operational efficiency challenges." Hence we can call it what we require and the digital transformation is like something for which so many executives engaged in legacy systems are struggling till now to get their heads around. Although start-ups succeed through their innovative methods of working style, creative use of data and approaches to integrate recent technologies, various traditional firms including public and private sectors are still facing difficulties in legacy system. Such organizations are stuck on their policies and process, rather than information and its insights. These firms which are moving slowly in the market getting left behind in the competitive race. Gartner says "two-thirds of business leaders believe their companies must pick up the pace of digitalization to remain competitive".

On the other hand, speeding up the development is quite tough. "Digital" is normally viewed as a complicated art which is understood by fewer experts. In so many cases, entrepreneur gets filled such knowledge gap through highly paid consultants who bring the publicity of digital transformation as a replacement for measurable business value.

4.3   Transformational Technology

In a current scenario, we are observing that the technologies are emerging, resurging and converging at once. Throughout the world organizations are trying to put themselves to beat its competitor through incorporating and practically applying inventive business models based on technology to make a distinction among others. Besides this framework, Technology Industry Innovation Survey was done in 2019 by KPMG and in that survey IoT (Internet of Things) was ranked the uppermost driver of business transformation for the upcoming three years. Everything whether it may be wearable health devices, homes and cities, are considered as "smart" in the current scenario and connects to a wide variety of devices and applications to assist the customers accordingly.

4.3.1   Internet of Things

The Internet of Things or IoT is one of the most demanding technologies among other key technologies required for digital transformation. With the addition of various sensors and devices in the network there is an exponential growth in the data also. Such stored data can also be utilized for business transformation through digital technologies. Utilization of tiny sensors has changed the world, which has allowed for rich information collection and well organized systems. Industries such as manufacturing and retailing have setup trucks, storage services, and factories with Internet of Things (IoT) devices and other smart tools which can be used together information about how they are used and provide insights and how the things can be optimized.

The other term i.e. Industrial Internet of Things (IIoT) which has become an expertise in separate field, allows the organizations to gather the data on their machines itself and tools which are based on machine learning or AI is used to analyze that data and give recommendations accordingly. Such systems can be utilized to improve the safety of employees at their workplaces and those places can be highlighted where costs could be reduced. Organizations can analyze and find the weak places and make out how to limit disruption in service or handle problems before they occur.

4.3.2   Robotic Process Automation

Robotic Process Automation (RPA) is a technology which lets the people to configure the software or a "robot" to integrate various actions of human who interacts with the digitalized system for running the business processes. The interface of RPA is used to gather the data and manipulate applications as humans do. Robotic Process Automation contains the software bots which assists to automate manual activities of business processes. RPA is treated as the fundamental step of intelligent automation which utilizes the strength of machine learning and true artificial intelligence. Various basic tasks related to offices are being performed by soft bots in all over the world and even they are involved in decision making processes also. RPA improves the performance of the system by adding up the humans capabilities in a machine.

4.3.3   Automation and Artificial Intelligence

Forrester recently said that organizations in all over the world are increasingly moving towards automation for various tasks which is used to be handled by human beings. It is bringing the change in the workforce at basic level, highlighting fears of mass job losses in the next coming decade. But this field is also improving the enterprises in better form in a several directions. Complicated and critical jobs, time-consuming jobs at factories being done by robots, keep people away from the positions which affect physical health of a worker. It has been also introduced into other areas like customer service, where so many companies are now using automated systems for responding to basic queries and complaints from the customers. Organizations are using AI for even everything ranging from security to human resources, which allow computers to handle jobs that have become expensive or redundant. Although uncertainties of automation and AI are in existence, recent reviews have proven that peoples are interested to adopt the automation and utilizing the capabilities of robots which can handle tedious tasks [18].

4.3.4 Blockchain

However, digital transformation is no longer a choice for businesses; it has become essential for the survival of business in the recent competitive environment. Blockchain as a new technology is likely to bring a dramatic change for business transformation in the coming decades. Blockchain technology came into the picture a few years back as a part of the bit coin revolution and at present it's a promising technology which can transform the business in various ways. It has given impact to almost every industry and every business which requires more organized business processes. As a crypto currency effort, blockchain was initially criticized but now it is in the initial implementation phase because of its wide applicability. The total investment for the blockchain solutions worldwide is predicted to touch the figure of $11.7 billion by 2022. Banks and other financial institutions have used blockchain technology for almost everything to simplify the processes like loan applications. One of the banking group in Canada have used blockchain for providing more power to individuals so that data collected by the financial institutions can be accessed by them. A large number of industries have started research for verifying the effectiveness of this technology, and it has a great impact on supply chain. Major business leaders like Walmart in retailing and McDonalds in fast food are now using blockchain to supply materials and food.

A well-known and one of the leading company in blockchain i.e. IBM has recently got the project of "blockchain system development" by Brazil which would be used to manage the country's birth and death records.

Google, Facebook, Twitter, and Amazon are some of the leading companies that have a great impact on our society and as a revolutionary innovation they have improved the actions which have changed the way of communicating with each other, way of thinking, ordering food online, or booking cabs. A large number of professional communities like scientists, developers, and researchers have contributed to the successful implementation of new technologies designed to address almost all the requirements of humans.

4.3.5   Cloud Computing

The recent concept of cloud computing has completely replaced the limitation of infrastructure and increased the capacity of companies whether it is small company or the bigger one. Companies need not to have the expensive IT infrastructure or not to invest for maintenance procedure. As per the survey of TechRepublic, around 70% of the companies are using cloud services or planning to use it. Businesses can move their most of the services to the cloud and can easily manage them. There is no headache for scaling up the infrastructure in case of the business expansion. The lesser prices available for cloud computing services have motivated the companies to adapt it. Hence, even smaller companies are able to access tools that were beyond the reach previously. Amazon Web Services (AWS), Google, Microsoft, and Alibaba are the biggest providers of cloud computing services in the market. As per the available models of cloud computing like Infrastructure as a Service (IaaS), Platform as a Service (PaaS), and Software as a Service (SaaS), cloud computing is gaining popularity and it will be one of the major elements in the next decade. According to the latest report of Forrester says that the cloud market will touch $411 billion by the year 2022. Additionally report says that the four leading vendors of cloud will produce 75% of the whole $75.4 billion cloud infrastructure market [19].

4.3.6   Smartphones and Mobile Apps

In a current scenario, technologies are getting changed frequently and as a result one more device has been introduced in the world of technologies as a new innovation. A large number of mobile users have been increased tremendously with the launch of smartphones which connects people on to the web. Hence, the popularity of smartphones has moved to other dimension of mobile apps development which is now became the part of lives. Uber and Ola have become verbs, while food delivery apps like Zomato and Swiggy are wildly admired. Peoples are using mobile apps for managing almost all the aspect of their lives through using calendar platforms, Google search engine, workout assistants, and voice memo programs. Way of communicating with each other has also been changed through heavy usage of smartphones. Mobile apps like WhatsApp, Signal and Facebook Messenger became the first choice of billions of peoples to communicate, through sending secure messages, images, videos, and voice messages all over the world in seconds. Google Maps and other Apps have made the people capable to explore geographically and made it to impossible to get lost. People can also book railway tickets, air tickets, movie tickets or can transfer money with each other in seconds with the palm size device.

4.3.7   4G and 5G

Fourth generation of mobile connectivity emerged in 2000s. Fourth generation (4G) enhanced the mobile internet speeds up to 500 times faster as compared to third generation (3G) and made capable to sustain HD quality video, making video calls and improved browsing speed. Currently 4G is popular throughout the globe but the Internet of Things (IoT) is getting popularity and hence the number of devices will increase exponentially and 4G will not be able to handle such system. To handle huge number of connections will require great capacity of network. Here fifth generation (5G) comes into picture. In business transformation almost every company is moving to adapt the recent technologies for changing their business processes and hence 5G can be adapted to use other technologies like IoT, Blockchain, and cloud computing.

4.3.8   Data Analytics

Excessive use of soft-wares and recent technologies which includes various devices is generating a variety of data. Various Apps like WhatsApp, Signal and Facebook Messenger are also generating the variety of semi-structured/unstructured data. Youtube is also one of the examples of having huge amount of data, IoT devices and sensors are generating the variety of data as well. Our data is becoming huge and more precious day by day. But the ability to analyse those data is required which can help in businesses transformation for adapting the changes. To analyze the different varieties of data very fast and accurate there is a need of expertise who can analyze the data with the help of various tools available in the market. As a result of analysis, better decisions can be made for business transformation. It is convenient for the companies to make long-term decisions when data is accurate and that has been analysed and sorted.

4.3.9   Social Media

Social media are commonly used in usual operations of many companies including every level of organization. It is changing the ways of communication and collaboration. Social media has changed the way of business ranging from marketing and operations to finance. Social media is used to improve relationship among employees and sharing the culture. In terms of business, it gives an opportunity to get your business popular among the people. No other technology provides the method to connect customers, employees, and others. Social networking sites and apps like Facebook, Twitter, Instagram are used for communication, sharing thoughts, photos, videos and many more. Hence they are having the huge number of users at present. All the market leaders are having their Twitter and Facebook accounts now days. Social media has the support of machine learning and AI concepts also, which is used for marketing purpose on the basis of users buying trends and gender. Social media has become the most essential ways for companies and business leaders to communicate with and getting reviews from people. As the number of users of smartphones is increasing day by day, the number of users on social media sites is also increasing simultaneously and it is predicted that it will bring billions of more users in the coming decade.

4.4   How to Get "Digital Transformation" in a Right Way for Any Business

A lot of executives have the idea about the threat from initial start-up competitors who are adapting digitalization, but how the existing companies can move fast, without any violation?

Approximately three-quarters of business leaders is alert about their organization which is prone to disruption, but a lot of leaders are not showing their interest to take the initiative of taking risk to transform. As per the analysis done on 500 executives belonging from UK and Ireland, fifty percent (50%) of the enterprises take the start-ups as a serious threat and approximately one-tenth of the enterprises do not gets agreed that they have any market competitor. Originally, seven percent (7%) of the executives said that the enterprises are not worried about the threat of digital disturbance. One of the experts, Kevin Hanley, who is the head of innovation at Royal Bank of Scotland, shares his three best practices for converting digital distraction into an advantage for the current competitive environment.

4.4.1   Look Beyond the Traditional Enterprise Firewall

Kevin Hanley is responsible for various types of activities at RBS, such as exploring innovative ideas worldwide, managing exploratory labs and applying the control process which supports to take creative ideas from theoretical to practical. He talked to some smart people globally and met around 1,500 companies in a year dealing with technologies ranging from larger organizations to smaller starts-up. He believes about the world, especially in finance, is getting changed exceptionally. The technology is getting changed so fast and it is becoming cheaper and ubiquitous which is representing a significant shift of the organization dealing with finance. The business operations related to traditional banking system has been broken into smaller one and most of them are being provided by the industries. Companies dealing with finance which are successful must identify and hold such change. To achieve success in the current scenario of disruption, large banks should merge their long-lasting skills with the knowledge of new entrants. Business executives are emphasizing to innovate, hence, should look ahead of the legacy enterprise firewall. Yet, Hanley warned the leaders and other executives about the change in cultural element are more complicated as compared to the technical transformation. Finance is turning to be more competitive and businesses should be more open. The success of the executive will be determined by the ability to work with others. There are various opportunities available for each type of organizations whether it is big or small but with the right skills. The organization must be able to adopt the changes technically and culturally [14].

4.4.2   Bring New Ideas From the Edge to the Core

As per the Kevin Hanley, those companies which are looking for transformation should make progress in two directions in parallel: (1) present and (2) the future. In first direction, organizations should emphasize on their existing traditional set-up, they must simplify the systems and build the technology efficient. Fix the complexity which you already have so that core can be improved. In the Second direction, executives must consider about their required aims and work backward from that state. Hanley advised that challenge yourself to think about the world just after ten years in advance and the activities you should do today to hold the opportunities which are getting emerged. He warned the executives not to make choices between these two directions i.e. present and future. Executives can simply emphasize on one or other but they must deal with both. If they emphasize on present, risk may increase; if they emphasize on innovation and creativity, basic operational concerns may fall down. RBS has established separate policies and control processes for the innovation which lets Hanley and his team members to experiment separately [14].

4.4.3   Define the Role of the CIO in the Innovation Process

We must have the answer of this question: who must lead the process of innovation? While 49% of senior executives thinks that CIOs (Chief

Information Officer) must be accountable for driving innovation in technology, as per the Dell EMC research, more than half (54%) of the executives feels that their IT leaders should make so many controls which restrict the potential for creativity. RBS considers innovation as an activity which covers all business units. Hanley considers that other businesses must adopt a similar stand and stay away from placing power for digital distraction in the hands of the IT department. As per Hanley—if innovation and creativity is especially the responsibility of the CIO, technology just becomes a hammer looking for a nail. If you are trying and changing your organization within normal business cycles, creativity of executive will be squashed. At RBS, Hanley is running short, sprint activity and there is a separate fund for it. They are presently exploring 40 innovation initiatives. Hanley runs monthly forums with chief executives at partner start-up organizations. These forums include the members of the RBS executive board [14].

4.5   Relevance of IoT in Digital Transformation

As a recent technology Internet of Things (IoT) is getting popularity and companies are trying to adapt it for their businesses. Hence, companies are required to have a plan to implement IoT in their business and to protect their data also. In the next coming five years, there is a prediction about the number of IoT devices and will reach around 50 billion. It means that you are putting the sensors on everything. It may be any devices, things, tractors or it may be anything you can think of.

Dignan think IoT is the very essential components which include digital transformation. It will transform the entire business by making changes in the way how you track your inventory and the supply chain, providing you more analytical data, and more insights. The best place where IoT will be most transformative can be seen under the smart city environment such as sensor based monitoring and controlling of traffic or supply of water or leakage. However, there is one challenge along with the collection of data generated by the sensors that deciding which data is important and should be kept for futures purpose, and which doesn't. Since storage is cheap, companies can keep data lying around. As per the Dignan, companies are putting a lot of sensors in most of the devices, and not aware or not having plans what to do with that data. Data which is collected and left lying around for potential use later can become vulnerable to attacks. As the data moves to the cloud, it needs to be secured. Dignan said that IoT is going to make everything smart, which is a little freaky yet also kind of cool.

4.6   Conclusion

Authors conclude that the recent trend of business transformation requires huge transformation in technologies as world is moving towards the concept of automation, implementing smartness in smart environment where the people are living and making efforts for the development. This paper covers the importance of business transformation, digital transformation and, technologies required for business transformation. Implementing digital transformation into a business doesn't mean that to apply technology which does the process digital, but it is more than that which includes the way that the employee works with such tools and works with teams. Hence digitalization is a method used to help in the business transformation. Digital transformation supports business transformation, but it doesn't mean that business transformation is dependent on digital transformation and vice-versa. Both the process must be implemented with the proper policies to achieve the success in the market. Apart from the various benefits of using recent technologies, some challenges related to maintaining the quality process of business, issues related to security of customers data and increasing the customer satisfaction and number of customers etc. are also there which we must handle in different domains.

References

1. Jarvenpan, S.L. and Ives, B., Introducing transformational information technologies: The case of the World Wide Web technology. *Int. J. Electron. Commer.*, 1, 1, 95–126, 1996.
2. Mukundan, P.M., Manayankath, S., Srinivasan, C., Sethumadhavan, M., Hash-One: A lightweight cryptographic hash function. *IET Inf. Secur.*, 10, 5, 225–231, Sep. 2016.
3. Gregor, S., Martin, M., Fernandez, W., Stern, S., Vitale, M., The transformational dimension in the realization of business value from information technology. *J. Strateg. Inf. Syst.*, 15, 3, 249–270, 2006.
4. Wan, J., Li, D., Zou, C., Zhou, K., M2M communications for smart city: An event-based architecture, in: *Proceedings—2012 IEEE 12th International Conference on Computer and Information Technology, CIT 2012*, pp. 895–900, 2012.
5. Development of Smart Cities and Its Sustainability: A Smart City framework. *International Journal of Innovative Technology and Exploring Engineering (IJITEE)* 8, 11, pp. 646–655, 2019.
6. Zanella, A., Bui, N., Castellani, A., Vangelista, L., Zorzi, M., Internet of things for smart cities. *IEEE Internet Things J.*, 1, 1, 22–32, Feb. 2014.

7. Berman, S.J., Digital transformation: Opportunities to create new business models. *Strateg. Leadersh.*, 40, 2, 16–24, 2012.

8. Andal-Ancion, A., Cartwright, P.A., Yip, G.S., The digital transformation of traditional businesses. *MIT Sloan Manag. Rev.*, 44, 4, 34–41, 2003.

9. Ismail, M.H., Khater, M., Zaki, M., Digital Business Transformation and Strategy: What Do We Know So Far? *Manuf. Artic.*, November 2017, 36, 2017.

10. https://flipboard.com/@techrepublic/digital-transformation-cb9mdcfkz

11. https://www.constellationr.com/research/constellation-research-2017-digital-transformation-study

12. https://www.techrepublic.com/resource-library/whitepapers/special-report-data-ai-iot-the-future-of-retail-free-pdf/

13. https://www.zdnet.com/article/why-iot-is-a-critical-part-of-digital-transformation/

14. https://www.zdnet.com/article/digital-transformation-three-ways-to-get-it-right-in-your-business/

15. https://www.techrepublic.com/article/the-top-technologies-that-enabled-digital-transformation-7. this-decade/

16. https://www.zdnet.com/article/what-is-digital-transformation-everything-you-need-to-know-about-how-technology-is-reshaping/

17. https://easternpeak.com/blog/key-steps-for-a-successful-digital-transformation/

18. https://assets.kpmg/content/dam/kpmg/ie/pdf/2019/05/ie-top-10-technologies-for-business-transformation.pdf

19. https://www.techrepublic.com/article/forrester-the-5-ways-cloud-computing-will-change-in-2020/

5

Future of Artificial Intelligence: Will People be at More of an Advantage Than They Are Today?

Priyadarsini Patnaik[1]* and Ravi Prakash[2]†

[1]Birla Global University, Bhubaneswar, India
[2]CBL University, Bhiwani, India

Abstract

Technological advancements continue to grow at an incredible speed which results an increased collaboration between humans and technology. Though the technology-based AI is relatively a new term but ground researches have already initiated on artificial intelligence. AI, has an ability to store huge amounts of data and process it with a very high speed, as well as has the ability to solve problems and could compete with human abilities. Today AI is nothing but a modern technology which studies how human brain thinks, learn, decide, and work while trying to solve a problem, and outcomes of the study is utilized for developing intelligent software and systems. AI will become an integral part of business houses and individuals, it might exceed human abilities but can it replace sophisticated behavior such as love, moral choice, emotions. In this study we will analyse and examine how humans and AI might evolve together and what would be the future of humans with the help of AI? Will people be at an advantage than they are today?

Keywords: Artificial intelligence, smart systems, automation

5.1 Introduction

As technological advancements continue to grow at an incredible speed the collaboration between humans and smart systems will be increased. Due to

*Corresponding author: pattnaikp2009@gmail.com
†Corresponding author: profraviprakash74@gmail.com

Parul Gandhi, Surbhi Bhatia, Abhishek Kumar, Mohammad Alojail and Pramod Singh Rathore (eds.) *Internet of Things in Business Transformation: Developing an Engineering and Business Strategy for Industry 5.0,* (61–70) © 2021 Scrivener Publishing LLC consumers high-demand of individualization and customization approach with modern consumers they prefer a degree of hands-on customization. In the post modernism era the people become more individualistic so that there is an earnest need to personalize the preference of the customer.

AI is a branch of computer science concerned with the study and creation of computer systems that exhibit some form of intelligence. AI systems can understand and perceive a natural language and comprehend a visual scene and systems which require human type of intelligence [1]. It is a study in the fields of psychology, physiology and cognitive science as these studies are required to understand human intelligence, human thought process and sensing process [2]. The objective of AI is to develop such smart computer systems which can be capable of performing tasks which require high levels of intelligence. In the year 1955, Newell and Simon designed the first AI program and John McCarthy, coined the term artificial intelligence and devoted to the development of intelligent machines [3–6].

AI works on psychological frame. The browsing pattern of the visitor allows AI to serve the need of the visitor or rather to create an interest to buy the product so that the visitor should convert into a customer. For instance, an unknown visitor tries to buy a shirt for him then he visits any online portal [7]. Now question arises what he will look into from the website? The cost, price range which his pocket allows, brand, color, fabric, design. Now AI work starts. AI will send the message to data centre to customize the needs of the visitor. So that he can be a potential buyer. Now AI works on the basis of databank and the experience he will provide the choice of the shirt before the visitors. Here AI will have a very sharp analysis on how consumer is behaving. The response of the consumer allows AI to provide the range of the product. So AI is nothing but it tries to read our mind so that it can customize the range of the product which suits the need of the customer [8].

AI may be one of the most developments of this century. The variety of AI tools includes knowledge representation, speech recognition, pattern recognition, search and matching, memory organization, robotics, understanding natural languages etc. AI drives data analysis, predicts lead scoring, and content personalization, which help to improve customers' experiences [9]. AI considers customer taste, browsing history, personal preferences, spending patterns to send highly customized and more relevant suggestions to their customers. Hyper-personalized artificial intelligence (AI) can deliver more relevant content, product, and service information to each user. This approach enhances personalized marketing. Business strategy which is equipped by AI is key to success, particularly for both today and tomorrow [10–13].

5.2   The State of Artificial Intelligence (AI)

AI is still in its infancy and we are on the direction of its growth and it will affect the lives of most individuals by the end of the centuries. The day will come soon when AI leaded countries will contribute towards the economic powers of the world. The countries that have recognized the potential of AI have already started investing the funds for resources to conduct further research programs in AI. Many leading countries including Canada, Italy, Austria, Singapore, Japan, USA and Britain have already initiated and announced plans for some AI research and development programs [14].

5.3   How Do Customers Interact with AI Nowadays?

AI has many applications in the areas like economics, medicine, banking, chemistry, marketing. AI has revolutionized the marketing. It allows consumers to locate the best prices for product or services. It creates sophisticated consumers by providing hyper personalized recommendations. Today's customers expect variety of products, with personalized recommendations without wasting their time. This is exactly what AI can achieve and deliver. When consumers visit any shopping sites, AI records every aspect of their visits, and the time spent on each activity. This enables AI to develop customized recommendations for the customers by gathering true behavioural data about the consumers [15].

5.4   AI as Digital Assistants

Digital assistants are the systems those have developed to perform many types of intelligent tasks. They can learn from past related experiences and can understand natural languages. They can recognize object from photograph, sensor and recommend better than human experts [16]. Though visual sensing and recognition, AI does provide impressive recommendations. The entire process takes place by four steps such as

- Step 1—Stimuli which is being produced by many objects are perceived by sensory devices. Attributes such as size, shape, color and texture have the abilities to produce strongest stimuli.
- Step 2—Attributes then get associated with the object classifications. Selected attributes then produce high and low class groupings.

- Step 3—Attribute values are being selected by forming generalized prototype descriptions and those are stored for subsequent recognition.
- Step 4—Recognition of familiar objects.

After recognition and by observing previous stimulus pattern, digital assistants provide familiar and personalized recommendations.

5.5 AI and Privacy, Data Security

Reports say we are witnessing many technological innovations which we never dreamed before. We have experienced smart systems which exceeds human capabilities. AI can solve varieties of problems and can adopt models of thinking and learning from psychology. Since AI is completely data driven, are the data we using are safe? Are they in safe hands? Do we know how our personal data is getting used? What about the confidentiality, integrity and security of huge numbers of personal data getting generated? We must ensure secure socket layer to protect our data [17]. Though we have many rules and regulations govern cyber security but there must be different modes of security operations to protect the personal data. Since there are two types of services namely AH (authentication to IP Packets) and ESP (service for encryption and authentication) which will build a secure system and can provide secure data system as well [18, 19].

We should adopt these measures to ensure data security. Such as

- Strong technical infrastructure
- Secure data protection laws
- Supporting services
- Cryptographic check

5.5.1 Artificial Intelligence and its Effect on Humans

In an survey, we have asked our respondent regarding how the human will be benefitted by AI. Our question: By 2030, do you think AI will empower human capacities? Will AI will lessen human independence? 63% of respondents said yes 2030, and 37% said no.

**Individuals will be
benefitted with
the help of AI**

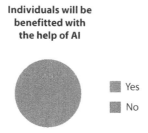

■ Yes
■ No

Respondents included that AI increased convenience (66.2% of respondents), reduce a shorter time of individual activities (59.9% of respondents), increased sense of control over efficiency (47.3% of respondents) as well as entertainment (44.6%).

Benefits Of AI

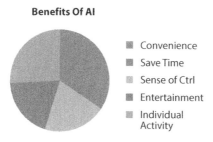

■ Convenience
■ Save Time
■ Sense of Ctrl
■ Entertainment
■ Individual
   Activity

What will decide on the dynamics and directions of development of AI to the greatest extent, in respondents' opinion, were actions implemented in that area in the world, which was indicated by above 55% of respondents as well as increased consumers' knowledge on new technologies, which will influence a change in their attitudes and preferences (47.3%) as well as needs and willingness to be innovative, automation, etc. 46.4%). What sccms interesting here is that only 23% of respondents admitted that it will be also influenced by actions undertaken by government institutions that popularize the concept of Artificial Intelligence. AI will enhance human competences. But AI systems can't work on our behalf. Human capacity to adapt our activities, empathy and an associated ethical framework, will be reduced by the disassociation. Deployment of AI is in the hands of civilization. We need to prepare an AI-literate public, we need to oversight in AI's development too [20].

**Which Factors will
Decide Dynamics Of AI**

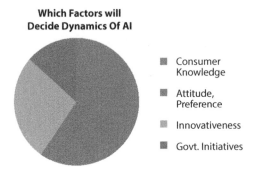

- Consumer Knowledge
- Attitude, Preference
- Innovativeness
- Govt. Initiatives

Here we can discuss these three points that draw from critical observations:

1) Human–AI evolution and the concern thereof
2) How to address AI's impact
3) Forecasting life in 2030

Human–AI evolution and the concern thereof

- Individuals' control over the lives will be reduced.
- Social disturbance will be created due to loss of human jobs by AI.
- Excessive dependent on AI will lead to skill diminishing of individuals.
- Vulnerabilities, cybercrime will be more.

People will be more too automated which leads to few problems like

1) Economic uncertainty, employment issues
2) People's privacy issue.

At the same time AI will support manhood to be more efficient, live safer and healthier. Importance will be given to how AI will be administered. AI will be used for improving our quality of life.

The biggest danger will be personalized recommendations. With more and more personalized recommendations, 'we will risk a loss of individual freedoms that we have fought for in the last decades and centuries'. Whether AI will mark our lives better depends on how it is executed on our decision-making practices [21, 22].

AI will enhance our abilities as humans and human autonomy will be diminished. Whether lives of people will be better than today depends on forthcoming technological developments especially it will depend on personal valuable data. More data means better AI, and data is exclusive and expensive to acquire. So there must be regulation and audit mechanisms on uses of our personal information [23].

Human-machines collaboration will bring many benefits to society over time which will extend our abilities. Machines will bring together different groups of people and communities to live together by leaving the big concern will these collaborations benefit everyone, or only a few? Humankind is not addressing the concern of educating people about potentials and threats of human-machine/AI collaboration [24]. Threat such as privacy violations can be detected in using big data where unawareness of using data where and how will lead to a serious concern.

Current developments do not forecast well for the fair progress of AI. Very few understand the technology and the implications of its safe use.

5.5.2 Conclusion

It's true that Artificial Intelligence is so powerful which can influence humans into taking actions. But what would be the next big challenges? AI is not meant to imitate human senses and thought processes. It cannot exceed human abilities too. Creativity within the human-machine has no limits [25]. Both research and public are interested in this promising field. Realism must be exercised because the human mind is far away from decoded, and it would be very dangerous to draw conclusion upon something so imprecise. But what can be concluded then, AI can conceptionally be connected in many elements and they can benefit from each other [26]. AI can be analyzed too to get brain responses for brands, products in the marketplace to get the success or failure for positioning a product. The day is not far when AI does not merely assist human beings in decision making but takes decisions on behalf of them. Predictably, despite its probability in empowering humans, the growing role of AI in the lives of them is troubled with conceptual, moral, ethical and regulatory dilemmas. India's economic diversity may pose challenges and deferral the mass consumption of AI, but such time needs to be sensibly utilized in conniving ethics, principles and frameworks to address related dilemmas [27].

References

1. Ambite, J.L. and Knoblock, C.A., Planning by rewriting. *J. Artif. Intell. Res.*, 15, 207–261, 2001.

2. Balazinski, M., Czogala, E., Jemielniak, K., Leslie, J., Tool condition monitoring using artificial intelligence methods. *Eng. Appl. Artif. Intell.*, 15, 1, 73–80, 2002.

3. Baldwin, H., *Artificial Intelligence Finds A Home In The Restaurant Industry Technology Can Help Restauranteurs Eliminate Costly Mistakes FSR*, NC, USA. 2016, Retrieved from https://www.foodnewsfeed.com.

4. Chan, C.W. and Huangb, G.H., Artificial intelligence for management and control of pollution minimisation and mitigation processes. *Eng. Appl. Artif. Intell.*, 16, 2, 75–90, 2003.

5. Chen, X. and Van Beek, P., Conflict-directed back jumping revisited. *J. Artif. Intell. Res.*, 14, 53–81, 2001.

6. Cristani, M., The complexity of reasoning about spatial congruence. *J. Artif. Intell. Res.*, 11, 361–390, 1999.

7. Devillers, L., Vidrascu, L., Lamel, L., Challenges in real life emotion annotation and machine learning based detection, in: *Neural Networks*, 1st ed., pp. 407–422, Elsevier, Orsay Cedex, France, 2005.

8. Franklin, J., The representation of context: Ideas from artificial intelligence. *Law Probab. Risk*, 2, 3, 191–199, 2003.

9. Goyache, F., Artificial intelligence techniques point out differences in classification performance between light and standard bovine carcasses. *Meat Sci.*, 64, 3, 219–331, 2003.

10. Halal, W.E., Artificial intelligence is almost here. *On the Horizon, The Strategic Planning Resource for Education Professionals*, pp. 37–3811, 2, 2003.

11. Hong, J., Goal recognition through goal graph analysis. *J. Artif. Intell. Res.*, 15, 1–30, 2001.

12. Kearns, M., Littman, M.L., Singh, S., Stone, P., ATTAC-2000: An adaptive autonomous bidding agent. *J. Artif. Intell. Res.*, 15, 189–206, 2001.

13. S., The future of fast food: KFC opens restaurant run by AI ROBOTS in Shanghai, 2016. Mail online. Retrieved from http://www.dailymail.co.uk-Lotfi A.

14. Zadeh, From Computing with Numbers to Computing with Words—From Manipulation of Measurements to Manipulation of Perceptions, in: *IEEE Transactions on Circuits and Systems I: Fundamental Theory and Applications*, 1st ed., p. 105119, IEEE Computer Society, Berkeley, CA 1999.

15. Masnikosa, V.P., The fundamental problem of an artificial intelligence realization. *Kybernetes*, pp. 71–80. 27, 1, 1998.

16. Metaxiotis, K., Ergazakis, K., Samouilidis, E., Psarras, J., Decision support through knowledge management: The role of the artificial intelligence. *Inform. Manag. Comput. Secur.*, pp. 216–221. 11, 5, 2003.

17. Newell, T., Artificial Intelligence Could Change the Fast Food Industry in a Major Way, FOODBEAST, 2017. Retrieved from https://www.foodbeast.com.

18. Peng, Y. and Zhang, X., Integrative data mining in systems biology: From text to network mining. *Artif. Intell. Med.*, 41, 2, 83–86, 2007.

19. Ramesh, A.N., Kambhampati, C., Monson, J.R.T., Drew, P.J., Artificial intelligence in medicine. *Ann. R. Coll. Surg. Engl.*, 86, 5, 334–338, 2004.

20. Raynor, W.J., The international dictionary of artificial intelligence. *Ref. Rev.*, 380. 14, 6, 2000.

21. Singer, J., Gent, I.P., Smaill, A., Backbone fragility and the local search cost peak. *J. Artif. Intell. Res.*, 12, 235–270, 2000.

22. Stefanuk, V.L. and Zhozhikashvili, A.V., Productions and rules in artificial intelligence. *Kybernetes: The International Journal of Systems & Cybernetics*, 817–826. 31, 6, 2002.

23. Tay, D.P.H. and Ho, D.K.H., Artificial intelligence and the mass appraisal of residential apartments. *J. Prop. Valuat. Invest.*, 525–540. 10, 2, 1992.

24. Toni, A.D., Nassmbeni, G., Tonchia, S., An artificial, intelligence-based production scheduler. *Integr. Manuf. Syst.*, 17–25. 7, 3, 1996.

25. Wang, S., Wang, Y., Du, W., Sun, F., Wang, X., Zhou, C., Liang, Y., A multi-approaches-guided genetic algorithm with application to operon prediction. *Artif. Intell. Med.*, 41, 2, 151–159, 2007.

26. Wongpinunwatana, N., Ferguson, C., Bowen, P., An experimental investigation of the effects of artificial intelligence systems on the training of novice auditors. *Manag. Audit. J.*, 306–318. 15, 6, 2000.

27. Zeng, Z., Pantic, M., Roisman, G.I., Huang, T.S., A Survey of Affect Recognition Methods: Audio, Visual, and Spontaneous Expressions. *IEEE Trans. Pattern Anal. Mach. Intell.*, 31, 1, 39–58, 2009.

6

Classifier for DDoS Attack Detection in Software Defined Networks

Gaganjot Kaur* and Prinima Gupta

Manav Rachna University, Faridabad, India

Abstract

Software Defined Networks has been emerged to transform the networking standards by making networking portable, programmable and autonomous by completely decoupling the standardised control and data planes. As SDN is assuring to provide more reliable and effective networking the challenges of providing a safe and secure network over the cloud is one of the most important target. The cloud performance gets affected by most of the cyber threats in which Distributed Denial of Service attacks (DDoS) are considered as one of the vulnerable threat over the cloud. These attacks generally make the cloud servers a victim and hence degrading the performance of the cloud. These attacks are normally intending the mitigating machines in synchronised way making the machines as victim of deliberate damage. The extensive work depicted here is the successful novel classifier that gives the best characterization precision by diminishing the order blunder rate for the KDD2000 informational index as is a powerful way to deal with recognizes DDoS assaults in SDN. The rising Software-Defined Networking (SDN) approach has demonstrated progressively encouraging upgrades in tending to DDoS flooding attacks. Finally, test outcomes display the recommended estimation that has an extraordinary execution, and the proposed structure changes with enhancing the security of the IoT with heterogeneous and feeble contraptions.

Keywords: Classifier, KDD 2000, Internet of Things (IoT), distributed denial of service attacks, software defined network, errors and attacks

Corresponding author: gaganjot@mru.edu.in

Parul Gandhi, Surbhi Bhatia, Abhishek Kumar, Mohammad Alojail and Pramod Singh Rathore (eds.) *Internet of Things in Business Transformation: Developing an Engineering and Business Strategy for Industry 5.0*, (71–90) © 2021 Scrivener Publishing LLC

6.1   Introduction

SDN is an advanced way that facilitates all the network nodes to administer the networking using programming, rather than existing system administration methods. SDN gives software the capability to control the network. It allows the network to virtualise the traffic based on how control plane and data plane are configured. SDN allows decoupling of the hardware from the software layer. SDN mainly emphasize the control over how the data is to be flowed along with the network traffic. SDNs guarantee overseers the capacity to shape the system any way they need. The SDN additionally enables heads to set the guidelines and controls through a product interface. SDN is depended upon to direct the way where that the stagnant architecture of standard frameworks is decentralized and complex while energy frameworks require continuously prominent adaptability and clear inquisitive about. SDN attempts to tie together coordinate comprehension in one system part by disassociating the sending procedure of information plane from the control plane. The control plane contains at any rate one controller which are considered as the cerebrum of SDN that masterminds where the whole understanding is intertwined. Software Defined Networking (SDN) is a system setup avenue which empowers the structure to be wonderfully and generally controlled, or 'changed', utilizing programming applications [1].

Figure 6.1 represents a product characterized that organize design of SDN which characterizes how a systems administration and figuring framework can be delivered utilizing a mix of open, programming based advances and thing orchestrating equipment that unmistakable the SDN control plane and the SDN information plane of the systems association stack. This assists administrators with managing the entire framework dependably and thoroughly, paying little brain to the concealed framework development. By isolating control and the executives from an assortment of gadgets, organize components and availability circuits that make up the system, an endeavour can make pool of absolute system limit from these circuits to use varying, while at the same time empowering deceivability all through the system. SDN controller has the overall point of view on the framework, yet it is feeble against DDoS assault. The territory of DDoS requires versatile and address classifier that does major activity from faulty data. It is in a general sense to perceive the ambushes in the controller at prior stage. SVM is exhaustively utilized classifier with high exactness and less phony positive rate. Recently, AI and ML information mining strategies are assuming a basic job in the recognition and the grouping

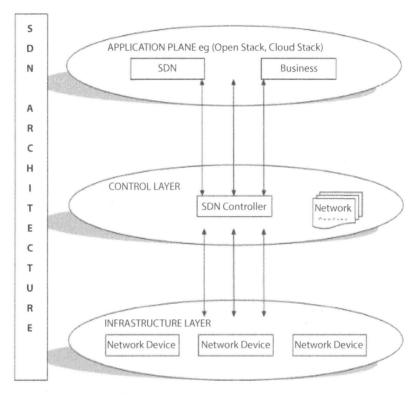

Figure 6.1 Architecture of SDN.

of interruption attacks. A few AI considers have been directed in various areas [2] but just a couple of these are on SDN. In SDN it is progressively hard to moderate the DDoS attacks because the switches handle the parcels just by stream passage got from the controller. They can't identify the malevolent streams. DDoS attacks are one of the genuine system security dangers confronting the Internet. DDoS attacks are propelled from the undermined hosts associated with the SDN switches. Continuous DDoS attacks have revealed that get away from statements are omnipresent in IoT, whichever is notwithstanding in the concealed stage. Outwardly safeguarding the prudent steps, by a wide margin the vast majority of IoT devices may unintentionally become aides to DDoS attacks. SDN is without a doubt the most perceived innovation, and its inside development is the segment of the control plane and data plane in the framework. It comprehends versatile control of framework traffic and gives a not too bad stage to the improvement of focus frameworks and applications. We examine the SVM classifier and balance it with various classifiers for DDoS area.

The straightforward technique behind a disavowal of administration (DoS) attacks is to preclude the utilization from securing framework assets to real clients and corrupt the framework accessibility. The essential instrument for DoS attacks execution is to send a surge of pointless system traffic to the objective with the goal that it can't react to certified solicitations for administrations or data. In the event that numerous sources are utilized by the attacker(s), it is called DDoS attacks, which is considerably more cataclysmic than DoS. The expansion of cell phones, yet in addition developing innovations, for example, the Internet of Things (IoT) will copy the amount of framework contraptions with front line at whatever point wherever benefits. SDNs decouple orchestrate control and sending limits enabling the framework to end up being truly procurable, and the principle structure that are distracted for pertinence and framework organizations. Framework information is authentically united trusted in formulating positioned auditors which accumulate up an overall point of view on the arrangement of hosts, and thing hardware and programming switches, which are imbecilic sending substances. With the methodology of Software Defined Networks (SDNs), there has been a quick progression in the territory of distributed computing. It is currently versatile, less expensive, and simpler to oversee. There is fundamental research on the best way to reinforce and upgrade the security of the IoT with SDN innovation. AI procedures are currently sent in the SDN framework for the location of malevolent traffic. AI approaches utilize the machine to pick up, following via preparing as indicated by the SDN in the stream peculiarities of the guide to secure the best acquirement model. In the conventional system architecture, the principle techniques for DDoS attacks identification innovation can be isolated into the attack location dependent on traffic qualities and attacks recognition dependent on traffic irregularity. The previous for the most part gathers a wide range of attributes data identified with the attacks and builds up a qualities database of DDoS attacks. By looking at and breaking down the information data of the present system information parcel and qualities database, we can decide whether it is attacks by DDoS or not. AI figurings like Naïve Bayes, K-Nearest neighbors (KNN), K-Means, K-Medoids have been used therefore [3]. The primary execution techniques are qualities coordinate, model thinking, state change, and master frameworks. The last is principally to set up influx illustration and investigation of anomalous stream transformation, to decide if the influx movement is irregular or not, in order to identify whether if the computing machines were invaded. DDoS attacks is most usually used to attacks the controller. DDoS attacks is an attacks wherein a few arranged PC structures attacks a goal, for instance, a site, server or other framework inventiveness provoking a renouncing of organization of the concentrated on measures for the customers. The objective machines are compelled to back off or here and there even crash and close somewhere near the flood of moving toward messages, affiliation requests or twisted bundles, therefore refusing assistance to genuine clients or machines. The aggressor utilizes traded off or arranged frameworks to introduce devices expected to attacks the server. Such undermined frameworks are known as bots or zombies. Shirking against DDoS assaults has been a critical point of convergence of the assessment organized. One response for perceiving such interferences and DDoS attacks is by masterminding the relationship into standard and idiosyncrasy [4].

6.2   Related Work

Latest investigations demonstrate that SDN assistance for IoT is accomplished as in getting brought together direct, reflection of system gadgets and adaptable, effective and mechanized reformation of systems. The joining of SDN and IoT is a conceivably doable answer for fortify the administration and control abilities of the IoT arrange [5] suggested a planning specified design for the SDN controller that prompts powerful attacks restriction during DDoS attacks outlined the execution, identification and relief of DDoS attacks in the SDN condition. Explored a stream rule flooding DDoS attacks, and concentrated a novel DDoS attacks focusing on the information plane of SDN. There is fundamental research on the most proficient method to reinforce and upgrade the security of the IoT with SDN innovation. Ref. [6] proposed a safe and disseminated design for IoT dependent on the SDN space. Costa-Requena *et al.* [7] proposed a planning based SDN controller engineering as far as possible attacks and ensure organizes in DoS attacks. In latest survey, numerous strategies have been acquainted with recognize and break down DDoS attacks. There has been a great extent of research on DDoS alleviation utilizing customary system insurance strategies and heuristics, for example, IP follow back, inconsistency recognition, entrance/departure sifting, ISP collective barrier, organize self-likeness [7]. These methodologies, nonetheless, have all demonstrated noteworthy constraints as suitable answers for relieving the DDoS attacks. A great extent of investigation on DDoS relief utilizing customary system insurance strategies and heuristics, for example, IP follow back, irregularity discovery, entrance/departure filtering, and ISP collective protection, organize self-closeness [8]. These methodologies, notwithstanding, have all demonstrated huge constraints as reasonable answers for alleviating the DDoS attacks. Most of current identification ventures rely on highlight determination from the IP parcels caught. Mouhammd Alkasassbeh *et al.* has taken all the 27 highlights within thought for an innovative dataset that encloses the cutting edge DDoS attacks in the distinctive system layers, for example, (SIDDoS, HTTP Flood). Sherif Saad *et al.* proposed another methodology for describing and distinguishing botnets utilizing system traffic practices. This methodology centers on identifying freshest and most testing kinds of botnets before they dispatch their attack. Distinctive AI methods have been used to reconcile the connected botnet recognizable identification necessities, to be specific flexibility, curiosity location, and early recognition. The aftereffects of the exploratory assessment subject to dataset taken exhibited that it is possible to perceive reasonably botnets during the botnet Command-and-Control (C&C) arrange and before they dispatch their assaults using traffic rehearses just [9]. SDN being a solitary essential issue of contact is effectively agreeable for attacks moreover. The most widely recognized and developing issue is DDOS attacks which develop as far as recurrence, volume and seriousness. This paper centers on breaking down the issue of attacks and further recommending the execution of AI calculations to arrange and distinguish the attacks. Crossover approach of Random backwoods calculation and Decision Tree Algorithm on Scapy Tool with substantial rundown of IPs have created exact after effects of distinguishing attacks. Additionally the downsides of usage of other AI calculations are indicated [10]. Ref. [11] suggested an affirmation plan improved for SDN against flood attacks reliant on the SVM classifier and another count called Idle-break Adjustment (IA). The makers scruti-nized the prospective arrangement and surveyed the estimations as indi-cated by the amount of streams, the CPU use of the SDN controller and of the Open v Switch. Dillon and Berkelaar [12] proposed an impedance affir-mation methodology by brushing SVM with underground frightening lit-tle creature settlement systems. They determined that CSVAC (Combining strengthen vectors with Ant zone) shows supported outcomes over SVM and Clustering dependent on Self-Organized Ant Colony Network (CSOACN). Multiclass SVM blueprint was finished utilizing one-against all procedure which trains N classifiers and course all N classifiers for testing dull model. This collects the testing time, which is basic for perceiving impedance at a previous stage. DDoS disclosure utilizing a troupe of adapt-able and cream neuro-delicate was suggested by Dillon and Berkelaar [12]. KDD 99 dataset is taken for assessment reason and NFBoost figuring gives high accuracy with less fake positive rate [13]. Tang *et al.* used MLP to recognize break in SDN, using six fundamental features easily obtained with OpenFlow limits. The MLP involves three disguised layers, with the structure and it is organized into two unquestionable classes, getting

75.75% of exactness in the best case. The examination was not acted in a real SDN condition, and despite the structure being given, nothing other than that with respect to the re-order condition was given [14]. In 2003, Ref. [15] used component assurance for interference acknowledgment applying neural frameworks (NNs) in addition, reinforce vector machines (SMVs) to gross the information countenances concurring with each specific class name. In 2009, Yao *et al.* [16] presented a wrapper-based data visage decision system to locate the maximum huge data features from the planning information administering unpredictable change slant escalating strategy, and by then uses straight assistance vector machine (SVM) to help the show of picked subset of information features. Jaur and Gupta [17] present a distinguishing proof methodology for DDoS attacks against SDN controller. They inject tremendous number of streams with very few groups (low-traffic streams). The acknowledgment system is proposed to discover the undermined interfaces where harmful attackers are related. Also, they show courses of action of DDoS attacks presented in standard framework that could create DDoS attacks against SDN controller. DDOS attacks on SDN are an undesirable assault to upset the conventional movement of the network bottlenecking the flattened movement of bundles on the framework thus sabotaging the redemption of the network. The paper demonstrates a prose system called Principal Component Analysis Recurrent Neural Network. According to this technique the framework peculiarities are perceived to portray the framework of the network. The structure is being expected for the recognizable proof and easing of DDOS attack for a colossal scale sort out accepting the definition to be cultivated for a splendid city. The current DDOS assault strategies accepts assured upsides and drawbacks and result is demonstrated contemplating the various specifications of precision, exactness and F score which is similarly differentiated and distinctive DDoS attack disclosure systems. PCA RNN is contemplated as one of the estimation decline strategy as it picks the yield estimations as per the genuine necessities. PCA RNN is similarly pre owned to improve the neural framework model. For forthcoming advertents the figuring can be taken a stab at progressively veritable educational files to consider continuously characteristic features of the identical [18]. At this moment outline is effected of Machine learning approaches used to complete SDN based Network Intrusion Detection System. For up and coming ramifications the troubles that are been discussed of giving increasingly critical exactness and flexibility can be cultivated using ML/DL strategies for NIDS. Disclosure of tremendous progressed DDoS attack from streak events using information estimations in programming described frameworks, 2018 IEEE International Conference [19], at the present time DDOS assaults are perceived by generally centralizing on the openflow enlighten-ment. As DDOS attacks are the essential collateral stress in the SDN the maker prescribes to recognize the attacks using a couple of estimations like General Entropy and Generalized Information Distance. The estimations regards are totally vulnerable on the movement of the network. The acknowledgment figuring is recommended by the movement of bundles and its instruction is taken care of in the header field that exists for SDN. The estimation regards are continuously reasonable for perceiving high rate DDOS assaults. For forthcoming endeavors it is obvious that as indi-cated by the certified traffic circumstance revelations can be made even more early and mitigations would be cultivated even more successfully [20]. In Ref. [21], the makers used a mix of SDN and AI systems to distin-guish and square upgrade contemplation attacks (DrDoS). The OpenFlow switch imitates the traffic to the disclosure administrator, which applies the assistance vector machine (SVM) method to arrange the groups as noxious or non-poisonous. On acknowledgment of malicious lead, the revelation administrator encourages the controller to frustrate the malignant bun-dles. Peng *et al.* [22] recommended a two-level weight altering game plan in SDN frameworks to manufacture perseverance time of a structure during DDoS attack. Their essential endeavour is encumbrance changing and in doing so they don't lighten DDoS attack anyway they had the alter-native to manufacture the continuance time by parcelling the heap. Hadianto and Purboyo [23] proposed a crossbreed countermeasure to hinder associ-ate mocking assaults in the SD-IoT controller [24] made two proactive shield frameworks for SD-IoT with non-patchable vulnerabilities. DDOS Attacks are in a general sense unavoidable and absurd use of benefits. SDN is a philosophy extensively preowned by the present framework where in it thinks the frame of references control so improving the ability to accumu-late the framework information. The current circumstance have used AI approaches to manage recognize DDOS attacks. At the present time is worked for revelation of inevitable movement of network stream using KNN procedure. The computation revealed right now higher precision rate, lower sham positive rate and better difference in acknowledgment of the assaults on SDN stood out from various figurings [25]. In this, the author proposes an identification plan to recognize DDOS attacks depen-dent on time highlight. The absolute first assignment for recognition is to examine the conduct of the attack on the system. Example acknowledg-ment of neural system procedure is utilized to perceive the attack and appropriately the move is made [26]. The outcome is assessed taking DARPA informational index and the outcome is then contrasted and suc-cessive likelihood proportion test. Subsequently after examination it's discovered that the arrangement which creator have offered assists with identifying attacks all the more rapidly and accurately. The trust the board protective cap (TMH) model plans to separate authentic clients from aggressors by enrolling four kinds of positiveness required to figure and accumulated as a major aspect of a permit at customers for session association with the server safely [27]. Research paper displays a traffic arrangement plan to enhance characterization execution when barely any preparation information are accessible is utilized. The traffic streams are depicted utilizing the factual highlights and traffic stream data is separated. A traffic grouping strategy is proposed to total the Naïve Bayes expectations of the traffic streams. Since order plot depends on the back restrictive probabilities, it can distinguish attacks happening in a questionable circumstance. The exploratory outcomes show that the proposed plan can productively arrange bundles than existing traffic grouping techniques and accomplished 92.34% exactness. In writing overview it has been examined that all things considered SDN being a rising worldview is utilized and required all over yet the significant worry to be taken consideration is the security. The significant concern is of DDOS attacks and there are different conventional strategies used to recognize the attacks. DDOS attacks on the controller bring the whole system at end and along these lines it's required to distinguish and moderate the dangers on the controller. SDN can streamline IoT's attachment and-play predefined strategies for arrange gadgets, naturally recognize and cure collateral amenableness, design edge registering and examine the earth of the information stream. The conveyed disavowal of administration (DDoS) attacks has expanded steeply with more gadgets to bargain and less secure focuses to attack. The IoT systems have been a significant casualty of the DDoS attacks because of their asset obliged qualities. Shielding IoT-empowered gadgets and systems from DDoS attacks and being undermined to play out the DDoS attack is a difficult undertaking [28].

6.3   DDoS Attacks Overview

DDoS attack is an attack which is focused by various traded off PCs called as bots or zombies concentrating on a solitary framework. Its inspiration is to make the target framework or system asset consumption, with the objective that the administration is by chance thwarted or quit, prompting administration inaccessibility. DDoS attack is detached into seven fundamental classes which are: flood attack, increase attack, core melt attack, land attack, TCP SYN attack, CGI request attack, and affirmation server attack. DDoS attacks are intended to debilitate the unfortunate casualty's assets, for example, organize transmission capacity, registering power, and working framework information structures. SDN is a system design in which the system traffic might be worked and oversaw powerfully as per client prerequisites and requests. Appropriated disavowal of administration attack targets impeding the accessibility of assets in the system. This errand is accomplished by a gathering of gadgets that are intentionally or unwittingly associated with the attack. Vindictive client floods the system assets with a lot of futile traffic to deplete them subsequently, noxious traffic gets served yet veritable parcels keep for administrations on the grounds that from bundle flood or clog. Research says that least complex possible and most fundamental stress of framework security is DDoS attacks. As indicated by Arbors organize report in 2014, "DDoS attacks against clients remain the main operational danger seen during the overview time frame 2013–2014, with DDoS attacks against foundation being the top worry for 2014." Attackers predominantly center on devastating the framework as opposed to attacking clients. As indicated by report [29], most basic focuses for attacks are ventures, Internet specialist co-ops, and web based gaming locales. DDoS attacks could be extensively named convention based attacks, volume-based attacks, and application layer attack [30]. Appropriated Denial of Service (DDoS) attacks have been a genuine danger in numerous parts of PC organizes and conveyed applications. The fundamental goal of a DDoS attack is to cut down the administrations of an objective utilizing numerous sources that are appropriated. For instance, assailants can move a large number of parcels to an unfortunate casualty to overpower its entrance data transmission with ill-conceived traffic, making on the web administrations inaccessible. The goal of a DDoS attack is to cut down the administrations of an objective utilizing various authorities that are conveyed. A commonplace case of this kind of attack is the flooding based attack in which an unfortunate casualty is overpowered with the monstrous measure of system traffic sent to it. The possibility of DDoS assaults rotates around a reality that countless sources dispersed over various areas are utilized to focus on an injured individual. There are various disavowals of administration (DoS) attack techniques being utilized to debase the presentation or accessibility of focused administrations on the Internet. Usually, these strategies can be delegated difficulties related with the SDN at each layer of the structure, application, control, and framework. Circulated Denial of Service (DDoS) attack is a sort of DoS attack that the barrage of concurrent information is getting to the server to shroud the accessibility of assets in the system. As per the condition of the web security, summer 2018 report, the biggest DDoS attack with a record top 1.35 Tbps was seen on Wednesday, February 28, 2018. Right now DDoS attack, the aggressors didn't utilize any botnet arrange. The DoS attacks normally develops as the traded off host spots single framework by sending surge of pointless deals. The primary objective of this attack is to diminish framework accessibility and keep real clients from getting to accessible administrations. In the event that assailants utilize numerous hosts rather than just one to target single framework which is the controller, this is called DDoS attacks [31].

6.4   Types of DDoS Attacks

Distinctive DDoS attack vectors target differing segments of a system association. All DDoS attacks include overpowering an objective gadget or system with traffic, attacks can be partitioned into three classifications: Volume Based, Protocol Based and Application Based. An aggressor may make utilize one or numerous distinctive attack vectors, or cycle attack vectors possibly dependent on counter estimates taken by the objective [32]. Figure 6.2 gives the representation of various DDOS attacks types.

Volume Based Attack—This type of DDoS attacks depend with respect to the volume of inbound traffic. The objective of this sort of attack is to over-burden the network's data transmission or cause CPU or IOPS use issues. The attacker utilizes a fundamental strategy—more assets dominate this match. On the off chance that they can over-burden your assets, the attack is fruitful. It is very simple for attackers to accomplish their objectives. Most site proprietors are utilizing imparted has and the ones to virtual private server (VPS) conditions are regularly set up in

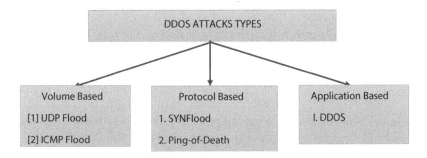

Figure 6.2 DDoS attacks types.

the littlest levels and arrangements. Volume based attacks include UDP floods, Ping floods and ICMP floods. In all the attacks the attacker attack the network based on the traffic flow and finally this kind of attack may also results in entire server breakdown of the network. Protocol Based Attack—The web depends on conventions. It's the manner by which things get from direct A toward point B. DDoS attacks dependent on conventions abuse shortcomings in Layers 3 and 4 convention stacks. This sort of attack devours the server assets, or some other system equipment, highly involved with handling limits. The outcome is administration disturbance. These attacks attempt to misuse your system stack by sending either a larger number of bundles than what your server can deal with or more transmission capacity than what your system ports can deal with. The convention abuse attack focuses on the gadget assets and application assets, that is it influences the primary working of the unfortunate casualty by depleting the assets, for example, memory, data transfer capacity, and so on. The different types of protocol based attacks are SYN flood and Ping of Death. These attacks results in server breakdown by affecting the three way handshake communication of TCP protocol between client, server and the host machine. Application based DDoS attack—The objective of these attacks is to deplete the assets of the destination. The attacks focus on the layer where site pages are produced on the server and conveyed because of HTTP demands. A solitary HTTP demand is modest to execute on the customer side, and can be costly for the objective server to react to as the server regularly should stack different records and run database questions so as to make a website page. Application level DDoS attacks come as HTTP GET floods. HTTP demand attacks are those attacks where assailants send HTTP GETs and POSTs to Web servers trying to flood them by expending a lot of assets [33]. These attacks are typically littler than the ones we have seen previously. By and by, the outcome of an application layer attack can be detestable, since they can go unnoticed until it is past the point where it is possible to respond. That is the reason they are classified "low and slow attacks" or even "moderate rate attacks". They can be quiet and little, particularly when contrasted with arrange layer attacks, yet they can be similarly as disruptive. Application assets essentially sends association demands and in the end over weights the injured individual bringing about neglecting to recognize any more association demands. Application-layer attacks (for the most part known as Layer 7 attacks) can be a piece of attacks which focus on the application, yet additionally the data transfer capacity and system. Attacks targeting the DNS server and HTTP flood attack are common application attacks which not only result in the server breakdown but also make the target machine unavailable and breaking the entire network [34].

6.5   DDoS Detection Techniques in SDN

Significant piece of the assurance against DDoS attacks is their recognition. There are numerous techniques identifying other attack classes, for example, recognition of Malware or Botnets. Since malware could make botnets and botnets are utilized for DDoS attacks, these location strategies can be assistance to the relief of DDoS attacks. The discovery of DDoS attacks can be founded on a few systems. SDN systems have unmistakable discovery strategies for various kinds of DDoS attacks. These strategies incorporate entropy-based, AI based, traffic design analysis, association rate, and procedures that consolidate the utilization of the IDS and OpenFlow. The most clear is a call from the person in question. In any case, this isn't the most exact strategy and don't scale well. Different procedures are increasingly logical dependent on have observing or organize stream checking. Checking of host markers, for example, utilized data transfer capacity, CPU use can bring up on progressing attack or an attack experiencing the system. This identification can show irregularities yet should be trailed by an examination of system traffic. The other technique dependent on organize stream observing is increasingly valuable and is progressively nitty gritty. Stream checking is widely portrayed by [35]. It is right now the most utilized innovation in Intrusion Detection Systems and abnormality detection. Approaches to recognizing and relieving DDoS attacks might be founded on measurable investigation, information base, or AI and information mining procedures. DDoS can be recognized when the volume of bundles in a system increment abruptly. There are different DDoS identification systems dependent on various methodologies [36].

6.6   Detection Using ML Techniques

AI based-arrangements are another way to deal with distinguished DDoS attacks in contrast to the controller in the SDN. ML is utilized to characterize of parcels. Calculations are prepared utilizing ordered dataset. In the wake of preparing it is competent to characterize structure ordinary to unusual bundles. Different ML calculations are utilized for interruption location. Calculations like Naïve Bayes, SVM, Decision Tree and so forth are utilized in bundle investigation. In these sorts of arrangements, the barrier system that was prepared by encouraging free attack streams (preparing) into AI calculation can recognize attack streams (testing) recommended a strategy to recognize DDoS attacks contrary to the controller by utilizing bolster vector machine (SVM) classifier [36]. SVM is one sort of huge edge classifier and sort of AI. It is utilized basically to discover the choice limit or a model that isolates focuses to at least two gatherings. For instance, let us accept that we have a dataset of preparing tests, and each purpose of these examples is set apart as have a place with some gathering. SVM makes a model to isolate these present information by drawing an unmistakable choice limit or whole that is as wide as could reasonably be expected. The information focuses that made this limit are known as the help vector focuses. At that point, this model classifies new datasets on a similar space as per which side of the hole they fall [37]. Mark based interruption discovery framework expect director to incorporate standards and marks to identify attacks. It requires a few worker hours to test, make and convey these marks and again make new for obscure attacks. Peculiarity put together IDS based with respect to AI method gives the answer for this issue they help in creating a framework that can gain from information and give expectation to the inconspicuous information dependent on the educated information. Machine Learning based methodologies can give progressively unique, increasingly proficient, and more brilliant answers for SDN executives, security, and improvement [38].

6.7   Proposed Work Using SVM Classifier

In the proposed work to detect DDoS attack a classifier used is a Support Vector Machine (SVM) discriminative classifier authoritatively portrayed by a disengaging hyper plane. So to speak, given checked getting ready data (directed learning), the figuring yields a perfect hyper plane which orchestrates new models. SVMs can deal with both straightforward, direct, order assignments, just as increasingly unpredictable, for example nonlinear, arrangement problems. It proposed Intrusion discovery strategy utilizing Support Vector Machine (SVM). This SVM the enormous edge classifier may help decline the mistakes in figuring. This improves the grouping task since focuses that are situated close to the choice limit have unsure characterization choice. At the end of the day, the vulnerability in the grouping choice might be diminished by making the edge sufficiently enormous. Second, as long as the edge is adequately tremendous, the model may have little alternatives of where data fit. Accordingly, as far as possible may be reduced, and this extends the ability to precisely portray data [39]. They additionally utilized component expulsion strategy to improve the effectiveness. The SVM classifier used is because the principle advantage for the same to be picked up in utilizing an enthusiastic learning technique, for example, a fake neural system, is that the objective capacity will be approximated internationally during preparing, subsequently requiring considerably less space than utilizing a sluggish learning framework. Energetic learning frameworks additionally bargain much better with clamour in the preparation information. Energetic learning is a case of disconnected learning, wherein present preparing questions on the framework have no impact on the framework itself, and in this way a similar inquiry to the framework will consistently create a similar outcome [40].

6.8   Data Set Used

The KDD informational index is a notable benchmark in the exploration of Intrusion Detection techniques. The unique KDD Cup informational index is a gigantic informational index for interruption location created by DARPA. The characteristic issue of KDD informational collection has prompted the improvement of new informational index known as NSL-KDD information set. This new informational index has beaten numerous issues like excess instances. KDD cup dataset anyway experiences different issues, for example, repetition, irregularity and it isn't standardized consequently we have utilized significantly better NSL-KDD informational index which and chose about 100K records with 42 properties and 22 Classes. The KDD informational index is a standard informational index utilized for the examination on interruption location frameworks [41].

6.9   Proposed Methodology

In the proposed work right now, DDoS guard frameworks are conveyed in the system to identify and forestall DDoS attacks autonomously. For that absolute initial step is to standardize the informational collection followed by building the classifier model on the informational collection and afterward playing out the calculation accordingly computing the weirdness and precision that gauges the appropriation of each component like likelihood of unusual conduct, mistake resilience, affectability, detection ratio. After the algorithm being implemented the result will also be evaluated in terms of accuracy rate, detecting false and true positive rate for the detection of attacks and checking the effect of time on the quantity of information packets received and number of packets lost. Also, it is essential to distinguish instruments that could be utilized in the examination of traffic.

6.10   Existing & Proposed Results

In the existing result for the parameters been used for detection of attacks in general using approach of KNN, Naïve Bayesian, Random forest the accuracy comes out to be 95.9, 91.4 and 99.5% respectively but using the proposed classifier of SVM for the detection of attacks for the 100K sample size the rate of detection is expected to be 99.8% and also specifying what kind of detects are harming the network. The expected outcomes specify that our calculation will definitely improve the exhibition of system and all the DDoS attacks will be identified much precisely.

6.11   Conclusion & Future Work

Security in actuality the hugest worries concerning the sending of SDN to tries needs real thought. Regardless of the way that SDN being concentrated programming use settle various issues that were accessible in the traditional framework, yet at some point or another, it transforms into the bottleneck for as a rule organize. Attack distinguishing is a wide subject of research for distributed computing that means to make the Cloud a safe and confided in stage for the conveyance of future Internet of Things. Our fundamental centre was to talk about conceivable DDoS dangers in SDN and alleviations which are been recommended till date. Right now work and its philosophy is examined which will be executed utilizing KDD informational index. The proposed model will refresh process sparing a lot of time contrasted with recovering a model while enduring barely any exhibition misfortune as far as location exactness. Later on, we mean to stretch out framework to totally beat the issue of DDoS with more effectiveness just as to improve the proposed work to distinguish the aggressors in any event, when they fulfill the known parameter value. Software-characterized arrange is the most recent engineering that has not yet been investigated totally. All the arrangements that have been recommended to verify it depend on its structure. Later on, it will be intriguing to perceive how assailants misuse SDN's helplessness to bargain the system. With focal engineering, defunctioning the system turns out to be very simple with simply trading off a solitary segment. In this way, early discovery of DDoS gets significant. Aggressors are thinking of new thoughts consistently to bargain the system. Subsequently, DDoS recognition plans must be with the end goal that they address new sort of dangers notwithstanding the distinguished ones. Future work will concentrate on usage of the proposed work and in addition will likewise concentrate on the most proficient method to proactively protect against DDoS assaults in SDN for IoT. For future perspective the parameters for the proposed work can likewise be grouped which can be explicitly implied for ongoing assault traffic identification and alleviation planned to security challenges [42].

References

1. J. N. Bakker, B. Ng, and W. K. G. Seah, Can machine learning techniques be effectively used in real networks against DDoS attacks? in *Proceedings - International Conference on Computer Communications and Networks, ICCCN*, 2018, https://ieeexplore.ieee.org/document/8487445.

2. S. Sezer *et al.*, Are we ready for SDN? Implementation challenges for software-defined networks, *IEEE Commun. Mag.*, 2013, https://ieeexplore.ieee.org/document/6553676.

3. Q. Li, L. Meng, Y. Zhang, and J. Yan, DDoS attacks detection using machine learning algorithms, in *Communications in Computer and Information Science*, 2019, https://doi.org/10.1007/978-981-13-8138-6_170

4. J. H. Jafarian, E. Al-Shaer, and Q. Duan, OpenFlow random host mutation: Transparent moving target defense using software defined networking, in HotSDN'12 - *Proceedings of the 1st ACM International Workshop on Hot Topics in Software Defined Networks*, 2012, https://doi.org/10.1145/2342441.2342467.

5. Open Networking Foundation, Software-Defined Networking: The New Norm for Networks white paper., ONF White Pap., 2012.

6. Open Networking Foundation, SDN Architecture Overview. version 1.0, ONF White Paper, 2013.

7. Open Networking Foundation, OpenFlow-enabled SDN and Network Function Virtualization. ONF Solution Brief, 2014.

8. M. H. Raza, S. C. Sivakumar, A. Nafarieh, and B. Robertson, A comparison of software defined network (SDN) implementation strategies, in *Procedia Computer Science*, 2014, https://doi.org/10.1016/j.procs.2014.05.532.

9. A. Darabseh, M. Al-Ayyoub, Y. Jararweh, E. Benkhelifa, M. Vouk, and A. Rindos, SDDC: A Software Defined Datacenter Experimental Framework, in *Proceedings - 2015 International Conference on Future Internet of Things and Cloud, FiCloud 2015 and 2015 International Conference on Open and Big Data*, OBD 2015, 2015, https://dl.acm.org/doi/10.1109/FiCloud.2015.127.

10. A. Akhunzada, E. Ahmed, A. Gani, M. K. Khan, M. Imran, and S. Guizani, Securing software defined networks: Taxonomy, requirements,

and open issues, IEEE Commun. Mag., 2015, https://ieeexplore.ieee.org/document/7081073.

11. B. Wang, Y. Zheng, W. Lou, and Y. T. Hou, DDoS attack protection in the era of cloud computing and Software-Defined Networking, Comput. Networks, 2015, https://dl.acm.org/doi/10.1016/j.comnet.2015.02.026.

12. R. Kandoi and M. Antikainen, Denial-of-service attacks in OpenFlow SDN networks, in *Proceedings of the 2015 IFIP/IEEE International Symposium on Integrated Network Management, IM 2015*, 2015, https://ieeexplore.ieee.org/document/7140489.

13. M. Dhawan, R. Poddar, K. Mahajan, and V. Mann, SPHINX: Detecting Security Attacks in Software-Defined Networks, 2015, https://www.ndss-symposium.org/ndss2015/ndss-2015-programme/sphinx-detecting-security-attacks-software-defined-networks/.

14. I. Sofi, A. Mahajan, and V. Mansotra, Machine Learning Techniques used for the Detection and Analysis of Modern Types of DDoS Attacks, *Int. Res. J. Eng. Technol.*, 2017.

15. Niketa Chellani, Prateek Tejpal, Prashant Hari, Vishal Neeralike , Enhancing Security in OpenFlow, Capstone Research Project Proposal, April 22, 2016.

16. L. Barki, A. Shidling, N. Meti, D. G. Narayan, and M. M. Mulla, Detection of distributed denial of service attacks in software defined networks, in 2016 International Conference on Advances in Computing, Communications and Informatics, ICACCI 2016, 2016, *https://ieeexplore.ieee.org/document/7732445*.

17. G. Kaur and P. Gupta, Hybrid Approach for detecting DDOS Attacks in Software Defined Networks, in *2019 12th International Conference on Contemporary Computing, IC3 2019*, 2019, *https://ieeexplore.ieee.org/document/8844944*.

18. N. Z. Bawany, J. A. Shamsi, and K. Salah, DDoS Attack Detection and Mitigation Using SDN: Methods, Practices, and Solutions, Arabian Journal for Science and Engineering. 2017, https://link.springer.com/10.1007/s13369-017-2414-5.

19. J. Liu, Y. Lai, and S. Zhang, FL-GUARD: A detection and defense system for DDoS attack in SDN, in *ACM International Conference Proceeding Series*, 2017, https://dl.acm.org/doi/10.1145/3058060.3058074.

20. A. Alshamrani, A. Chowdhary, S. Pisharody, D. Lu, and D. Huang, A defense system for defeating DDoS attacks in SDN based networks, in *MobiWac 2017 - Proceedings of the 15th ACM International Symposium on Mobility Management and Wireless Access, Co-located with MSWiM 2017*, 2017, https://dl.acm.org/doi/10.1145/3132062.3132074

21. J. Suarez-Varela and P. Barlet-Ros, Towards a NetFlow Implementation for OpenFlow Software-Defined Networks, in *Proceedings of the 29th International Teletraffic Congress, ITC 2017*, 2017, *https://ieeexplore.ieee.org/document/8064355*.

22. K. S. Sahoo, M. Tiwary, and B. Sahoo, Detection of high rate DDoS attack from flash events using information metrics in software defined networks, in 2018

10th International Conference on Communication Systems and Networks, COMSNETS 2018, https://www.researchgate.net/publication/322976769.

23. J. Cui, J. He, Y. Xu, and H. Zhong, TDDAD: Time-based detection and defense scheme against DDoS attack on SDN controller, in Lecture Notes in Computer Science (including subseries Lecture Notes in Artificial Intelligence and Lecture Notes in Bioinformatics), 2018, https://link.springer.com/chapter/10.1007/978-3-319-93638-3_37.

24. Y. Yu, L. Guo, Y. Liu, J. Zheng, and Y. Zong, An efficient SDN-Based DDoS attack detection and rapid response platform in vehicular networks, *IEEE Access*, 2018, https://ieeexplore.ieee.org/document/8408784.

25. H. D'Cruze, P. Wang, R. O. Sbeit, and A. Ray, A software-defined networking (SDN) approach to mitigating DDoS attacks, in Advances in Intelligent Systems and Computing, 2018, https://link.springer.com/chapter/10.1007/978-3-319-54978-1_19.

26. R. Hadianto and T. W. Purboyo, A Survey Paper on Botnet Attacks and Defenses in Software Defined Networking, *Int. J. Appl. Eng. Res.*, 13, 1, 483–489 2018.

27. H. Peng, Z. Sun, X. Zhao, S. Tan, and Z. Sun, A Detection Method for Anomaly Flow in Software Defined Network, *IEEE Access*, 2018, https://www.researchgate.net/publication/325303704.

28. J. Costa-Requena *et al.*, SDN and NFV integration in generalized mobile network architecture, in *2015 European Conference on Networks and Communications, EuCNC 2015*, 2015, *https://ieeexplore.ieee.org/document/7194059*.

29. X. Zhao, Y. Lin, and J. Heikkila, Dynamic texture recognition using multi-scale PCA-learned filters, in *Proceedings - International Conference on Image Processing, ICIP, 2018*, https://www.researchgate.net/publication/323351912.

30. S. Scott-Hayward, S. Natarajan, and S. Sezer, A survey of security in software defined networks, IEEE Communications Surveys and Tutorials. 2016, https://ieeexplore.ieee.org/document/7150550.

31. D. Kreutz, F. M. V. Ramos, and P. Verissimo, Towards secure and dependable software-defined networks, in HotSDN 2013 - Proceedings of the 2013 ACM SIGCOMM Workshop on Hot Topics in Software Defined Networking, 2013, https://doi.acm.org/10.1145/2491185.2491199.

32. M. Antikainen, T. Aura, and M. Särelä, Spook in your network: Attacking an SDN with a compromised openflow switch, in *Lecture Notes in Computer Science (including subseries Lecture Notes in Artificial Intelligence and Lecture Notes in Bioinformatics), 2014*, https://link.springer.com/chapter/10.1007/978-3-319-11599-3_14.

33. A. Akhunzada, E. Ahmed, A. Gani, M. K. Khan, M. Imran, and S. Guizani, Securing software defined networks: Taxonomy, requirements, and open issues, *IEEE Commun. Mag.*, 2015.

35. L. Schehlmann, S. Abt, and H. Baier, Blessing or curse? Revisiting security aspects of Software-Defined Networking, in *Proceedings of the 10th*

International Conference on Network and Service Management, CNSM 2014, 2014, https://link.springer.com/chapter/10.1007/978-3-319-11599-3_14.

34. B. Krebs, Study: Attack on KrebsOnSecurity Cost IoT Device Owners $323K — Krebs on Security, Brian Krebs's cyber-security blog, 2016. 37. KDD-CUP, "KDD-CUP," ACM Special Interest Group on Knowledge Discovery and Data Mining, 2016.

35. S. Shin, L. Xu, S. Hong, and G. Gu, Enhancing Network Security through Software Defined Networking (SDN), in *2016 25th International Conference on Computer Communications and Networks, ICCCN 2016*, 2016, *https://ieeexplore.ieee.org/abstract/document/7568520.*

36. N. Handigol, B. Heller, V. Jeyakumar, D. Maziéres, and N. McKeown, Where is the debugger for my software-defined network?, in *HotSDN'12 - Proceedings of the 1st ACM International Workshop on Hot Topics in Software Defined Networks*, 2012, https://dl.acm.org/doi/10.1145/2342441.2342453.

37. Shin S, Porras P, Yegneswaran V, Fong M, Gu G, Tyson M. FRESCO: modular composable security services for software-defined networks. ISOC NDSSS, http://faculty.cse.tamu.edu/guofei/paper/FRESCO_NDSS13.pdf 2013.

38. R. T. Kokila, S. Thamarai Selvi, and K. Govindarajan, DDoS detection and analysis in SDN-based environment using support vector machine classifier, in *6th International Conference on Advanced Computing, ICoAC 2014*, 2015, https://ieeexplore.ieee.org/document/7229711.

39. S. Shin and G. Gu, Attacking software-defined networks: A first feasibility study, in *HotSDN 2013 - Proceedings of the 2013 ACM SIGCOMM Workshop on Hot Topics in Software Defined Networking*, 2013, https://dl.acm.org/doi/pdf/10.1145/2491185.2491220.

40. S. Nanda, F. Zafari, C. Decusatis, E. Wedaa, and B. Yang, Predicting network attack patterns in SDN using machine learning approach, in *2016 IEEE Conference on Network Function Virtualization and Software Defined Networks, NFV-SDN 2016*, 2017, https://ieeexplore.ieee.org/document/7919493.

41. W. Navid and M. N. M. Bhutta, Detection and mitigation of Denial of Service (DoS) attacks using performance aware Software Defined Networking (SDN), in *2017 International Conference on Information and Communication Technologies, ICICT 2017*, 2018, *https://ieeexplore.ieee.org/document/8320164.*

42. J. Pan and Z. Yang, Cybersecurity challenges and opportunities in the new 'edge computing + iot' world, in *SDN-NFVSec 2018 - Proceedings of the 2018 ACM International Workshop on Security in Software Defined Networks and Network Function Virtualization, Co-located with CODASPY 2018*, 2018, https://dl.acm.org/doi/10.1145/3180465.3180470.

7

IoT-Based Optimized and Secured Ecosystem for Energy Internet: The State-of-the-Art

Shilpa Sambhi[1]*, Shikhar Sambhi[2]† and Vikas Singh Bhadoria[3]‡

[1]Independent Researcher
[2]Stanadyne India Pvt. Ltd, Chennai, India
[3]ABES Engineering College, Ghaziabad, U.P., India

Abstract

In India, the concept of smart cities and Internet of Everything is taking shape with a faster pace, so the dependence on electrical energy is increasing day by day. Renewable energy is being adopted rapidly to overcome the power shortages and to meet the power demand of households, which are still not connected to the country's electricity grid. If we consider India's transmission & distribution losses, power theft, power equipment failure, payment default by consumers, the total average losses are still significantly high. The volatile electrical energy scenario, amid India's growing electricity demand and efficiency can be optimized by adoption of new technologies like Internet of Things (IoT) in Indian distribution companies. When Energy is integrated with internet, then it is known as Energy Internet. This technology will help to collect real-time information of power production, distribution & transmission. Therefore, the energy world will make a transition towards decentralized, digitized and de-carbonized system for creating a smart transaction platform that gives rise to true 'prosumers'. Such a system will be able to collect information of connections, metering and billing, management of equipment in case of maintenance, energy audit and customer services, etc. The benefits will be extended to utilities and grid operators, as they will be able to balance supply and demand in real-time by engaging these prosumers directly.

*Corresponding author: shilpasambi@gmail.com
†Corresponding author: shikhar_sambhi@yahoo.com
‡Corresponding author: vikasbhadoria@gmail.com

Parul Gandhi, Surbhi Bhatia, Abhishek Kumar, Mohammad Alojail and Pramod Singh Rathore (eds.) *Internet of Things in Business Transformation: Developing an Engineering and Business Strategy for Industry 5.0*, (91–126) © 2021 Scrivener Publishing LLC

IoT also supports renewable energy integration into the grid in a fruitful way. IoT provides two techniques for making this system autonomous—Blockchain and Software defined networking. Both technologies have their pros and cons, which are discussed in detail in this chapter. The issues related to inter-operability, reliable communication and cyber security in Indian utilities are also addressed in this chapter.

Keywords: Energy internet, Internet of Things, web of things, blockchain, software-defined networking

7.1   Introduction

The Smart Cities Mission was launched by the Government of India in 2015. The objective is to develop an ecosystem with four pillars—institutional, physical, social and economic infrastructure. Basically, the core elements of smart city are optimum water & electricity supply, efficient mobility & public transport, affordable housing, effective waste management, Wi-Fi connectivity & digitalization, sustainable environment, safety & security of the citizens, health and education [1]. All these core elements are connected to each other using sensor technology for better management. This is known as Smart City 1.0; this means the cyber-physical systems like public transport system, water system, car parking, street lights and other required amenities are interconnected with sensorics technology. The next phase of smart city aims to improve the services of city, in addition to improvement in quality of life. This is known as Smart city 2.0; this means that city will be able to make service decision intelligently by using the 3Ds—data, digital, and (human-centered) design [2]. Therefore, now we can observe the shift from *smarter things* to *smart decisions*. Apart from providing better quality of life to residents, smart city is also working towards economic competitiveness and sustainable environment. This will help to engage government, citizens, and businesses in an intelligently connected ecosystem. The decisions are made according the data submitted by citizens to the end users, where city officials can analyze this real-time data to amend the use of energy, water management, waste management, etc. for improving or re-developing the system [3]. For instance, to streamline the waste management system, the officials can track vehicles, so that garbage trucks can be redirected to the routes where garbage collection has skipped because of some reason. Another instance is that citizens can check real time traffic and the time of next bus for a particular destination; an asthmatic patient can follow an alternative route by avoiding high pollution areas; families can plan their day-out by accessing information about beaches and parks. All such instances mean that smart cities will be connected, networked, and collaborative.

As India is dealing with the problem of over-population, smart cities provides a good solution for efficient usage of space and resources to facilitate quality life [4]. This calls for the need of enhancement of connectivity between citizens and administration. This connectivity can be effectively provided by combination of IoT, advanced ICT, machine learning and big data. A network of sensors, continuously monitoring a system, for instance, weather/environment conditions, can help to find measures to improve air quality and other parameters affecting life. Similarly, sensor network can help to improve and maintain public properties like roads, bridges, hospitals and schools. Hence, smart cities fulfill the social and psychological needs of the population [5].

The smart city will be driven by electrical energy; this energy will be consumed by the households (lights, air-conditioners/heaters, geyser, refrigerator, microwave, charging of mobile phone, laptop, electric vehicles, etc.), individual (use of App to control devices, etc.), street & park lights, CCTV, sensors and other devices to control and maintain different operations of smart city [6]. This means that the energy consumption will increase, so more energy has to be produced. This increased energy demand can be easily met from thermal power plants. Here, we must understand the problems associated with thermal power plants. The generation of electricity in thermal plants is done through burning of coal. The problems associated with coal burning are: (i) it requires large amount of water; (ii) it discharges arsenic and lead into surface waters, causing water pollution; (iii) coal burning releases carbon dioxide, sulfur dioxide, nitrogen oxides and mercury into the air, leading to air pollution. In the current scenario, we are facing the worst environmental conditions [7]. Renewable source of energy like solar energy can be a solution to this issue. Solar energy is clean and does not contribute to climate changes [8]. As per the directions of Government of India, public buildings have to install solar panels to generate part of electricity required for the functioning of various operations [9]. If the solar plant generates more than the energy consumed by the building, then it can send the excess energy to the power grid, to generate revenue. Now, the role of Power Grid system comes in to picture.

An electric power grid is a network of electrical energy providers and consumers which are connected by transmission and distribution lines from various locations [10]. If case of repair work during any fault or maintenance routine scheduled in the grid, it has to shut down. This means that the consumers connected to this grid will not receive any power during the repair/maintenance time and this becomes a major disadvantage of the grid system. A solution to this problem is a micro-grid. It is a small-scale power grid which functions as decentralized energy production and distribution system [11]. Generally, a micro-grid comprises of distribution generators and renewable wind & solar energy resources. It is also integrated with main power grid to meet the high energy consumption demands and shut downs during repair work; the ease in maintenance/repair work is now done using thermal imaging [12]. Energy generation through solar power is being employed rapidly in places like public buildings and societies. The excess energy generated can be send back to a micro-grid to generate revenue, in addition to giving flexibility and ability to the micro-grid. If these grids are joined together using IoT technology, then it becomes Smart Grid [13]. The deployment of smart grid improves the functioning, repair/maintenance work and forecasting by automating process. The tools of IoT ensure that different grids can communicate with each other effectively.

The traditional energy trading model has few problems associated with securing data of energy generation by different power generating units and consumption pattern of energy by different consumers [14]. The associated problems are: (i) less transparency in transactions; (ii) risk of tempering of transaction data; (iii) privacy protection of historical data of energy generation & consumption from cyber-attacks; (iv) complexity in meeting the dynamic energy demands. In order to make the system flexible, safe, secure, and optimize the operations, an intelligent energy management system can be implemented with smart grids. Adoption of IoT technologies like artificial intelligence, machine learning, blockchain and software defined network will help to make optimal power flow strategies [15]. This way energy trading will progress from centralized system to distributed/decentralized system. So, in case of data loss from one computer system will not affect the entire operation of grid system, as the data will be available at other computer systems. Smart transaction platform will give rise to 'prosumers', which means the same person can play the role of both supplier and consumer in a smart grid [16]. In other words, a smart grid together with renewable energy resources can help to make the system clean, secure and efficient.

This chapter is organized as follows. In Section 7.2, the difference between home automation and smart home is presented. In Section 7.3, the reasons for energy generation shift towards renewable resources are given. In Section 7.4, the benefits of applying IoT for energy management are presented and the role of IoT in smart grid is given in Section 7.5. The bottleneck areas of the existing system are presented in Section 7.6. In Section 7.7, the solution provided by IoT technology for secured transactions is stated. In Section

7.8, the fusion of energy internet with IoT and blockchain is presented. In Section 7.9, the chapter is concluded with discussion on challenges for safe and secured ecosystem in energy internet.

7.2   Distinguishing Features Between Home Automation and Smart Home

Different devices are automated by installing a suitable sensor along with a controller. The software program embedded in the controller operates the device in accordance to the signal received from the sensor. This makes the device 'intelligent' [17]. For instance, room lights can be automatically switched on or off, depending on the presence of people in the room. If no one is there in a particular room, then lights will be switched off, else it will be switched on. This is possible with the use a passive sensor called, infrared sensors, connected in a room. This sensor will be connected to a controller, which will switch on or off the lights, as per the signal received from the sensor. Similarly, consumer appliances like TV, washing machine, refrigerator, air conditioner, geyser, water pump, etc. can be intelligent. This is home automation, where each device is working independently as shown in Figure 7.1. The appliance is automated and controlled by means of interfacing a sensor and appropriate software programming [18]. Here, a conclusion is drawn that in home automation, appliances work automatically but it cannot be controlled or monitored with a mobile app or a web page.

In smart home, appliances work automatically; it can be controlled or monitored from a remote location with a mobile app or a web page also, as shown in Figure 7.1. These appliances are made 'intelligent' using IoT tools [19]. For instance, if water pump is left on, accidentally, then the status of it can be checked through a suitable app and switch off. Power analyzer is installed at the socket of appliance and it measures the power consumed by the respective appliance. The sensor is connected to a controller, which sends the data to the cloud; the user can access this data through a mobile app or a webpage, from where the appliance can be monitored and controlled. The different sensors, controllers and devices used in smart home may have different communication protocols [20]. In order to collect data of these devices at a common protocol, to make smart devices communicate synchronously, we can build an operating system to satisfy this protocol requirement. But this process may add to the complicacy of the system. Therefore, the already available platform can be used to bring data at a common platform. This available platform is 'the

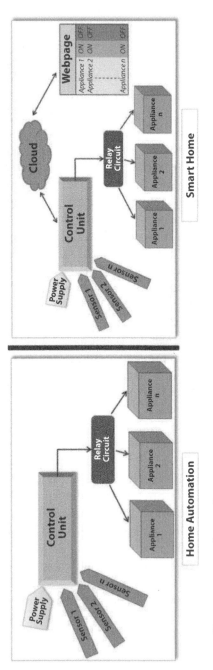

Figure 7.1 Home automation & smart home.

web/internet'. The plan is to bring the entire data from different sensors to a cloud. The user can access the data from the cloud and use it suitably to control and monitor the device from a remote location. As the sensor data is being sent to the cloud and monitored from cloud, this is known as Web of Things (WoT) [21]. This can be referred from Figure 7.2. For instance, if air-conditioner/geyser can be switched on, few minutes before reaching home; a smart camera can send the pictures of installed area and the pictures can be saved to the cloud for future purpose. Generally, power analyzer is installed at the socket of appliance and it measures the power consumed by the interfaced appliance. The sensor is connected to a controller, which sends the data to the cloud; the user can access this data through a mobile app or a webpage, from where the appliance can be monitored and controlled.

In a similar way, IoT tools can provide efficient surveillance systems, used for real time monitoring of a building from remote location [22]. Suitable gas and smoke sensors can be installed in building at different points, to sense fire. Apart from raising an alarm, the sensor can be connected to the internet through a controller. When the sensor senses smoke above a threshold level, then signal can be sent to the nearest fire station by means of message. This will help to take the timely action. Another instance can be considered for elevator monitoring system. A building can have multiple numbers of elevators. The signal from the controller of each elevator can be sent to the cloud through internet and the maintenance

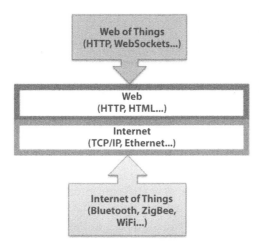

Figure 7.2 Internet-of-Things & Web-of-Things.

personnel can monitor the status of all elevators to check safe and secured operation.

The power consumed by smart home is monitored with a smart energy meter. The typical energy meter displays the energy consumed and some person has to note the reading for generating the bill. This means that there is an additional cost of meter reading. Moreover, the reading can be subjected to error and safety issues because energy meters are generally installed inside the home premises. A smart energy meter overcomes such issues. The smart meter sends the real-time power consumption data to the cloud [23]. The user as well as the authorities can monitor the data of energy consumed through a mobile app or a web page. This may help the user to monitor the energy consumption on regular intervals of time [24]. Further, if this system is interfaced to the bank account or an e-wallet then electricity bill dues can be deducted automatically. This system may prove to be consistent, robust, efficient and cost effective system, and is part of Advanced Monitoring Infrastructure (AMI). So, smart energy meter is an essential part of smart grid.

Apart from smart homes, a smart city will have smart street lighting, water supply & storage supply, and an effective surveillance system [25]. The street lights are interfaced with sensor to detect light and movement in the surroundings, related circuitry for interfacing with a controller with real-time clock can be controlled and monitored through IoT tools. The controller is responsible for sending the data to the cloud through internet. The sensor can switch on/off and adjust the brightness of lights, depending on the surrounding/sunlight, number of people and weather condition [26]. Similarly, suitable distance measuring sensors can be used to check water level in the storage tank on real-time basis. The signal from the sensor can be sent to the valves of the storage tank to control the opening and closing of the water supply. Flow rate sensors can be installed at various points to check the flow rate and leakage of water from the pipes. This will help to reduce the wastage of water. A surveillance systems based on IoT tools can be installed at different locations in the city, so as to monitor the events in real time [27]. In case of any mishap, the security personnel can take the required action on time. For effective surveillance, smart cameras can be installed and the events can be captured in video. This video can be saved in the cloud for future action. The hospitals/police station in the city can also be intimated so that they can prepare themselves before the patient/victim arrives. So far, the parameters discussed for the smart city are limited, but it can be extended further as per the requirement.

Let us consider an instance of charging station for electric vehicles. Each smart city has to equip charging station for electric vehicle (EV) as its numbers are increasing in India [28]. The energy is stored and provided by the battery of EV to drive. The state of charge (SoC) of the battery can be measured and the data can be sent to cloud. IoT based remote monitoring of SoC can help the user to make decision of either charging the battery with Grid to Vehicle (G2V) system or sell stored energy back to the grid with Vehicle to Grid (V2G) system [29]. This way not only the energy utilization has been optimized but clean energy has also been produced and it has not contributed to pollution by any means. The energy demand is rising rapidly in India and shift towards renewable form of energy together with IoT tools implemented in smart grid will prove to be reliable, robust and cost-effective. The data of real time demand and supply of energy can be gathered using sensors. This dataset can be analyzed for studying the load pattern, by using IoT tools such as machine learning and artificial intelligence, to increase efficiency.

7.3 Energy Generation Shift Towards Renewable Sources

The hydro-thermal power plants generate electricity using fossil fuels like coal and natural resources like water. But with the increase in demand of energy, these resources are depleting fast. More over use of coal for generating energy leads to air pollution and India is going through worst phase of air pollution. The water resources are also depleting at a faster rate. Therefore the Government of India has taken an initiative to motivate renewable source of energy especially, solar energy, by granting benefits to the prosumers.

Generation of electricity from renewable source of energy like solar energy has few benefits. The main advantage is that it is a non-polluting energy source, so the solar panels for generating electricity can be located within the residential and commercial areas. This is known as grid. As the load is close to the grid, so transmission and distribution losses are low, as compared to that of thermal plants [30]. Therefore, power can be purchased directly from grid and the cost of energy is much lower than that received from traditional thermal plants. This means that external economies of scales also drive the motivation for adopting solar energy.

A grid is an inter-connected network to transfer electrical energy from producers to consumers. The Government is promoting participation from private players for generating electricity through renewable generation, but weather fluctuations can bring variability in renewable resources [31]. The electricity generation from individual generation assets using renewable resources, can be subjected to uncertainty. This uncertainty can be due to two factors: (i) variability in energy supply, and (ii) variability in energy demand. The fluctuations in weather conditions can bring up to 70% uncertainty in daytime solar capacity (due to clouds) and 100% of wind capacity on days with still air; the variation in energy supply can be measured on the scale of seconds, days and hours. Based on the historical data, predictive analyses can be done to understand the consumption pattern/ energy demand of the consumers. New technologies and approaches, integrated with smart grid, can enable to deal with variation of energy supply and demand on a minute-by-minute and hourly basis. Large scale storage can be installed on the grid and, if required, long distance transmission lines of renewable electricity can be set up so that energy from other grids can also be accessed to balance regional energy demand and supply. It is the need of the hour to enhance electricity generation through renewable sources, in order to make it cost effective [32].

An effective weather monitoring and forecasting system will help in predicting: (i) the energy generation through renewable sources on daily or hourly basis; (ii) improve the reliability of the grid; (iii) reduce the energy generation from thermal power plant, thereby, reducing coal burning & hence, air-pollution, and (iv) savings in capital & operating cost, thereby, making the energy cheaper.

7.4   Robust Energy Management with IoT Technology

A network of physical systems, connected to each other through internet is called *Internet of Things* (IoT). These physical systems could be any electronic device, on which sensors and related software is embedded. The device is connected to wired or wireless network so that it can communicate with other electronic devices. Such devices can be used for monitoring, locating and analyzing many activities [33]. All such devices have to use same internet protocol (IP) that is connected to internet (refer Figure 7.3). The essential properties of IoT are:

(i)   *Intelligent system*: Different smart devices are embedded with different software, so to make the data compatible for each device, a common platform is required – internet. This seamless connectivity makes the system intelligent enough to analyze the environment;

(ii)   *Sensor network*: The sensors allow devices/machines to imitate the human ability to recognize and assess an event.

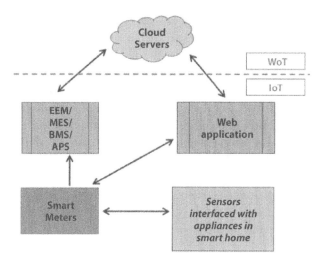

Figure 7.3 Devices communicating through cloud servers.

This information is stored in cloud for analyses and further action;

(iii) *Machine-to-Human communication*: The system becomes smart with seamless machine-to-machine communication and machine-to-human communication. Such communication enables interaction of device with the real world environment;

(iv) *Energy efficient and robust*: Smart devices work in real environment, which can be harsh enough to make the conditions tough for the device. The IoT device must have good reliability for maintaining the energy efficiency;

(v) *Secured system*: The data from a device is passed on to the cloud and then to other access points, either through wired or wireless system. This data can be prone to security threats. Hence, it is important to adopt suitable safety measures for data security like device authentication, firewall, IPS (Intrusion prevention system), blockchain, SDN (software defined network), etc.

In order to improve the overall efficiency, IoT tools help to analyze the power generation and consumption, with pre-defined algorithms. Sustainability of the energy generation and efficient distribution of electricity is possible because of ad hoc monitoring and supervision of energy consumption, using high-end IoT tools such as data mining. This analysis may help to get the comprehensive information about energy wastage. The combination of smart appliances such as bulbs, switches, television, power outlets, etc. with internet, enables energy generation companies to produce energy more efficiently. As the energy usage data is send to the cloud, the consumers are able to control the appliances from remote location. This means that the consumer is able to centrally manage different appliances in his home through a cloud-based interface. In other words, the collective approach by sensors and actuating system, coupled through internet, may help to optimize the overall energy consumption. The key intention behind the fusion of IoT and energy management system is to permit the allied entities to communicate with each other through a common information model [34]. It is important to understand the practices in energy management, which are mentioned in the form of three layers as follows:

- *Bottom layer*: This layer includes sensors with electrical appliances and smart meter to measure energy consumption which are connected to each other through internet for seamless communication. The benefit of using smart meter is that it measures the power factor and maximum/minimum peak voltage, based on which it monitors and analyze the energy consumption pattern. It is to be noted that smart meters can be deployed with a home to study the consumption pattern in different time slots, or in industries either with a single machine or a production line. Such data can be used for optimum utilization of energy.

- *Middle layer*: This layer is responsible for data transmission and acts as a medium between different devices to communicate & perform the desired task. The data is collected from different sensors integrated with smart devices and is send to the cloud using standard communication protocols like HyperText Transfer Protocol (HTTP), TCP/IP, etc.

- *Top layer*: The energy consumption data collected by smart energy meters can be transferred to suitable energy management software. This software can be EEM (Enterprise Energy Management), Manufacturing Execution Systems (MES), Building Management Systems (BMS) or Advanced Production and Scheduling systems (APS). A detailed analysis can be done to check energy wastage and optimize energy consumption at different points.

7.5   Solution from IoT Technology for Secured Transactions

The entire data collected by different varieties of sensors is utilized for some analysis by an organization. For example, by collecting the consumption pattern of electricity of particular region, the organization can plan further load scheduling and predictive maintenance schedule of its machines or transmission lines. In this way, the organization would be able to plan to keep the inventory of material/components usually required in case of maintenance and breakdown. The data of different faults occurring at different locations and different point of time will help the organization to understand the major cause of failure. Such analysis may help them to modify the design of the components, so as to reduce further losses and bring down the replacement/maintenance cost. In the era of digital transformation, it is really important that the captured data must not be lost or hacked. Hence, IoT cyber security solutions are relevant to understand [35]. The solution for secured and safe transactions provided by technology of Internet-of-Things (IoT) can be categorized as follows:

7.5.1   Category I: Centralized Approach

The security solutions available for wireless sensor network and machine-to-machine (M2M) communications are categorized as cryptographic based techniques [36]. This technique was adapted for IoT communications, and it ensures security and privacy of the data. As part of security, the data is available to authenticated users only. It is worthwhile to note here that these solutions work in centralized environment. The central trusted entities ensure smooth functioning of the smart systems, but in case, the system faces technical issues, the entire data can be lost. Moreover as the number of smart devices increases, this classical approach is subjected to scalability issues and data management becomes a big challenge.

7.5.2   Category II: Decentralized Approach

To overcome the scalability issues and fear of data loss, new security solutions have come up. These solutions are provide decentralized solution, which means it can handle high scale of devices interconnected and the data is distributed to each and computer available in the network. Therefore, if the data is lost from one computer, then it can be retrieved from other computer. The following two emerging technologies may provide the decentralized approach for security solution [37]. Both approaches have their pros and cons which are explained next.

7.5.2.1 Blockchain Technology

This technology works on peer-to-peer architecture, without the need of any central trusted server. Also, it is not necessary that the two entities participating in transaction trust each other. Once the transaction is verified, it becomes practically impossible to contradict performed transactions. The challenges of data privacy and access control are addressed by this technology.

This technology is particularly used for digital transaction over an open distributed network [38]. It allows secured transaction of smart contracts over peer-to-peer network, without the need of a central authority like banks, lawyers and accountants. Therefore, we can say that blockchain provides independent transactions. Rest other participants serve the purpose of a witness to every transaction carried out between two entities. These transactions are time-stamped and are stored on a digital ledger, in the form of blocks. A series of such transactions taking place in a particular interval of time make up different blocks, which are interlocked with each other, forming a blockchain. This process can be referred from Figure 7.4. This blockchain is duplicated in every computer on the network, so it is known as distributed ledger; which means if the data of one computer is lost due to any reason then the entire data can be retrieved because the data is decentralized. Transactions recorded in blockchain can be verified at any

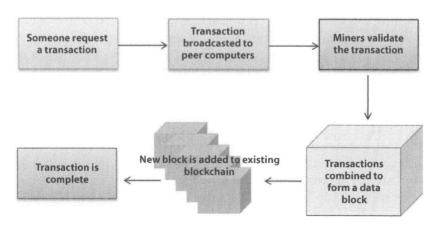

Figure 7.4 Process of secured transaction using blockchain.

point of time as the records are permanently stored in a digital ledger. The interlocking is done by using the hash values of blocks, which is generally the time stamp when the transaction takes place. These hash tags can be considered as a security tag. This means that if any data has to be changed in a particular transaction then a new block will be formed, which will also contain the information of the previous transaction. In other words, the blockchain will be rehashed again and the changes will be observed in the new blockchain. Hence, the previous block cannot be modified by any means. So, we can say that the transaction is completely tamper proof and safe. If any attacker tries to hack, modify or erase any transaction, then he has to change all the hashes in the successive blocks, which is computationally infeasible as blockchain is immutable.

Another important feature of blockchain is that it is neither controlled nor legally claimed by a single entity [39]. A computer code, popularly known as consensus protocol, is developed between the entities of the blockchain. The purpose is to empower the entities with decision making using the information stored in blockchain. This protocol establishes the trust between the entities and removes the need of intermediary entity like lawyer and accountant. This feature is known as 'smart contracts'. So we can say that a smart contract is like a legal agreement between the entities which is formulated by the lawyers and accountants. All the transactions or applications performed in blockchain are considered genuine decentralized application, if it is accepted and verified by smart contract. The blockchain is validated using a decentralized and automated verification method known as proof-of-work (PoW). In case of public blockchain, hashing is done by special nodes known as 'miners'. A pre-specified mathematical puzzle has to be solved to put a block in the blockchain. This puzzle is known as proof-of-work (PoW). The miner, who solves the PoW first, gets some monetary incentive. But this model has a major drawback. The miners need high computational power of computer to compete in solving PoW. At times, such high computational power is considered to be wastage and incentives are not paid appropriately paid to the miners. To overcome these drawbacks, public blockchain was changed to private blockchains for other potential applications like implementation of blockchain in smart grid system and industry 4.0 [40].

Private blockchain is popularly known as industrial blockchain. Unlike public blockchain, it is possessed and controlled by an individual entity [41]. Now, private blockchain can also be consortium-based, permissioned blockchain and is a localized event. Consortium blockchain is possessed and controlled by a group of companies, while permissioned blockchain provide special permission to verified user for performing a specific task.

Such private blockchain are applicable for service sectors like smart grid & power distribution, smart homes, healthcare, smart manufacturing, industry 4.0 etc. It is worthwhile to note here that in private blockchains, miners are replaced by individual entity or group of members and PoW is swapped with a suitable protocol, called proof-of-stake (PoS). The entities are required to frequently prove ownership of their own stake and the process of validation is allocated as per the percentage of stake of the individual entity. For instance, if an entity holds 20% of the stake of the total blockchain assets, then that entity will have to carry out 20% of the required mining activity. Therefore, this approach of PoS can result is large savings on computational energy and operating costs as the complexity is reduced in the process of decentralized validation process.

Let us try to understand the working of blockchain technology. Consider three entities as A, B and C. In the initial state, suppose 'A' has Rs. 100, 'B' has Rs. 70 and 'C' has Rs. 120. This will be reflected in their centralized ledger maintained by the bank. Here is the sequence of events taking place while one entity transfers some money to other:

# Case	# Transactions	Status of bank ledger
1	'A' transfers Rs. 30 to 'B'	'A' has Rs. 70 & 'B' has Rs. 100
2	'A' promises 'C' to give Rs. 80	As per last updated bank ledger, this transaction is not possible
3	'B' returns Rs. 30 to 'A'	'A' has Rs. 20 & 'C' has Rs. 200

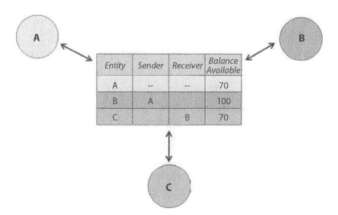

Figure 7.5 De-centralized banking system using blockchain.

In this process of money transfer, all three entities have to update their account balance. They spend considerable amount of time & effort on coordination, synchronization and checking to ensure successful transaction. On using blockchain technology, a single ledger is maintained and validated with transaction entries of all the entities. This ledger is decentralized, which means the entities have right to access this ledger at any point of time. So in blockchain, there is a single version of records and not different databases. The case of decentralized banking system can be referred from Figure 7.5.

7.5.2.2 Software Defined Networking (SDN)

This is a new paradigm to develop flexible network solutions and control the network resources using centralized SDN controller [42]. The motive is to separate the network control plan and data plan programmatically. This way the configuration and dynamics of network traffic can be controlled using centralized SDN controller. The task of this controller is to dictate the set of rules to the devices of SDN architecture. These devices could be routers, switches, gateways and related IoT devices. SDN architecture devices cannot make control decisions, but learn these rules from SDN controller. In case where devices have limited network resources, SDN architecture provides an efficient and flexible solution for overcoming challenges of scalability, security & reliability in IoT environment. In reference to the heterogeneity in security issues, different types of SDN architectures have been proposed. In one type of architecture, emphasis has been given on multiple SDN domains so as to manage the security policies between them. In other words, each SDN controller follows the security policy inside its domain and also coordinates with the security policies outside its domain provided by other SDN controllers. Another type of architecture proposes to use Openflow protocol. Here, IoT nodes act as SDN gateways to identify malicious attacks from compromised devices and apply an appropriate mitigation action. Openflow protocol provides sufficient computation energy along with the advantages like: (1) validate node in the same segment; (2) implement satisfactory security rules. This way SDN gateways exchange the security rules to establish secure connections between nodes of different segments. Other advanced and customized architectures are available depending upon the application area. The traditional network and software-defined network is shown in Figure 7.6.

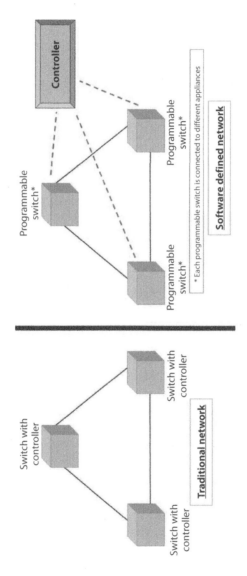

Figure 7.6 Traditional network and software-defined network.

SDN is an emerging technology and is not established enough to deal with the security issues in IoT [43]. The potential challenges with SDN architecture are:

(1) As SDN controllers operate in centralized architecture and dictate the rules to the devices, so these controllers are the potential points of attack.

(2) In case of an attack to the SDN controller, the data plan is also exposed to threats, which will degrade the performance of the network.

(3) As the number of IoT devices increases, SDN approach will suffer from scalability issues and the efficiency of the network will degrade.

(4) A vehicular network like that of automated guided vehicles (AGV) provides a highly dynamic environment. The frequency of changes in network topology is high as lot of data is exchanged between AGV. While transferring some data from one AGV to another, the SDN controller has to check & validate the security policy and other related configurations. In such a case, the approach of centralized SDN controller will be a time consuming.

7.6   Role of IoT in Smart Grid

Referring to the benefits of IoT, the technology can be implemented in various sectors such as cities, transportation, irrigation, homes, health, industries, logistics etc. It is estimated that there will be approximately 41 billion connected IoT devices in the year 2025, generating about 80 ZB of data. Integration of IoT with a grid makes it smart, robust and efficient [44]. Several configurations of architectures are available for implementation of IoT tools in smart grid. A basic architecture using blockchain is presented below (refer to Figure 7.7). The operation of smart grid can be divided in four segments—power generation, transmission, distribution and most important, consumption pattern of consumers [45, 46].

7.6.1   Power Generation

The existing system—Increasing energy demands and pollution created by existing thermal power stations needs an immediate attention. This is causing a rapid shift in generating electricity through renewable sources

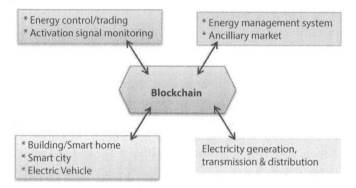

Figure 7.7 Energy transaction through blockchain.

of energy like solar and wind. The region receiving abundant sunlight throughout the year is chosen for installation of photo-voltaic (PV) panels, so as to generate electricity using solar energy. Generating stations based on solar energy can be seen in the form of solar farm and solar tree. In the similar way, a number of wind turbines are installed in the regions where velocity of wind is high. Therefore, we can say that (i) geographic location is a matter of concern for setting up of electricity generating station through renewable energy sources; and (ii) sunlight and wind velocity are irregular in nature as it depends on weather conditions. In other words, we can say that generating electricity through renewable sources is subjected to fluctuations in reliability and predictability of power supply.

Benefit of implementing IoT—A reliable weather forecasting system together with IoT based system, can help to predict the availability of power supply through renewable energy sources in future. Sensoric system using temperature, humidity and wind velocity, collects weather information, which is send to the cloud for such analysis. Considering the energy generation through solar energy, the system work as follows: (i) The PV panel, DC boost converter output and battery is equipped with current and voltage sensors; (ii) These sensors are connected to a controller; (iii) On receiving signals from different sensor, the controller sends this data to a cloud database for storage; (iv) This data can be analyzed in two ways by prosumers from a remote location either through web interface or a mobile app; (v) In first type of analysis, the prosumers can make decision to sell the excess stored energy back to the grid by using the concept of net metering; (vi) In second type of analysis, the end-user can monitor the health of machinery, which helps to create a predictive maintenance schedule.

In the similar way, IoT tools can be adopted while generating power through wind, hydroelectric and thermal power plants.

7.6.2   Power Transmission

The traditional system—The transmission lines are spread over thousands of kilometers to reach out the consumers. Earlier, these lines were monitored periodic by manual visits, but the system is subjected to challenges for checking the lines spread in remote locations. This is an unreliable system of monitoring transmission lines. The problems associated with related equipment and towers are damages due to weather condition like cyclone, thunderstorm and earthquake. The towers may tilt or vibrate due to extreme weather conditions.

Benefit of implementing IoT—An online monitoring system can be created with the integration of IoT tools, which can provide information regarding early detection of faults, conductor temperature, wind velocity and other weather conditions. This information may help to monitor transmission line performance and its working status. Deployment of power analyzer at each tower will facilitate to identify the loss of energy. One of the prime reasons for loss of energy could be power theft, so timely action can be taken to prevent the same. Therefore, we can say that monitoring system for components of power system together with IoT tools may prove to be robust and reliable.

7.6.3   Power Distribution

The existing system—Trained persons are required to keep check on machinery of generation, transmission and distribution. But the problem with such a human-depended system is that if a machine fails to operate then the transmission and hence, distribution of energy may get affected. In other words, we can say that the availability of power supply will be disturbed.

Benefit of implementing IoT—It is important to have an effective maintenance schedule for any machine, so that it can work optimally in its life span. Good maintenance schedules always help to improve reliability and cost effectiveness. Online monitoring system proves to be beneficial in the following terms: (i) It helps to identify the equipment requiring immediate attention, along with its location; (ii) Reports like maintenance schedule, equipment health & weather monitoring can be saved on cloud database for future analysis; (iii) Manual monitoring system is reduced. Moreover, deployment of smart energy meters will collect the energy consumption data and send it to cloud database. This way information about load consumption in each region can be collected and distribution of energy can be optimized. Therefore, in smart grid sensors will be installed to measure temperature, humidity, noise, vibration, current and voltage. The towers supporting transmission lines tilt in due to high wind velocity, cyclone and other such natural calamities, so tilt sensor can be installed on tower to take timely action.

7.6.4   Consumer Consumption

Combination of smart grid with distribution system and demand side load can prove to be an efficient plant-to-plug ecosystem. This combination is known as smart electricity. This concept is made effective by the use smart electrical equipment. The smart devices, connects to each other through internet and form an intelligent distribution network. Such network offers grid benefits like lowering energy losses, enhancing uptime of electrical appliances, robust power quality, optimizing energy usage and reducing consumer electricity bills. With deployment of IoT tools, this ecosystem will become a two way system between power supply and demand loads, which is expected to benefit the electricity producers, distributors and consumers.

7.7   Bottleneck Areas of Existing System

- Transmission line losses: The transmission lines are spread in kilometers from generating station till distribution points. The voltage level has to be stepped up and down at different points, which result in power losses. These losses are considerable and the burden goes to the consumer pocket.
- Low reliability: In India, we have centralized, utility-based model of electrical grid. This means that the reach of such infrastructure of grid is limited, especially in rural areas. Also, it is noticed that most often load shedding is done in rural areas.
- Power tariffs are expensive: The more the transmission line losses, the more expensive power tariffs will be. This means that rural markets are not able to afford high power costs, so problems of electricity tapping and theft are also rising.

- Discrepancies in net metering: More than 23 states in India have approved renewable energy generation units. This means that if a person has installed rooftop solar system, then excess power can be send back to the grid under net metering system. The credits of the excess power are adjusted in the bill of the customer. In other words, the same person has acted like a consumer of generated solar energy and a producer by sending back the excess energy back to the grid. This person is known as prosumer. At times, the credits are not adjusted in the bills, may be due to system error. This leads to distrust among the consumers about using solar energy.
- Challenges in rural market: The foremost challenge is the dependence on manual efforts for meter reading to generate electricity consumption bills and its collection on regular basis. The consumers of rural market often fail to make regular payments due to employability issues and expensive cost of electricity.

7.8   Fusion of Energy Internet with IoT and Blockchain

Conventional grids are centralized and it creates inefficiencies in distribution of energy, like unutilized energy surplus. This means the areas affected by power outages will not receive electricity. So, it is important to balance the supply and demand in real time for efficient operation of the grid and related utilities. Another point is that it must engage the prosumers directly. Grid also integrates renewable energy in a cost-effective approach. A peer-to-peer blockchain based energy trading system from local grids through blockchain can be formulated to reduce the requirement for energy storage [47]. In other words, the decentralized nature of blockchain can permit distributed energy producers to sell energy seamlessly to consumers in their local area. This mechanism is known as Group Net-Metering [48]. It is important to note here that the requirement of long distance power transmission lines and the losses related to it will also reduce. The blockchain technology together with smart energy meters (IoT), when connected to smart grid and distribution network, provides many efficient opportunities for energy distribution.

Smart energy meters act as the nodes from where the energy consumption data is collected. Blockchain uses decentralized, digitized and de-carbonized data storage to record such digital transactions. This data is replicated and synchronized, which is open to all the users in the network [49]. Each transaction will be documented through smart contracts, which form the legal procedure as decided by the authorities. The participants of smart grid network can make energy purchase decision. According to the energy produced and used, funds are transferred between prosumers based on the energy consumed and surplus produced as recorded by smart energy meter. This will result in more competition in energy price and better reliability from public opinion. As blockchain technology does not require any middleman or central authority for performing the transactions between millions of users, hence, it creates a trusted system for managing billing and payment due settlement in energy transactions [50]. Blockchain technology makes the system flexible, speed up the process and reduces overall cost of the system. The system makes a transition from centralized system (like energy companies, trading platforms, and banking) to decentralized system, which is popularly known as peer-to-peer transaction. Still, the stakeholders of the system will be the energy companies and the Government to form the legal procedures and decide the price of energy from time to time.

Basically, the concept of group net-metering is beneficial in smart micro-grids in a localized area [51]. This area can supply energy to residential loads or industrial loads. The rural areas in India offer vast possibility to develop local smart grids, as the rural areas are worst hit when decision for load shedding is made. Using permissioned blockchain based infrastructure; the energy market of rural sector can prove to be cost effective and durable. The facility of peer-to-peer energy exchange in rural micro-grid can benefits in the following ways:

(i) The integration of IoT technology i.e., smart meters and embedded blockchain technology provides secure information of energy consumed, surplus energy produced and the payment made by an individual user. This data is preserved forever and is available for audits at any point of time.

(ii) The access to the blockchain information can be provided with the help of a suitable mobile application.

(iii) The verification of prosumers can be done through aadhar numbers automatically and due payment can be enabled through the bank account linked with aadhar number.

(iv) In rural areas, the facility of pre-paid mode of payment can be deployed as it will tackle the problem of non-payment or late payment by the users.

(v)   In case the payments are made in due time, subsidies can be provided to economically weaker section of society through their linked aadhar numbers.

(vi) Based on the amount of surplus energy from renewable sources, send back to the grid, the users can be provided suitable incentives.

(vii) Blockchain based system can facilitate seamless integration of rural micro-grid to the regular grid and provide incentives accordingly.

(viii) As the transactions are transparent and secured with smart meters, it reduces the risk of power theft and help in recovery of debt.

Another important parameter is to consider the carbon footprint of each energy generation plant. As the carbon footprint have an environmental impact, so this must be factored into energy cost. But there is little incentive for the consumers as well as energy companies to but energy with low carbon footprint. The tracking of carbon footprint from each power plant is possible with blockchain technology. This data will be protected from tampering, so the penalty of carbon tax can be charged at the point of sale. The energy with large carbon footprint will be expensive to buy, so these energy producing companies have to restructure in order to meet the environmental friendly standards. There are popular platform for peer-to-peer transactions of energy using blockchain technology and these are as follows:

(i)   *Transactive Grid*: It is collaboration between ConsenSys and LO3 Energy, which intends to reduce the need of energy storage by supplying the surplus energy to the needy one.

(ii) *SunContract*: This grid is particularly for energy trading of solar and other forms of renewable energy. A high capital investment is required for installation of renewable energy power plants. It is expected that with implementation of blockchain technology, the organizations will get good return on investment.

(iii) *EcoChain*: This is a blockchain App which provides a platform to prosumers to invest in energy generation from renewable sources and get back good return on investment.

(iv) *ElectricChain*: This platform provides incentives for solar energy generation plants.

Here, we see observe the emergence of Microsystems based on number of prosumers in particular area. Prosumers mean the individuals, who are acting as consumers by producing electricity, especially using renewable source like solar and also acting as producer of electricity by sending back the surplus energy back to local grid. Blockchain offer a wider opportunity to increase the number of prosumers by providing flexible and trusted platform with high degree of autonomy for energy trading. In other words, we can say that blockchain provides a transparent market where prosumers can make their energy buy and sell decisions and do the peer-to-peer transactions securely.

The Government has plans to shift to electric vehicles by 2030 [52]. As of now, there are 150 charging stations in India for electric vehicles. The electric vehicles can be charged in any charging station with the use of smart plug. The car owner can be billed for the energy consumed with the decentralized, flexible and trusted system provided by blockchain technology. The electric vehicles can interact with the charging stations automatically, which will make an autonomous billing system. The benefits of such a blockchain based system can be as follows:

(i)   The use of smart plugs will enable the electric vehicles to be charged at any charging station.

(ii) There is no requirement of third party to maintain the legal proceedings, as it will be handled by smart contracts in blockchain.

(iii) Interoperability issues will be resolved automatically.

(iv) Transparency of the transactions, i.e., energy units consumed and payment made, is available to users of the network.

(v)   The authentication, charging and billing will be carried out by a simple blockchain system. The validation and audit report can be generated at any point without manual efforts.

Association of smart blockchain technology with Internet of Things (IoT) proposes an example of public blockchain, which maintains a secured transaction between users, who are known to each other. Therefore, multiple *Smart Blockchain Networks* can be established on local and regional basis.

7.9   Challenges for Safe and Secured Ecosystem in Energy Internet

At this stage, it is important to understand the difference between safety and security of a system. Both terms relate to the risk factor associated with the system, which could be intentional or accidental. This risk factor can have impact on different parameters related to environment, finance, human error etc. Typically, the safety of the system could be defined as an agreement that the system does not harm its environment. Safety is related to accidental risks like damages occurring from natural disasters and human error. The security of the system consists in protecting it from the intentional attacks that come from its environment. So, security is related to malicious attacks performed by humans to hack the relevant data. Both the terms—safety and security have an impact on each other. For instance, if the data exchanged between the smart grid and maintenance personnel is compromised by the security attack then the maintenance personnel will not be able to perform scheduled maintenance, which may lead to shut down of the grid.

The components included in Internet of things are sophisticated sensors, particularly wireless sensor networks (WSN), actuators and chips embedded in the physical things, to make them smart. These things are connected together and exchange huge data between them and with other digital components without any human intervention. An efficient security system may have an intention to not only protect and reinstate, but also assure the safety of the information in the computer from malicious attack. In other words, an efficient security system must have the following features:

(i) Secrecy: According to this feature, if any unauthorized entity or a process tries to access some confidential information, then the data becomes meaningless to that entity or process.

(ii) Data integrity: This feature ensures that data has not been accidentally or intentionally modified by a third party.

(iii) Validation: This performs verification of data source.

(iv) Non-repudiation: This is a legal aspect, where any entity sending a message will not be able to refuse it in the future.

(v) Accessibility: It is ensured that the services of the system are available to the valid entities.

(vi) Privacy policy: The aim of such a policy is to ensure that the identity of authorized users cannot be traced by any means.

7.9.1   The Case of Smart Grids

Automation is possible because of electrical energy, so it has a relevant role in the overall economic development. The concept of smart grid came into existence when electrical distribution line was integrated with information technology to collect the data of consumer demand [53]. This data has helped to optimize the generation of electricity. The smart grid consists of a network, popularly known as, advanced metering infrastructure (AMI), the purpose of which is to synchronize the generation and consumption of electricity. This optimization is possible with IoT technology. The major aspects required for security and privacy are mentioned below:

(i) Accessibility: The integrated network consisting of sensor network and smart meters, along with real time optimization queries handled by central control system, must be available continuously. The network must be secured enough so that intruders cannot perform malicious attack.

(ii) Secrecy: As the information exchanged between smart meters and the central control system is sensitive, it must not be disclosed to the unauthorized third parties.

(iii) Reliability: The data exchanged between smart meters and the central control system is required for making optimized decisions based on consumption pattern of different users in a particular region. If the data is corrupted due to any intentional or accidental malicious attack then the reliability of the data is questioned. The corrupted data in AMI network could give wrong decision for optimization of electrical energy usage.

(iv) Non-repudiation: Keeping in-line the legal aspects, any entity or process of AMI cannot deny that it has not received control commands or related information from the central control unit.

(v) Privacy policy: The information contained in AMI network is very sensitive. So, it becomes relevant to protect the information related to electrical energy consumption pattern of the household and industries. Such information must be made untraceable.

Apart from security and privacy policies, smart grids are subjected to the following security challenges:

(i) Different devices integrated in IoT system follow different communication protocols. This means the information has to be made compatible with each other to make the system work automatic.

(ii) Increasing scalability: As the number of smart devices like smart energy meters and other smart electrical appliances are increasing rapidly, the consumption of electrical energy is also growing. So, increase in scalability may lead to security challenges.

(iii) Susceptibility to malicious attacks: Information technology is more prone to data theft or hacking. In smart grids, we are basically collecting the data from various nodes and using it for optimization of electrical energy supply & demand. Because smart grids have open infrastructure, so the reliability and secrecy of data in AMI network is prone to attacks such as injection, IP spoofing and DoS/DDoS attacks.

(iv) Privacy policy for data: Lot of data is exchanged between smart meters and central control unit. This data includes information regarding energy consumption/real-time usage of energy by each household and other payment details. For security reasons, this data must not be hacked or leaked by the intruders. If the data is hacked, then intruders can manipulate with the operation of the smart grid and with the sensitive details of the consumers payment methods.

7.9.2 The Case of Smart Cities

The emerging concept of smart cities is targeted to boost up the usage of public resources and the quality of life [54]. Therefore, different sensors are installed at various points like along the road sides, buildings, smart devices and smart cars. In public places, this sensor network can help to manage traffic and monitor weather conditions to manage flights. In households, sensor network can be either used to position solar panels so as to supply optimum electrical energy to the devices or generate alarm in case of any incident. Consider an example of charging station of electric vehicle (EV) [55]. With the help of a mobile application, the owner of EV can locate the nearest charging station. After charging, he can pay the bill using any one of the digital banking methods. Here, it becomes relevant to safely secure the data regarding units consumed while charging the EV, time taken to charge and the details of payment made by the user. Such data can help to make an analysis regarding the energy usage so that improvements can be made in the future. Similarly, it is very important to secure the data regarding payment details made by the user. A concept of smart car is shown in Figure 7.8. The security requirements of the smart cities can be generalized are mentioned below:

(i)   Maintaining information privacy by providing limited access to relevant data.
(ii) Maintaining record of source of information and user authentication.
(iii) Reliability of data collected is relevant as this data can be used for analysis and other decision making process, which helps to improve daily lives of citizens.
(iv) Availability of specific data to the authenticated users and decision makers.

Despite of the security policies, smart cities face the following security challenges:

(i)   Smart devices vary in terms of its application, capability and characteristics. So, the foremost challenge in smart city is to make these diverse smart devices communicate with each other. Moreover, no communication standard has been formulated for the devices dedicatedly working for different applications.
(ii) As the number of smart devices is increasing daily, this creates a challenge regarding scalability.
(iii) There is huge amount of data from different smart devices being collected in web cloud. The challenge is to locate the source of data, then control it from unauthorized usage and secure its reliability and privacy.

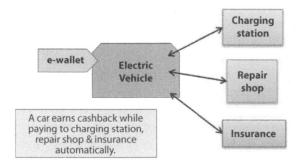

Figure 7.8 Smart car performing secured transactions through blockchain.

References

1. An, J., Li, G., Ning, B., Jiang, W., Sun, Y., Re-sculpturing Semantic Web of Things as a Strategy for Internet of Things' Intrinsic Contradiction, in: *Artificial Intelligence in China. Lecture Notes in Electrical Engineering*, vol. 572, Q. Liang, W. Wang, J. Mu, X. Liu, Z. Na, B. Chen (Eds.), Springer, Singapore, 2020.

2. Lau, B.P.L., Wijerathne, N., Ng, B.K.K., Yuen, C., Sensor Fusion for Public Space Utilization Monitoring in a Smart City. *IEEE Internet Things J.*, 5, 2, 473–481, April 2018.

3. Balaji, S., Nathani, K., Santhakumar, R., IoT Technology, Applications and Challenges: A Contemporary Survey. *Wireless Pers. Commun.*, 108, 363, 2019. https://doi.org/10.1007/s11277-019-06407-w.

4. Bhattacharyya, R., Das, A., Majumdar, A., Ghosh, P., Sharma, N., Chakrabarti, A., Balas, V. (Eds.), Real-Time Scheduling Approach for IoT-Based Home Automation System, in: *Data Management, Analytics and Innovation. Advances in Intelligent Systems and Computing*, vol. 1016, Springer, Singapore, 2020.

5. Zhang, C., Wu, J., Long, C., Cheng, M., Review of Existing Peer-to-Peer Energy Trading Projects. *Energy Procedia*, 105, 2563–2568, May 2017. https://doi.org/10.1016/j.egypro.2017.03.737.

6. Datta, A. and Odendaal, N., Smart cities and the banality of power. *Environ. Plan. D: Society and Space*, 37, 3, 387–392, 2019. https://doi.org/10.1177/0263775819841765.

7. de Falco, S., Angelidou, M., Addie, J.-P.D., From the "smart city" to the "smart metropolis", Building resilience in the urban periphery. *Eur. Urban Reg. Stud.*, 26, 2, 205–223, 2019. https://doi.org/10.1177/0969776418783813.

8. Rohit, G. and Anandarajah, G., Energy for Sustainable Development, Assessing the evolution of India's power sector to 2050 under different CO_2 emissions rights allocation schemes. *Energy for Sustainable Development*, 50, 2019, 126–138. https://doi.org/10.1016/j.esd.2019.04.001.

9. Mohammad, F.A. and Alam, S., Assessment of power exchange based electricity market in India. *Energy Strateg. Rev.*, 23, 163–177, January 2019. https://doi.org/10.1016/j.esr.2018.12.012.

10. Al-Sakran, H., Alharbi, Y., Serguievskaia, I., Framework Architecture for Securing IoT Using Blockchain, Smart Contract and Software Defined Network Technologies. *2019 2nd International Conference on new Trends in Computing Sciences (ICTCS), Amman, Jordan*, pp. 1–6, 2019.

11. https://economictimes.indiatimes.com/news/economy/policy/transition-to-e-vehicles-may-take-longer-than-2030-teri-chief/articleshow/70265140.cms?from=mdr (Accessed on date: 20-12-2019)

12. https://economictimes.indiatimes.com/the-twin-problems-that-in-dias-thermal-power-sector-must-overcome/articleshow/51056423.cms?from=mdr (Accessed on date: 22-08-2019)

13. https://smartcityhub.com/collaborative-city/smart-cities-1-0-2-0-3-0-whats-next/ (Accessed on date: 06-08-2019)

14. https://www.businesstoday.in/sectors/energy/green-energy-push-now-cpwd-government-buildings-will-run-on-solar-panels/story/228866.html (Accessed on date: 07-09-2019)

15. https://www.energymatters.com.au/misc/peer-to-peer-solar-energy-trading-guide/(Accessed on date: 25-10-2019)

16. https://www.powergridindia.com/one-nation-one-grid (Accessed on date: 06-06-2019)

17. https://www.powergridindia.com/smart-grid (Accessed on date: 14-10-2019)

18. https://www.tatapower.com/products-and-services/micro-grids.aspx (Accessed on date: 06-06-2019)

19. Marín, J., Rocher, J., Parra, L., Sendra, S., Lloret, J., Mauri, P.V., Autonomous WSN for Lawns Monitoring in Smart Cities. *2017 IEEE/ACS 14th International Conference on Computer Systems and Applications (AICCSA)*, Hammamet, pp. 501–508, 2017.

20. Akkaya, K., Guvenc, I., Aygun, R., Pala, N., Kadri, A., IoT-based occupancy monitoring techniques for energy-efficient smart buildings. *2015 IEEE Wireless Communications and Networking Conference Workshops (WCNCW)*, New Orleans, LA, pp. 58–63, 2015.

21. Biswas, K. and Muthukkumarasamy, V., Securing Smart Cities Using Blockchain Technology. *2016 IEEE 18th International Conference on High Performance Computing and Communications; IEEE 14th International Conference on Smart City; IEEE 2nd International Conference on Data Science and Systems (HPCC/SmartCity/DSS)*, Sydney, NSW, pp. 1392–1393, 2016.

22. Gai, K., Wu, Y., Zhu, L., Qiu, M., Shen, M., Privacy-Preserving Energy Trading Using Consortium Blockchain in Smart Grid. *IEEE Trans. Ind. Inf.*, 15, 6, 3548–3558, June 2019.

23. Kaur, J., Sood, Y.R., Shrivastava, R., Emerging Green Energy Potential: An Indian Perspective, in: *Applications of Computing, Automation and Wireless Systems in Electrical Engineering. Lecture Notes in Electrical Engineering*, vol. 553, S. Mishra, Y. Sood, A. Tomar (Eds.), Springer, Singapore, 2019.

24. Lohan, V., Singh, R.P., Kolhe, M., Trivedi, M., Tiwari, S., Singh, V. (Eds.), Home Automation Using Internet of Things. In: Advances in Data and Information Sciences, in: *Lecture Notes in Networks and Systems*, vol. 39, Springer, Singapore, 2019.

25. Akbar, M.A. and Azhar, T.N., Concept of Cost Efficient Smart CCTV Network for Cities in Developing Country. *2018 International Conference on ICT for Smart Society (ICISS)*, Semarang, pp. 1–4, 2018.

26. Mylrea, M. and Gourisetti, S.N.G., Blockchain for smart grid resilience: Exchanging distributed energy at speed, scale and security. *2017 Resilience Week (RWS)*, Wilmington, DE, pp. 18–23, 2017.

27. Samaniego, M. and Deters, R., Blockchain as a Service for IoT. *2016 IEEE International Conference on Internet of Things (iThings) and IEEE Green*

Computing and Communications (GreenCom) and IEEE Cyber, Physical and Social Computing (CPSCom) and IEEE Smart Data (SmartData), Chengdu, pp. 433–436, 2016.

28. Molderink, Bakker, V., Bosman, M.G.C., Hurink, J.L., Smit, G.J.M., Management and Control of Domestic Smart Grid Technology. *IEEE Trans. Smart Grid*, 1, 2, 109–119, Sept. 2010.

29. Muzammal, S.M. and Murugesan, R.K., A Study on Secured Authentication and Authorization in Internet of Things: Potential of Blockchain Technology, in: *Advances in Cyber Security. ACeS 2019. Communications in Computer and Information Science*, vol. 1132, M. Anbar, N. Abdullah, S. Manickam (Eds.), Springer, Singapore, 2020.

30. Nidhi, N., Prasad, D., Nath, V., Different Aspects of Smart Grid: An Overview, in: *Nanoelectronics, Circuits and Communication Systems. Lecture Notes in Electrical Engineering*, vol. 511, V. Nath and J. Mandal (Eds.), Springer, Singapore, 2019.

31. Nitnaware, D., Smart Energy Meter: Application of WSN for Electricity Management (February 24, 2019). *Proceedings of International Conference on Sustainable Computing in Science, Technology and Management (SUSCOM)*, February 26–28, 2019, Amity University Rajasthan, Jaipur, India, Available at SSRN: https://ssrn.com/abstract=3356286 or http://dx.doi.org/10.2139/ssrn.3356286.

32. Noura, M., Atiquzzaman, M., Gaedke, M., Interoperability in Internet of Things: Taxonomies and Open Challenges. *Mobile Netw. Appl.*, 24, 796, 2019. https://doi.org/10.1007/s11036-018-1089-9.

33. Flauzac, O., González, C., Hachani, A., Nolot, F., SDN Based Architecture for IoT and Improvement of the Security. *2015 IEEE 29th International Conference on Advanced Information Networking and Applications Workshops*, Gwangiu, pp. 688–693, 2015.

34. Novo, O., Blockchain Meets IoT: An Architecture for Scalable Access Management in IoT. *IEEE Internet Things J.*, 5, 2, 1184–1195, April 2018.

35. Prasad, R. and Rohokale, V., Internet of Things (IoT) and Machine to Machine (M2M) Communication, in: *Cyber Security: The Lifeline of Information and Communication Technology. Springer Series in Wireless Technology*, Springer, Cham, 2020.

36. Du, R., Santi, P., Xiao, M., Vasilakos, A.V., Fischione, C., The Sensable City: A Survey on the Deployment and Management for Smart City Monitoring. *IEEE Commun. Surv. Tutorials*, 21, 2, 1533–1560, Second quarter 2019.

37. Das, R.K. and Misra, H., Smart city and E-Governance: Exploring the connect in the context of local development in India. *2017 Fourth International Conference on eDemocracy & eGovernment (ICEDEG)*, Quito, pp. 232–233, 2017.

38. Hinrichs-Rahlwes, R., Renewable energy: Paving the way towards sustainable energy security: Lessons learnt from Germany. *Renewable Energy*, 49, 10–14, January 2013. https://doi.org/10.1016/j.renene.2012.01.076.

39. Hossain, Md A., RoyPota, H., Squartini, S., Abdou, A.F., Modified PSO algorithm for real-time energy management in grid-connected microgrids. *Renewable, Energy,* 136, 2019, 746–757 https://doi.org/10.1016/j.renene.2019.01.005.

40. Spanias, S., Solar energy management as an Internet of Things (IoT) application. *2017 8th International Conference on Information, Intelligence, Systems & Applications (IISA), Larnaca,* pp. 1–4, 2017.

41. Sanjay Kumar, S., Khalkho, A., Agarwal, S., Prakash, S., Prasad, D., Nath, V., Mandal, J. (Eds.), Design of Smart Security Systems for Home Automation, in: *Nanoelectronics, Circuits and Communication Systems. Lecture Notes in Electrical Engineering,* vol. 511, Springer, Singapore, 2019.

42. Caraguay, Á.L.V., Peral, A.B., López, L.I.B., SDN: Evolution and Opportunities in the Development IoT Applications, First Published May 4, 2014. Review Article, *International Journal of Distributed Sensor Networks,* Volume: 10 issue: 5, 1–10. https://doi.org/10.1155/2014/735142.

43. Garg, S., Yadav, A., Jamloki, S., Sadana, A., Tharani, K., IoT based home automation. 261–271, Published online: 06 Feb 2020. Journal of Information and Optimization Sciences, Volume 41, 2020 - Issue 1: Recent trends in Optimization, Signal Processing and Automation. https://doi.org/10.1080/0 2522667.2020.1721581.

44. Sambhi, S., Thermal Imaging Technology for Predictive Maintenance of Electrical Installation in Manufacturing Plant—A Literature Review. *2nd IEEE International Conference on Power Electronics, Intelligent Control and Energy Systems (ICPEICES-2018),* IEEE.

45. Ahram, T., Sargolzaei, A., Sargolzaei, S., Daniels, J., Amaba, B., Blockchain technology innovations. *2017 IEEE Technology & Engineering Management Conference (TEMSCON), Santa Clara, CA,* pp. 137–141, 2017.

46. Del Carpio-Huayllas, T.E., Ramos, D.S., Vasquez-Arnez, R.L., Feed-in and net metering tariffs: An assessment for their application on microgrid systems. *2012 Sixth IEEE/PES Transmission and Distribution: Latin America Conference and Exposition (T&D-LA), Montevideo,* pp. 1–6, 2012.

47. Ku, T., Park, W., Choi, H., IoT energy management platform for microgrid. *2017 IEEE 7th International Conference on Power and Energy Systems (ICPES), Toronto, ON,* pp. 106–110, 2017.

48. Tang, Q., Xie, M., Yang, K. *et al.,* A Decision Function Based Smart Charging and Discharging Strategy for Electric Vehicle in Smart Grid. *Mobile Netw. Appl.,* 24, 1722, 2019. https://doi.org/10.1007/s11036-018-1049-4.

49. Tanwar, S., Tyagi, S., Kumar, S., The Role of Internet of Things and Smart Grid for the Development of a Smart City, in: *Intelligent Communication and Computational Technologies. Lecture Notes in Networks and Systems,* vol. 19, Y.C. Hu, S. Tiwari, K. Mishra, M. Trivedi (Eds.), Springer, Singapore, 2018.

50. Caragliu, A. and Del Bo, C.F., Smart innovative cities: The impact of Smart City policies on urban innovation. *Technol. Forecasting Social Change.* Volume 142, 2019, Pages 373-383. https://doi.org/10.1016/j.techfore.2018.07.022.

51. Telang, A.S., Bedekar, P.P., Wakde, S.D., Towards Smart Energy Technology by Integrating Smart Communication Techniques, in: *Techno-Societal 2018*, P. Pawar, B. Ronge, R. Balasubramaniam, A. Vibhute, S. Apte (Eds.), Springer, Cham, 2020.

52. Hamidi, V., Smith, K.S., Wilson, R.C., Smart Grid technology review within the Transmission and Distribution sector. *2010 IEEE PES Innovative Smart Grid Technologies Conference Europe (ISGT Europe), Gothenberg*, pp. 1–8, 2010.

53. Viriyasitavat, W., Da Xu, L., Bi, Z. *et al.*, Blockchain-based business process management (BPM) framework for service composition in industry 4.0. *J. Intell. Manuf.*, 2018. https://doi.org/10.1007/s10845-018-1422-y.

54. Su, Z., Wang, Y., Xu, Q., Fei, M., Tian, Y., Zhang, N., A Secure Charging Scheme for Electric Vehicles With Smart Communities in Energy Blockchain. *IEEE Internet Things J.*, 6, 3, 4601–4613, June 2019.

55. Zikria, Y.B., Kim, S.W., Hahm, O., Afzal, M.K., Aalsalem, M.Y., Internet of Things (IoT) Operating Systems Management: Opportunities, Challenges, and Solution. *Sensors*, 19, 1793, 2019.

8

A Novel Framework for Intelligent Spaces

Deepali Kamthania

School of Information Technology, Vivekananda Institute of Professional Studies, Delhi, India

Abstract

With the amplified availabilities of smart sensors and context aware appliance, ispace have wide range of application. In order to transform a space to ispace communication and information exchange sensors, modeling tools for understanding user's intention and narration coordination are required. In this paper the framework for implementation of ispace has been proposed considering various design and implementation issues. The basic issues of an intelligent space that need to be taken care and handled by pervasive computing environment have also been discussed.

Keywords: Intelligent space (ispace), radio frequency identification (RFID), pervasive computing, robustness, context-based awareness

8.1 Introduction

Intelligent space (ispace) intend to design system entrenched with wisdom for understanding, monitoring, controlling [1] and communication with the users and environment. Humans communicate with the environment through accent, touch, gestures, smell and motion besides unique characteristics fascia, speech, finger prints, physics, etc. The CCTV (close circuit TV), sensors, microphones, actuators and many gadgets are available that helps in achieving interaction. The ubiquitous computing goes behind the scene, to keep sensors and actuators in collaboration to achieve pervasive computing with the goal to provide hassle free uninterrupted quality life to individual. The various objects in the environment are wirelessly

Email: deepali102@gmail.com

Parul Gandhi, Surbhi Bhatia, Abhishek Kumar, Mohammad Alojail and Pramod Singh Rathore (eds.) *Internet of Things in Business Transformation: Developing an Engineering and Business Strategy for Industry 5.0*, (127–140) © 2021 Scrivener Publishing LLC

connected and continuously keep collecting and processing data to adapt to various circumstances [2]. Many gadgets are available helps in achieving the ubiquitous environment through Internet of Things (IOT) sensor technology and Radio Frequency Identification (RFID) technology [3]. The systems based on tethered interfaces provide virtual reality but untethered interfaces are applied for stable natural interactions. As the users moves from places to places the interaction of the devices of the users and the computing environment goes region specific and it also depends on the preferences and likes of the local users. In this scenario it is therefore necessary to develop a framework in which different devices and users are able to communicate, without any extra efforts and loading on the computing of the user's computer. In the last few years for tracking people in image sequences articulated model-based techniques are applied [4–8]. In this Chapter the authors have tried to put forward a solution of a future smart retail store fitted with various gadgets and devices and has proposed a framework for intelligent space. The basic issues of a retail store that need to be taken care and handled by pervasive computing environment have also been discussed.

8.2   Intelligent Space

The design of ispace should be devised as a fulltime uninterrupted service which works even if the user requirements are not completely defined. The system should be self-adaptive in case of device failure [9, 10] and equipped to make smart choice along with constant monitoring of environmental state. The interaction in ispace is dynamic and based on abstract services rather than resources with the ability to map a service to wide range of solutions and choose the best based on minimized cost and resource. In order to transform a space to ispace for communication and information exchange sensors and modeling tools for understanding user's intention and narration coordination are required. The people driven narrative spaces use sensing modality to recognize and comprehend real time surrounding data to identify people and theirs action in space.

8.2.1   Sensing

In real time scenario the unencumbered virtual reality interfaces requires uninterrupted tracking of person features like hand position, location, unique characteristics, etc. which are identified using computer vision techniques [11, 12]. The mathematical algorithms are applied to interpret hand gestures used in managing various electrical domestic devices controlled using hand gestures [13] have used map estimator and Kalman filter to track real time human body motion considering 2D human body as a set of color areas. In order to have pointing direction and accurate depth maximum likelihood approaches are quite effective for locating body features in 3D space. Hidden Markov Models (HMMs) and Bayesian networks are used to classify human movements and gestures [14, 15]. HMMs based method is used for dynamic gesture trajectory modeling and recognition using Adaboost algorithm with condensation and partitioned sampling [16].

8.2.2   Multimodal Perception

Understanding user intention is the key for successful implementation of a smart space. Robust sensing is the basis for the accurate understanding of the user's purpose and context. For understanding user objective it is essential that there is complete tracking and data collection of individual movement and based on data analysis appropriate action are taken. The user can be tracked with the help of sensors. Single sensor like camera, radar or electric field sensor provide single view which will not be very useful in understanding user intention so in most of the cases multi sensor are preferred to tackle real time situation. The collection of data from multi-sensors results in redundancy which need to resolved for accurate perception [17].

8.2.3   Context-Based Data Interpretation

For accurate measurement of about user location it is essential to construe the dimensions in respect to user action and context. The same action or gesture can have different meaning, so the system should be capable enough to understand expectation based on user's action and intelligent enough to differentiate among the actions based on the previous data. The model should be flexible and adaptive revised by learning the user's interaction profile [18, 19].

8.2.4   Narrative Engines

In interactive environment direct mapping of sensor input with digital output works is not very effective as it involves series of coupling between user input and system responses. To create narrative spaces it is essential to simulate encounter between public and digital media acting as character which requires taking user's intentions and context of interaction into consideration [18] to develop a story based on how the user's actions match the system's expectations about those actions, and the system's goals.

8.3   Product Identification

There are various technologies available for product identification, among them bar code and Radio Frequency Identification (RFID) is popular. RFID technology can be used to manage the inventory, billing and product identification. There are various telecom technologies available in the market that can be used to communicate and track objects wirelessly. Spread spectrum radios are available in the market that can be used over small distances to transfer position data within the store. This can be used in position identification and tracking of the customer. If the customer position can be measured and moves are tracked in the retail store he can be guided by the smart shopping tool in choosing appropriate product as well as guiding him to suitable racks and aisles. RFID has demonstrated its efficiency in providing automated data capture and serialized identification capabilities and turnout to be a pervasive technology. Earlier experiments have shown that RFID can deliver significant results in consumer experience and retail operation. In RFID system the data carrying information related to article or entity identification, location etc. is transmitted through transponders and received by machine readable tag readers which facilitates the scenario where humans and things are linked and contactable i.e. "anytime and anywhere" ICT and can be tracked using tiny radio transmitters, or tagged with embedded hyperlinks using various frequency bands. Some examples of application of frequency range are as follows: Less than 135 kHz is used for animal tagging and tracking. The frequencies like 1.95, 3.25, 4.75, and 8.2MHz can be used in retail stores for Electronic Article Surveillance (EAS) systems. The 27 MHz frequency and above is used for ISM (Industrial, Scientific and Medical) applications. The frequency range 902–916 MHz can be applied for Railcar and Toll road applications whereas 5.85–5.925 GHz band for Intelligent Transportation Services. The data transfer rate between tag and reader is directly affected by the carrier wave frequency and is linked to bandwidth in the frequency spectrum. For better performance channel bandwidth should be double the bit rate. To take care of noise bandwidth plays an important role. The tags or transponder (TRANSmitter/resPONDER) and a reader or interrogator are main component of RFID system the availability of power determines the range for wireless communication considering noise to signal ratio for higher frequencies. The tags are designed for interfacing to external coil having stamp, location and data for communication. The transponder memory (RAM, ROM or nonvolatile programmable) depend on the type of device for data storage. EROM is used in transponder to store data even in sleep state. The operating system instruction processing logic for delay, data flows, etc. are available with transponder to perform basic functioning of device and RAM supports intermediate storage during the process [19].

8.4   Position Measurements

The prospect digital surroundings need to intelligent enough to understand the human need and provide quick response. It requires precise positioning of individual and items with Global Positioning System (GPS) [20]. Pervasive Computing involving precise information of indoor location make electronic devices responsive [21] involves radio frequency (RF) transmissions. To understand the time and distance between transmitter and receiver 2-D position triangulation can be considered using different range transmitters for coordinates [22–24].

Figure 8.1 shows receiver as proximity detector. The signal s (t) of BS bandwidth arrive receiver rec (t) having propagation time (T_0), carrier frequency (ω_c) and noise component noise (t) having θ phase shifting

$$rec(t) = rec_1(t) + noise(t) = s(t - T).e^{jw_c t + \theta} + noise(t) \qquad (8.1)$$

where

$T_0 = R/c$ = (distance between transmitter and receiver/propagation speed in free space).

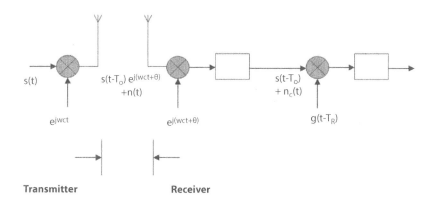

Figure 8.1 Transmitter and receiver.

The transmitted signal is mixed with ω_c to generate $R\{s(t).e^{jw_c t}\}$. The received signal baseband is lowered by mixing with a local oscillator signal $e^{jw_c t + \theta}$ but still the noise component as given Equation (8.2) exists so the gating functions $g(t - T_R)$ are applied at receiver end (where T_R is the estimated arrival time) to check whether range given in Equation (8.3).

$$n_c(t) = noise(t).\cos(w_c t + \theta) \qquad (8.2)$$

$$R_R = c.T_R \qquad (8.3)$$

If the signal is outside the range the error is generated.

Mallinckrodt and Sollenberger proposed optimum gating function $T_R - T_0$ for time measurement error minimization. Mallinckrodt's gating function differentiates $s(t)$ and differentiation function as parts of matched filter. The optimum receiver has gating of matched filter having differentiator at time T_R. Equation (8.4) shows minimum time measurement error for optimum setup.

$$\partial T_R = \frac{1}{\beta \sqrt{\left(2E \middle/ N_0 \right)}} \ where \ \beta^2 = \frac{1}{E} \int_{-\infty}^{\infty} (2\pi f)^2 / R_1(f)^2 \, df \qquad (8.4)$$

where,

β^2: mean-square bandwidth or Gabor bandwidth of the signal.

E: energy in the received signal $r_1(t)$ having signal bandwidth β.

$$E = \int_{-\infty}^{\infty} |R_1(f)|^2 \, df$$

The above factor is depended on the shape of the signal spectrum along with receiver bandwidth.

The root-mean-square range error

$$\partial R_R = c.\partial T_R \qquad (8.5)$$

The range error of an optimal receiver is determined by the energy received, the noise floor, and the effective bandwidth β for transmitted signal $s(t)$.

Helstrom observed that in case different observations of match filter are considered having independent noise contributions $n_0(T_R)$ are combined before differentiation it results in significant increase in range.

Considering the independent measurements (P) the reduction in time measurement variance can be expressed as follows

$$\partial T_R^{'2} = \cfrac{1}{\beta^2 \sum_{K=1}^{P} \left(\dfrac{2E}{N_0} \right)_k} = \cfrac{1}{\beta^2 \left(\dfrac{2E_T}{N_0} \right)} \tag{8.6}$$

where, $(E/N_0)_k$ is kth measurement of energy to noise density and E_T is the total received energy over all the k measurement periods.

The position of an item can be defined in terms of coordinates or distance. For day to application exact coordinates are not required rather relative position are of greater significance in indoor environment for context-aware intelligent systems. In the indoor environment, pseudo range measurement is due to reflection of surroundings along with receiver and transmitter signal. The multipath introduces error as distance is given by line of sight path and reflected components. For intelligent environment ideal receivers are considered which perform averaging of radio energy and remove the effect of fast fading to identify the line-of-sight component from amongst the multipath components [25].

The root-mean-square (RMS) range error in ideal Direct Sequence Spread Spectrum receiver is given as follows

$$\delta R_R = \sqrt{\frac{B}{f_c}} \frac{c}{2B\sqrt{E_T/N_0}} \tag{8.7}$$

where

c, propagation signal speed in free space, E_T, total received signal energy from several measurements, N_0, thermal noise, B, bandwidth of the pulse-shaping filter and f_c, chipping rate [26].

The performance of ideal receiver in Ref. [27] is calculated starting from the theoretical RMS error of Equation (8.7) in terms of the accuracy with which a given range can be measured, and the largest range that can be measured to a specified accuracy.

Plug and play positioning technology block translates the raw coordinates into logical descriptor in real time applications. The signal measurement take place at the physical layer and the information delivery is handled by the application layer. The details are discussed in next section.

8.5 Proposed Framework

Figure 8.2 shows the multilayer architecture of ispace. The observation collection is done at Reader level and outside IP network. The event manager at network edge performs observation processing and event translation. The mediation layer exists between network core edges. The network service and event consumer application resolve identifiers into entity description and subsequent query for associated context data. The application layer provides interface with the users. Application logic: Network core (Data center) level. The service management and tasking layer: the service

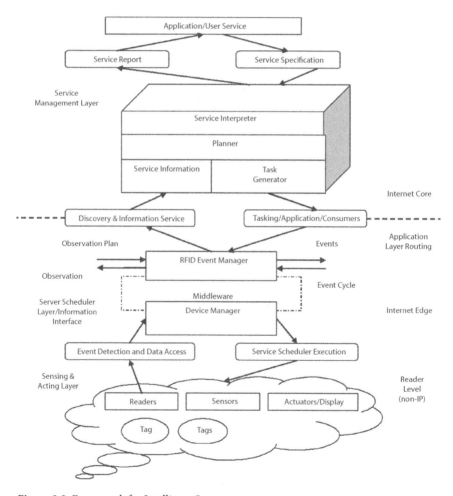

Figure 8.2 Framework for Intelligent Spaces.

manager scheduler conveys semantic information to application or system to make intelligent decision based on interference algorithm for extracting relevant information from data pool. The middleware layer is responsible for service scheduling. The sensing and acting layers have sensors and actuators connected by wireless network. For ispace state estimation the information collection and sensing of events are performed by sensors based on which control algorithms are executed by actuators. For event discovery, management and reporting event manager in RFID stack provide application programming interface. The events have to be processed in the specific time intervals [28]. The event manager provides RFID-specific context translation, required for pervasive computing systems [29].

Smart devices interact with physical world through embedded sensors connected to wireless self-organizing and configuring stable network which also requires good processing and storage capacity along with high resolution smart cameras to collect image and video data for analysis and GPS to get the location coordinates. Intelligent Retail spaces is characterized by multimodal sensory observation as user is changing the state continuously for searching the required items in the store, it requires mapping of sensory information using probabilistic and statistics techniques. IRS requires computational communication and interaction among items with PDA. The coordinates are required between item and user, timely information about each product/agent/item in the surrounding environment (racks) is essential so as the customer can response swiftly with the timely information. PDA has communication capacity with sensors and CPU. The context analysis is implemented using machine learning to make system more effective in IRS [30]. The Bayesian inference method has been applied on the signal information for distribution conditioning. The dynamic Bayesian network has been used to computer distribution conditioning on signal information and to take case of missing and noise measurement 30 and time is synchronization is required for sensing and actuation in the environment between computational controls and processing. The communication delays, data loss in sensing and actuation may cause insatiability or unpredictable behavior.

In automatic object identification system radio wave communication between reader and tag is required. The RFID tags can be active, passive or semi passive. The unique ID serial number (electronic product code) is broadcasted through radio frequencies by RFID tag to a nearby RFID reader. RFID systems can operate at different frequencies [31].

For automatic object identification UHF is used for identification of tag in the field at a given time minimizing collisions [32, 33]. The far field carrier wave operate using backscatter method, the tag reflects a part of electromagnetic wave emitted by reader to transmit information by examining reflection cross section of wave component sent back to reader for comparison with original. The data is encoded turning on and off the load connected. RFID tags are integrated with sensors. RFID readers communicate with sensors, read ID's from tag for transmitting information to host for inventory tracking and management. It enables monitoring of tagged objects in specified local area for location management and logistics operation. To prevent misuse data is encrypted and the distance between tag and reader is bounded and shielded during transmission [34, 35]. Due to denser system and presence of metal interference or collision between tags transmission occurs because of external radio frequency which can result in RFID read errors. The collision problem can be taken care by using variants of an anti-collision and singulation technique for orderly access of a specific tag [36]. RFID supports automatic identification of tagged entities in pervasive environment. It increases data collection and storage capacities immediately and accurately minimizing human efforts. Item level tagging improves inventory management support self-service payment and smart shelving. IRS takes advantage of tagged item as they can effectively tack and trace products accurately account for received and assembled products which in turn speed up the process and save time [37].

8.6 Conclusions

In this paper an attempt has been made to propose a framework of intelligent space, the different components that make an intelligent space and various software modules required to run behind them have been discussed along with RFID technology application in for inventory management in any other field.

References

1. Mallinckrodt, A.J. and Sollenberger, T.E., Optimum Pulse-Time Determination. *IRE Trans.*, PGIT-3, 151–159, 954.
2. Azarbayejani, A. and Pentland, A., Real-time self-calibrating stereo person tracking using 3-D shape estimation from blob features. *Proceedings of 13th International Conference on Pattern Recognition*, 1996.
3. Liu, B., Wang, F.-Y., Geng, J., Yao, Q., Gao, H., Zhang, B., Intelligent spaces: An overview. *2007 IEEE International Conference on Vehicular Electronics and Safety*, 2007.

4. Bregler, C. and Malik, J., Tracking People with Twists and Exponential Maps. *Proceedings of the IEEE Computer Society Conference on Computer Vision and Pattern Recognition (CVPR '98)*, IEEE Computer Society, Washington, DC, USA, p. 8, 1998.

5. Floerkemeier, C. and Lampe, M., RFID middleware design—Addressing application requirements and RFID constraints, in: *Proc. SOC-EUSAI, in: ACM International Conference Proceeding Series*, vol. 121, pp. 219–224, 2005.

6. Marinagi, C., Belsis, P., Skourlas, C., New Directions for Pervasive Computing in Logistics. *Procedia-Soc. Behav. Sci.*, 73, 495–502, 2013.

7. Helstrom, C.W., *Statistical Theory of Signal Detection*, Pergamon Press Oxford, England, 1960.

8. Gavrila, D.M. and Davis, L.S., 3-D model-based tracking of humans in action: a multi-view approach, in: *Proceedings of the 1996 Conference on Computer Vision and Pattern Recognition (CVPR '96) (CVPR '96)*, IEEE Computer Society, Washington, DC, USA, p. 73, 1996.

9. Darrell, T., Moghaddam, B., Pentland, A.P., Active face tracking and pose estimation in an interactive room, in: *Proceeding of CVPR '96 Proceedings of the 1996 Conference on Computer Vision and Pattern Recognition (CVPR '96)*, p. 67, 1996.

10. Katsiri, E., Bacon, J., Mycroft, A., Linking sensor data to context-aware applications using abstract events. *J. Pervasive. Comput. Syst.*, 3, 4, 347–377, 2007.

11. Kaplan, *Understanding GPS principles and applications*, Artech House, Boston & London, 1996.

12. Roussos, G. and Kostakos, V., RFID in pervasive computing: State of the art and outlook. *Pervasive Mob. Comput.*, 5, 110–131, 2009.

13. Goldman, R.P., Musliner, D.J., Krebsbach, K.D., Managing Online Self-adaptation in Real-Time Environments. *Lect. Notes Comput. Sci.*, 2614, 6–23, 2003.

14. Hall, D.L. and Llinas, J., An introduction to multisensor data fusion. *Proc. IEEE*, 85, 1, 6–23, 1997.

15. https://www.advancedmobilegroup.com/blog/whats-the-deal-with-rfid-frequencies

16. Item-level RFID Tagging and the Intelligent Apparel Supply Chain. RFID journal, 2011, Piscataway, New Jersey, http://www.rfidjournal.com/whitechapters/1.

17. Finkenzeller, K., *RFID Handbook: Fundamentals and Applications in Contactless Smart Cards and Identification*, John Wiley & Sons, London, 2003.

18. Römer, K., Schoch, T., Mattern, Dübendorfer, T., Smart identification frameworks for ubiquitous computing applications. *Wirel. Netw.*, 10, 6, 689–700, 2004.

19. Kakadiaris, I.A. and Metaxas, D., Three-Dimensional Human Body Model Acquisition from Multiple Views. *Int. J. Comput. Vision*, 30, 3, 191–218, 1998.

20. Laddaga, R., Robertson, P., Shrobe, H., Introduction to Self-adaptive Software: Applications. *Lect. Notes Comput. Sci.*, 2614, 1–5, 2003.

21. Yamamoto, M. and Yagishita, K., Scene constraints-aided tracking of human body, in: *Proceedings of Computer Vision and Pattern Recognition (CVPR'00)*, pp. 151–256, 2000.

22. Skolnik, M.I., *Introduction to Radar Systems*, Second Edition, McGraw-Hill, New York, 1981.

23. Marinagi, C., Belsis, P., Skourlas, C., New Directions for Pervasive Computing in Logistics. *Procedia—Soc. Behav. Sci.*, 73, 495–502, 2013.

24. Subhash Chandra, N., Venu, T., Srikanth, P., A Real Time Static & Dynamic Hand Gesture Recognition System. *Int. J. Eng. Inventions*, 4, 12, 93–98, 2015.

25. Porcino, D., & Wilcox, M., Empowering' ambient intelligence' with a direct sequence spread spectrum CDMA positioning system, Location Modeling for Ubiquious Computing, Workshop Proceedings Ubicomp, p11, 2001.

26. Oh, S. and Sastry, S., Distributed Networked Control System with Lossy Links: State Estimation and Stabilizing Communication Control. *Proceedings of the 45th IEEE Conference on Decision and Control*, 2006.

27. Remagnino, P. and Foresti, G.L., Ambient Intelligence: A New Multi-disciplinary Paradigm. *IEEE Trans. Syst. Man Cybern.-Part A*, 35, 1, 1–6, 2005.

28. Pavlovic, V.I., *Dynamic Bayesian Networks for Information Fusion with Applications to Human–Computer Interfaces*. PhD Thesis, University of Illinois, Urbana-Champain, 1999.

29. Peeters, R., Singelee, G., Preneel, B., Towards More Secure and Reliable Access Control. *IEEE Pervasive Comput.*, 11, 3, 76–83, 2012.

30. Caneel, R. and Chen, P., *Enterprise Architecture for RFID and Sensor Based Services*, Oracle Corporation, Redwood Shores, Calif., 2006.

31. Sparacino, F., Davenport, G., Pentland, A., Media Actors: Characters in Search of an Author. *IEEE Multimedia Systems '99, International Conference on Multimedia Computing and Systems (IEEE ICMCS'99)*, 7–11 June 1999, Centro Affari, Firenze, Italy.

32. Sparacino, F., Oliver, N., Pentland, A., Responsive Portraits, in: *Proceedings of the Eighth International Symposium on Electronic Art (ISEA 97)*, Chicago, IL, USA, September 22–27, 1997.

33. Starner, T. and Pentland, A., Visual Recognition of American Sign Language Using Hidden Markov Models. *International Workshop on Automatic Face and Gesture Recognition (IWAFGR)*, Zurich, Switzerland, 1995.

34. Thing Magic, *Getting a Read on Embedded UHF RFID: Why RFID Modules are the Smart Choice for Developing Next Generation Solutions*, Cambridge, 2012, http://www.thingmagic.com.

35. Wang, X., Xia, M., Cai, H., Gao, Y., Cattani, C., Hidden-Markov-Models-Based Dynamic Hand Gesture Recognition. *Math. Prob. Eng.*, special issue, 1–11, 2012.

36. Want, R., An introduction to RFID technology. *IEEE Pervasive Comput.*, 5, 1, 25–33, 2006.

37. Wren, C.R., Azarbayejani, A., Darrell, T., Pentland, A.P., Pfinder: Real-time tracking of the human body. *IEEE Trans. Pattern Anal. Mach. Intell.*, 19, 7, 780–785, 1997.

9

Defense and Isolation in the Internet of Things

Ravi Kumar Sharma[1]*, Tejinder Pal Singh Brar[1]† and Parul Gandhi[2]‡

[1]Chandigarh Group of Colleges, Landran, Punjab, India
[2]Manav Rachna International Institute of Research and Studies, India

Abstract

The Internet of Things refers to a type of network to connect anything with the Internet based on stipulated protocols through information sensing equipments to conduct information exchange and communications in order to achieve smart recognitions, positioning, tracing, monitoring, and administration. Internet of Things is a platform where every day devices become smarter, every day processing becomes intelligent, and every day communication becomes informative. While the Internet of Things is still seeking its own shape, its effects have already stared in making incredible strides as a universal solution media for the connected scenario. Architecture specific study does always pave the conformation of related field. Directly or indirectly, the presented architectures propose to solve real-life problems by building and deployment of powerful Internet of Things notions. Further, research challenges have been investigated to incorporate the lacuna inside the current trends of architectures to motivate the academics and industries get involved into seeking the possible way outs to apt the exact power of Internet of Things. A main contribution of this it summarizes the current state-of-the-art of Internet of Things architectures in various domains systematically.

Keywords: IoT protocols, network layer, transport layer, IoT gateways, routing attacks, IoT OAS, cryptography, public-key

*Corresponding author: ravirasotra@yahoo.com
†Corresponding author: tpsbrar@hotmail.com
‡Corresponding author: gandhi2110@gmail.com

Parul Gandhi, Surbhi Bhatia, Abhishek Kumar, Mohammad Alojail and Pramod Singh Rathore (eds.) *Internet of Things in Business Transformation: Developing an Engineering and Business Strategy for Industry 5.0*, (141–168) © 2021 Scrivener Publishing LLC

9.1   Introduction

The Internet of Things prompts another processing worldview. It is the aftereffect of moving processing to our continuous condition. The IoT gadgets, other than associating with the Internet, additionally need to converse with one another dependent on the arrangement setting. All the more absolutely, IoT isn't just about carrying savvy items to the Internet, yet in addition empowering them to converse with one another. This will have direct ramifications to our life, and change the manner in which we live, learn, and work. Along these lines, it gives an enormous chance to programmers to bargain security and protection. Note that we ought not just verify IoT frameworks from perils that may assault it over the open Internet, yet in addition secure a coopting gadget or respectful hub from an awful hub in a similar system. Today, we have sensibly secure and safe online monetary exchanges, web-based business, and different administrations over the Internet. Center to these frameworks is the utilization of cutting edge cryptographic calculations that require significant figuring power. Brilliant articles have restricted capacities regarding computational force and memory, and may be battery-controlled gadgets, along these lines raising the need to receive vitality proficient innovations. Among the striking difficulties that building interconnected brilliant items presents are security, protection, and trust. The utilization of Internet Protocol (IP) has been anticipated as the standard for interoperability for shrewd items. As billions of savvy objects are required to spring up and IPv4 addresses have in the long run arrived at exhaustion, the IPv6 convention has been distinguished as a contender for keen article correspondence. The difficulties that must be defeated to determine IoT security and protection issues are huge. This is essentially a direct result of the numerous requirements connected to the arrangement of security and protection in IoT frameworks. The arrangement of the IoT raises numerous security issues emerging because of the accompanying viewpoints:

- The very nature of smart objects, for example, the adoption of lightweight cryptographic algorithms, in terms of processing and memory requirements
- The use of standard protocols, for example, the need to minimize the amount of data exchanged between nodes
- The bidirectional flow of information, for example, the need to build an end-to-end security architecture.

9.1.1   IoT Reference Model

Today, there is no institutionalized theoretical model that portrays and institutionalizes the different elements of an IoT framework. Cisco Systems Inc. has proposed an IoT reference model [1] that contains seven levels. The IoT reference model permits the handling happening at each level to extend from minor to complex, contingent upon the circumstance. The model likewise depicts how errands at each level ought to be taken care of to look after effortlessness, permit high adaptability, and guarantee supportability. At last, the model characterizes the capacities required for an IoT framework to be finished. The seven levels and their short qualities are appeared in Table 9.1. The crucial thought is to display a degree of deliberation and proper practical interfaces to give a total arrangement of IoT. It is the soundness of a start to finish IoT engineering that permits one to process volume of setting explicit information focuses, cause important data, to oversee characteristic element of enormous scope, and at last plan astute reactions.

The significant structure factor is that IoT should use existing Internet correspondence framework and conventions. Level 3 is broadly alluded to as Edge Computing or Fog Computing. The essential capacity is to change

Table 9.1 IoT world forum reference model.

IoT reference model	
Levels	**Characteristics**
Physical devices and controllers	End point devices, exponential growth, diverse
Connectivity	Reliable, timely transmission, switching, and routing
Edge computing	Transform data into information, actionable data
Data accumulation	Data storage, persistent and transient data
Data abstraction	Semantics of data, data integrity to application, data standardization
Application	Meaningful interpretations and actions of data
Collaboration and processes	People, process, empowerment, and collaboration

information into data, and perform restricted information level investigation. Setting explicit data preparing is done at this level with the goal that we acquire significant information. A significant element of mist registering is its capacity of continuous handling and figuring. All the more absolutely, levels 1, 2, and 3 are worried about information moving, and the more elevated levels are worried about data got from the information things. It prompts a phenomenal worth zone wherein individuals and the procedures are engaged to make significant move from the underneath universe of IoT. The center target is to robotize the majority of the manual procedures, and engage individuals to improve and more intelligent.

At each degree of the reference model, the expanding number of substances, heterogeneity, interoperability, unpredictability, versatility, and circulation of elements speak to an extending assault surface, quantifiable by extra channels, strategies, on-screen characters, and information things. Further, this extension will essentially build the field of security partners and present new reasonability challenges that are exceptional to the IoT.

9.1.2 IoT Security Threats

There are three general classes of dangers: Capture, Disrupt, and Manipulate. Catch dangers are identified with catching the framework or data. Upset dangers are identified with denying, crushing, and disturbing the framework. Control dangers are identified with controlling the information, character, time-arrangement information, and so on. The most straightforward kind of uninvolved dangers in the IoT is that of listening in or checking of transmissions with an objective to get data that is being transmitted. It is additionally alluded to as catch assaults. Catch assaults are intended to oversee physical or sensible frameworks or to access data or information things from these frameworks. The omnipresence and physical dispersion of the IoT items and frameworks give assailants extraordinary chance to deal with these frameworks. The circulation of keen items, sensors, and frameworks brings about self-ads, reference points, and work interchanges, giving assailants more noteworthy chance to block or intervene in data transmission inside the earth. Also, the recurrence of the information transmissions, information models, and configurations help assailants in cryptanalysis.

A portion of the notable dynamic dangers are as per the following: Masquerading: an element claims to be an alternate substance. This incorporates disguising different items, sensors, and clients. Man-in-the-center: when the aggressor subtly transfers and potentially modifies the correspondence between two elements that accept that they are straightforwardly speaking with one another. Replay assaults: when an interloper sends some old (bona fide) messages to the beneficiary. On account of a communicate connection or guide, access to past transmitted information is simple. Disavowal of-Service (DoS) assaults: when an element neglects to play out its legitimate capacity or acts in a manner that keeps different substances from playing out their appropriate capacities.

Dynamic dangers, for example, disguising, replay assaults, DoS assaults are, all in all, nearly simple in an IoT domain. One model is the execution of cloned reference points from an untrusted source. Reference points are little remote gadgets that constantly transmit a straightforward radio sign saying, "I am here, this is my ID." In many cases, the sign is gotten by close by cell phones utilizing Bluetooth Low Energy (BLE) innovation. At the point when the cell phone distinguishes the guide signal, it peruses the reference point's recognizable proof number (ID), computes the separation to the guide and, in light of these information, triggers an activity in a signal good versatile application. In the writing [2], the IoT dangers are specified as cloning of brilliant articles by untrusted makers, falsifying/substitution of the IoT gadgets by the outsiders, pernicious firmware substitution, and assaults on generally unprotected gadgets by listening stealthily or extraction of accreditations or security properties, notwithstanding the standard risk vectors such Man-in-the-center and DoS assaults. The security and protection necessities are controlled by the idea of assaults in an IoT domain.

9.1.3   IoT Security Requirements

This area exhibits a review on the security prerequisites of the IoT. The essential security properties that should be executed in IoT are recorded straightaway. Classification: transmitted information can be perused distinctly by the correspondence endpoints; accessibility: the correspondence endpoints can generally be come to and can't be made out of reach; honesty: got information are not altered during transmission, and guaranteed of the precision and culmination over its whole lifecycle; genuineness: information sender can generally be checked and information beneficiaries can't be ridiculed and approval: information can be gotten to just by those permitted to do as such and ought to be made inaccessible to other people. The prerequisites for verifying the IoT are unpredictable, including a mix of approaches from versatile and cloud models, joined with mechanical control, computerization, and physical security. A considerable lot of the security necessities for the IoT are like the prerequisites for the IP convention based Internet. The innovations and administrations that have been utilized to verify the Internet are material by and large with reasonable adjustment required at each degree of the IoT reference model. Other than the standard security prerequisites, and from the dangers talked about, the accompanying security necessities can be determined.

9.1.3.1 Scale

The significant necessity is the scale wherein an IoT domain is relied upon to develop. The number of inhabitants in elements is required to develop exponentially as clients grasp increasingly keen and associated items and gadgets, more sensors are conveyed, and more articles are implanted with knowledge and data. Every element, contingent upon its inclination, attributes, conveys with it a related arrangement of conventions, channels, strategies, information models, and information things, every one of which is dependent upon potential danger. This expanded scale has the impact of extending the objective surface. As noted before, the scale and multifaceted nature at each degree of the IoT model decide the measure of process and capacity prerequisites, and thus the expense and force spending plan. The exchange off among cost and assets decides the accessibility of assets for framework security, cryptographic calculations, key size, and strategies.

9.1.3.2 IP Protocol-Based IoT

The utilization of IP advances in IoT brings various essential points of interest, for example, a consistent and homogeneous convention suite, and demonstrated security design. It likewise rearranges the systems to create and convey imaginative administrations by expanding the tried IP-based structures. It prompts a marvel called "development of assault surface." It suggests that when we interface the beforehand detached—by presenting new gadgets that stream setting delicate information, by putting information in versatile cloud, or by pushing figuring to edge gadgets—new purposes of entrance for security dangers unavoidably emerge. As the systems of shrewd items and IP converge, there is a high likelihood of security vulnerabilities because of convention interpretations, contradictory security frameworks, and so forth. The undertaking security model has been set apart by two boss principles:

- Security has been centered around best-of-breed applications and apparatuses: answers for firewall, for organize security, for information security, for content security, etc.
- Security has been edge based, which means associations verified the end gadget and the server, and responded to perceived interruptions or dangers, for example, infections

or DoS assaults. With regards to IoT, border based security instruments have little pertinence. The assault surface is a lot more extensive, regularly borderless, and includes heterogeneous frameworks.

9.1.3.3 Heterogeneous IoT

Another significant structure thought in the IoT is the way the associated things can cooperate to make esteem and convey creative arrangements and administrations. IoT can be a twofold edged sword. In spite of the fact that it gives a potential answer for the development basic, it can likewise altogether support operational multifaceted nature if not appropriately coordinated with key hierarchical procedures. Security procedures ought to likewise be appropriately intended to line up with the association forms. The complex operational innovations make it hard for structuring a strong security design in IoT. It is a typical sentiment that in the near future IP will be the base normal system convention for IoT. This doesn't suggest that all articles will have the option to run IP. Conversely, there will consistently be small gadgets, for example, minor sensors or Radio-Frequency Identification (RFID) labels, that will be composed in shut systems actualizing basic and application-explicit correspondence conventions and that in the end will be associated with an outside system through an appropriate door. To put it plainly, the heterogeneous qualities of the systems make it harder to execute certain IP-based security frameworks, for example, symmetric cryptosystems.

9.1.3.4 Lightweight Security

The remarkable estimation of IoT is acknowledged just when keen objects of various qualities interface with one another and furthermore with back-end or cloud administrations. IPv6 and web administrations become the basic structure squares of IoT frameworks and applications. In obliged organized situations, shrewd articles may require extra conventions and some convention adjustments so as to improve Internet interchanges and lower memory, computational, and power necessities. The utilization of IP advancements in IoT brings various fundamental focal points, for example, a consistent and homogeneous convention suite, and demonstrated security design. It additionally disentangles the systems to create and convey inventive administrations by broadening the tried IP-based structures. In any case, it likewise presents new difficulties in receiving certain systems in its present condition. The IoT gives interconnectedness of individuals and things for a tremendous scope with billions of gadgets. It is without a moment's delay a tremendous open door for better proficiency and better administrations, just as an immense open door for programmers to bargain security and protection.

It might be noticed that one of the key components of the cutting edge security in the Internet is the utilization of cutting edge cryptographic calculations requiring significant preparing power. Many, if not most, IoT gadgets depend on low-end processors or microcontrollers that have low handling force and memory, and are not structured with security as a need plan objective. Protection implemented through encryption, verification to acclimate personality, and Information validation by utilizing carefully marked declarations are the key security instruments in the Internet today. These instruments depend on the accompanying cryptographic figures, for example, Advanced Encryption Standard (AES), Secure Hash Algorithm (SHA2), and the open key figures RSA and elliptic-bend cryptography (ECC). Transport Layer Security (TLS) convention, and forerunner Secure Sockets Layer (SSL) convention, which give confirmation and data encryption utilizing the figures referenced. Public-Key Infrastructure (PKI) gives the structure squares to confirmation and trust through a computerized endorsement standard and Certificate Authorities (CA).

Current IoT executions have holes as far as actualizing the above security systems, despite the fact that these instruments have across the board reception in the IP systems. For instance, there are various business and open-source TLS executions that can be embraced in an IoT gadget. These libraries commonly expend in excess of 100 KB of code and information memory, which isn't a ton for a traditional figuring gadget, yet is illogical for an IoT gadget, for example, a restorative sensor. The cryptographic figures utilized by the TLS convention are a wellspring of noteworthy computational burden on the low end CPU of the regular IoT gadget. This computational burden brings about higher force utilization too. For instance, the information rate bolstered by a 32 piece MCU executing AES-128 may tumble from 3 Mbps to 900 Kbps if the MCU is subbed with a 16 piece processor. Note that this thus prompts circuitous impacts like longer dynamic time, more force channel, and a shorter battery life. Basically the test is to make the asset compelled IoT systems interoperate with the ingenious IP systems.

The present standards of IT security should be deconstructed by reconsidering and overhauling conventions, calculations, and procedures considering the advancing IoT design. All the more definitely, organize scale, heterogeneous, power limitations, and portability modify the assault surface on an a lot bigger scope and in more noteworthy broadness. It requires reevaluation and adaption of IP-based conventions and presentation of IoT explicit conventions.

9.2   IoT Security Overview

This area presents important foundation on the IoT control conventions, for example, ZigBee, IPv6 over Low-power WPAN (6LoWPAN), Constrained RESTful Environments (CoRE), CoAP, and security conventions, for example, IKEv2/IPSec, TLS/SSL, Datagram Transport Layer Security (DTLS), Host Identity Protocol (HIP), Protocol for Carrying Authentication for Network Access (PANA), and Extensible Authentication Protocol (EAP). It additionally talks about the key ideas on IoT security that incorporates personality the board, confirmation, approval, protection, trust, and administration for IoT systems. The scientific categorization of security assaults, dangers, and security instruments is exhibited in Table 9.2.

9.2.1   IoT Protocols

It examined the security methods for obliged IoT gadgets with use cases. It begins with the portrayal of general security design alongside its essential techniques, and afterward talks about how its components collaborate with the obliged correspondence stack and investigates upsides and downsides of well known security approaches at different layers of the ISO/OSI model. Additionally, the materialness and constraints of existing Internet conventions and security designs with regards to IoT are talked about in Ref. [3]. It gives a review of the organization model and general security needs. It displays the difficulties and prerequisites for IP-based security arrangements and feature explicit specialized impediments of standard IP security conventions (IPSec). There are right now IETF working gatherings concentrating on expanding existing conventions for asset compelled arranged situations. These are: CoRE [4], 6LoWPAN [5–7], Routing Over Low force and Lossy systems (ROLL) [8], and the Light-Weight Implementation Guidance (LWIG) working gatherings. Huge purposes behind appropriate convention advancements and adjustments for asset compelled objects are focused toward convention pressure to fit into littler Maximum Transmission Units (MTU), consequently decreasing force utilization with littler bundles, disposal of discontinuity, and diminishing the

Table 9.2 Security mechanisms to mitigate the threats in the IoT networks.

Threats/security mechanism	Data privacy	Data freshness	Source authentication	Data integrity	Intrusion detection	Identity protection
Capture						
Physical systems						X
Information	X			X		X
Disrupt						
DoS attack		X	X		X	
Routing attack					X	
Manipulate						
Masquerading	X		X	X		X
Replay attack		X	X	X	X	
Man-in-the-middle			X	X	X	

handshake messages. A run of the mill IoT layer for a Bluetooth shrewd empowered gadget convention stack is appeared in Table 9.3.

IPv6 essentially grows the quantity of accessible IP addresses for use by giving 2,128 locations. This implies, if vital, each gadget can have its own special IPv6 address. Measures, for example, 6LoWPAN have made it conceivable to coordinate sensors in a vehicle skeptic way. 6LoWPAN empowers sensors to converse with IP Protocols locally. Besides, new application layer conventions, for example, CoAP and Message Queue Telemetry Transport (MQTT) [9] guarantee ideal utilization of transmission capacity and assets of obliged IoT gadgets. Bluetooth Smart is an open standard that is explicitly intended for the requirements of battery fueled sensors and wearables. Presently controlled with the 6LoWPAN IETF draft, Bluetooth Smart is very much put to address advancing necessities of sensors associating with the cloud without the requirement for astute portals. The Internet Protocol Service Profile (IPSP) characterizes setting up and dealing with the Bluetooth coherent connection control and adjustment convention (L2CAP) association arranged channel. IPSP and Bluetooth Smart 6LoWPAN standard guarantees ideal IP stack execution over Bluetooth Smart as a physical layer. 6LoWPAN characterizes the formation of an IPv6 address of a gadget from its Bluetooth Smart gadget address. It additionally packs the IP header where conceivable to guarantee ideal utilization of RF data transfer capacity for power sparing purposes. A static profile of an IoT object speaks to the information by its very own endpoint assets, (for example, character, battery, processing power, memory size, and so on) and the security settings it expects to utilize or needs from the system. The static profile can be perused just (preset by merchant), compose once (set by producer), or rewritable (client empowered). Note that specific security natives might be computationally restrictive for IoT objects; an exchange is in this manner required before the foundation of a safe channel with the goal that the concerned endpoints can concur upon a cryptographic suite.

Table 9.3 Bluetooth smart device protocol stack.

Application layer	CoAP mqtt
Transport layer	UDP TCP
Network layer	IPv6 ICMPv6 RPL
Adaptation layer	Bluetooth Smart 6LoWPAN
Physical and link layer	IPSP

9.2.2 Network and Transport Layer Challenges

The IPSec [10] utilizes the idea of a Security Association (SA), characterized as the arrangement of calculations and parameters, (for example, keys) used to encode and validate a specific stream one way. To set up a SA, IPSec can be preconfigured (determining a preshared key, hash capacity, and encryption calculation) or can be progressively haggled by the IPSec Internet Key Exchange (IKE) convention. The IKE convention utilizes hilter kilter cryptography, which is computationally overwhelming for asset compelled gadgets. To address this issue, IKE augmentations utilizing lighter calculations ought to be utilized. Information overhead is another issue for IPSec usage in IoT situations. This is presented by the additional header exemplification of IPSec AH and additionally Encapsulating Security Payload (ESP) [11], and can be alleviated by utilizing header pressure.

CoAP proposes to utilize the DTLS convention [12] to give start to finish security in IoT frameworks. The DTLS convention gives a security administration like TLS, yet over UDP. This is exceptionally reasonable for IoT situations because of its utilization of UDP as transport convention. This outcomes in evasion of issues from the utilization of TCP in organize obliged situations that are caused because of the incredibly factor transmission postponement and misfortune joins. DTLS is a heavyweight convention and its headers are too long to even think about fitting in a solitary IEEE 802.15.4 MTU. 6LoWPAN gives header pressure components to lessen the size of upper layer headers. 6LoWPAN header pressure systems can be utilized to pack the security headers also [13] proposed another 6LoWPAN header pressure calculation for DTLS is proposed. It interfaces the packed DTLS with the 6LoWPAN standard utilizing institutionalized systems. It is demonstrated that the proposed DTLS pressure fundamentally diminishes the quantity of extra security bits [14] presented a two-way confirmation security conspire for the IoT dependent on DTLS. The proposed security plot depends on the broadly utilized open key based RSA cryptography convention and takes a shot at top of standard low force correspondence stacks.

9.2.3 IoT Gateways and Security

Availability is one of the significant difficulties in planning the IoT arrange. The assorted variety of end focuses makes it exceptionally hard to give IP network. It is significant that non-IP gadgets also have an instrument to interface with IoT. The IoT passages can disentangle IoT gadget configuration by supporting the various ways hubs locally associate, regardless of whether this is a changing voltage from a crude sensor, a flood of information over an internal incorporated circuit (I2C) from an encoder, or intermittent updates from a machine by means of Bluetooth. Doors viably moderate the incredible assortment and decent variety of gadgets by solidifying information from dissimilar sources and interfaces and connecting them to the Internet. The outcome is that singular hubs don't have to tolerate the multifaceted nature or cost of a rapid Internet interface so as to be associated. There are a few different ways that an IoT passage can stretch out network to hubs as portrayed underneath.

- The system hubs interface with the IoT by means of a door. The hubs themselves are not IP-based and consequently can't legitimately associate with the Internet/WAN. Or maybe, they utilize either wired or remote PAN innovation to interface with the entryway with a more affordable and less intricate method of network. The portal keeps up an IoT specialist for every hub that deals with all information to and from hubs. Right now, insight can likewise be situated in the door.
- The hubs can likewise interface straightforwardly to the Internet utilizing a WAN association, for example, Wi-Fi or Ethernet. The passage serves principally as a switch; truth be told, it very well may be basically a switch when hubs have their own IoT operator and self-sufficiently oversee themselves.
- Alternatively, the hubs can interface straightforwardly to the Internet utilizing a PAN association, for example, 6LoWPAN. Right now, passage fills in as an interpretation point between the PAN and WAN. Numerous IoT applications handle possibly delicate information. Information gathered from area administrations, for instance, should be shielded from hacking. So also, therapeutic gadgets need to keep up the security of people. With regards to the IoT portal engineering, the security preparing and components can be offloaded from hubs to the entryway to guarantee appropriate verification, ensuring trades of information, and defending protected innovation. This empowers IoT hubs to execute more noteworthy security than could be monetarily actualized in singular end focuses.

9.2.4 IoT Routing Attacks

Dangers emerging because of the physical idea of IoT gadgets can be alleviated by proper physical security shields, while secure correspondence conventions and cryptographic calculations are the main method for adapting to the way that they emerge due to IoT gadgets speaking with one another and the outer world. For the later, IoT gadgets can either run the standard TCP/IP convention stack, if their computational and force assets permit, or can run adaptions which are upgraded for lower computational and power utilization. There are some notable steering assaults that can be misused by aggressors. The 6LoWPAN systems or an IP-associated sensor systems are associated with the customary Internet utilizing 6LoWPAN Border Routers (6LBR). The Routing Protocol for Low-Power and Lossy Networks (RPL) is a novel steering convention institutionalized for 6LoWPAN systems. RPL makes a goal situated coordinated non-cyclic chart (DODAG) between the hubs in a 6LoWPAN. It underpins unidirectional traffic toward DODAG root and bidirectional traffic between 6LoWPAN gadgets and among gadgets and the DODAG root (normally the 6LBR). RPL empowers every hub in the system to decide if parcels are to be sent upwards to their folks or downwards to their youngsters.

Attacks on sensor networks that are applicable to IoT are discussed in Refs. [15, 16]. Some well-known routing attacks on IoT are as follows:

- Selective-forwarding attacks
- Sinkhole attacks
- Hello flood attacks
- Wormhole attacks
- Clone Id and Sybil attacks

With selective-forwarding attacks, it is possible to launch DoS attacks where malicious nodes selectively forward packets. This attack is primarily targeted to disrupt routing paths. For example, an attacker could forward all RPL control messages and drop the rest of the traffic. This assault has severer outcomes when combined with different assaults, for example, sinkhole assaults. One of the answers for prepare for specific sending assaults is to make disjoint ways between the source and the goal hubs. Another successful countermeasure against particular sending assaults is to ensure the aggressor can't recognize various kinds of traffic, in this way compelling the assailant to either advance all traffic or none.

In sinkhole assaults, a noxious hub publicizes a deceitful directing way with an apparently great course metric and pulls in numerous close by hubs to course traffic through it. An interruption discovery framework could be facilitated in the 6LBR and can use data from different DODAGs to recognize sinkhole assaults.

In the welcome flood assault, the HELLO message alludes to the underlying message a hub sends when joining a system. By communicating a HELLO message with solid sign force and a great steering metric, an aggressor can acquaint himself as a neighbor with numerous hubs, potentially the whole system. A basic answer for this assault is for every HELLO message the connection is checked to be bidirectional.

A wormhole is an out-of-band association between two hubs utilizing wired or remote connections. Wormholes can be utilized to advance bundles quicker than through ordinary ways. A wormhole made by an aggressor and joined with another assaults, for example, sinkhole, is a genuine security danger. One methodology is to utilize separate connection layer keys for various portions of the system. This can balance the wormhole assault, as no correspondence will be conceivable between hubs in two separate sections. Likewise, by restricting geographic data to the areas it is conceivable to beat a wormhole.

In a clone-ID assault, an assailant duplicates the personalities of a legitimate hub onto another physical hub. This can, for instance, be utilized so as to access a bigger piece of the system or so as to defeat casting a ballot plans. In a Sybil assault, which is like a clone ID assault, an assailant utilizes a few coherent substances on the equivalent physical hub. Sybil assaults can be utilized to assume responsibility for enormous pieces of a system without conveying physical hubs. By monitoring the quantity of examples of every character it is conceivable to identify cloned personalities. It would likewise be conceivable to distinguish cloned personalities by knowing the land area of the hubs, as no character ought to have the option to be at a few places simultaneously.

9.2.5   Bootstrapping and Authentication

Bootstrapping and verification controls the system passage of hubs. Confirmation is exceptionally pertinent to IoT and is probably going to be the main activity did by a hub when it joins another system, for example, after portability. It is performed with a (for the most part remote) validation server utilizing a system get to convention, for example, the PANA [17]. For more noteworthy interoperability, the utilization of the EAP [18] is imagined. Upon effective confirmation, higher layer security affiliations could likewise be set up, (for example, IKE followed by IPSec [19]) and propelled between the recently validated endpoint and the entrance control specialist in the related system.

The Internet Key Exchange (IKEv2)/IPSec and the HIP [20] live at or over the system layer. The two conventions can play out a validated key trade and set up the IPSec changes for secure payload conveyance. Right now, there are likewise progressing endeavors to make a HIP variation called Diet HIP [21] that considers misfortune low-influence systems at the confirmation and key trade level.

9.2.6 Authorization Mechanisms

The present day benefits that run over the Internet, for example, famous web based life applications, have confronted and taken care of security related issues when managing individual and ensured information that may be made open to outsiders. Later on, the IoT applications will confront comparative issues, and others that might be one of a kind to the area. The OAuth (Open Authorization) convention has been characterized to take care of the issue of permitting approved outsiders to get to individual client information [22]. OAuth 2.0 [23] is an approval system that permits an outsider to get to an asset possessed by an asset proprietor without giving decoded qualifications to the outsider. For instance, expect that a social insurance sensor or versatile application needs to get to a Facebook profile to post announcements. There is no compelling reason to give the Facebook certifications to the application; rather, the client signs into Facebook, and accordingly the application is approved to utilize Facebook for the client's benefit. The client can likewise disavow this approval whenever by erasing the benefit in the Facebook settings. The OAuth 2.0 convention characterizes the accompanying four jobs.

9.2.6.1 Resource Owner

It is an entity capable of granting access to a protected resource. When the resource owner is a person, it is referred to as an end user. In the above example, this could be the end user of the healthcare device.

9.2.6.2 Resource Server (Service Provider, SP)

It is the server hosting the protected resources, capable of accepting and responding to protected resource requests using access tokens. In the example, this is the Facebook server.

9.2.6.3 Client (Service Consumer, SC)

It is the application making protected resource requests on behalf of the resource owner and with its authorization. The term client does not imply any particular implementation characteristics (e.g., whether the application executes on a server, a desktop, or other devices). In this case, it is the healthcare sensor or mobile application.

9.2.6.4 Authorization Server

It is the server issuing access tokens to the client after successfully authenticating the resource owner and obtaining authorization. In this example, it would be the Facebook authorization server.

9.2.7 IoT OAS

Note that the IoT gadgets may have difficulties in usage of OAuth because of the CPU concentrated nature of cryptographic calculations [24] proposed an adjusted engineering called IoT-OAS. Right now, related capacities are assigned to an outside IoT-OAS approval administration, so as to limit the memory and CPU necessities on the IoT gadget itself.

An approaching OAuth verified solicitation is sent to an IoT-OAS administration for check of the entrance token contained in the solicitation. The IoT-OAS administration registers the advanced mark of the approaching solicitation utilizing the proper plan (PLAINTEXT/HMAC/ RSA) and matches it with its inside store to confirm the client and customer accreditations and authorizations for asset get to. It at that point gives a fitting reaction back permitting or denying the mentioned access from the customer. This methodology empowers the IoT gadget to concentrate alone assistance rationale and opens up computational assets from being overpowered by security and cryptographic usage. The security conventions at each layer between various systems are appeared in Figure 9.1.

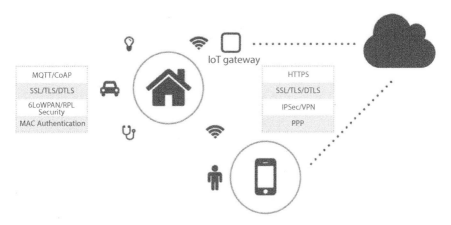

Figure 9.1 An overview of IoT and IP security protocols.

9.3   Security Frameworks for IoT

Right now, examine a portion of the particular structures utilized for understanding a safe IoT framework. The low capacities of IoT gadgets as far as their vitality and figuring abilities, remote nature, and physical defenselessness are examined to be the contributing variables to some novel security vulnerabilities. Specifically, we spread the tight asset requirements, convention interpretation, for example, HTTP ↔ CoAP, and start to finish Security. Other significant points incorporate the engineering structure viewpoints: Distributed versus Centralized methodology, bootstrapping character and key exchange, security mindful distinguishing proof, versatility, and IP arrange elements. In the period of inescapable registering with huge systems of asset compelled IoT gadgets, Moore's law can be deciphered diversely [25]: as opposed to a multiplying of execution, we see a splitting of the cost for consistent figuring power like clockwork. Since many predicted applications have incredibly tight cost requirements after some time, for example, RFID in tetra packs, Moore's law will progressively empower such applications. Numerous applications will process delicate wellbeing observing or biometric information, so the interest for cryptographic parts that can be productively executed is solid and developing.

9.3.1   Light Weight Cryptography

The term lightweight cryptography alludes to a group of cryptographic calculations with littler impression, low vitality utilization, and low computational force needs. Each originator of lightweight cryptography must adapt to the exchange offs between security, cost, and execution. It is commonly simple to upgrade any two of the three structure objectives: security and cost, security and execution, or cost and execution; be that as it may, it is hard to advance every one of the three plan objectives on the double.

At the point when we look at lightweight cryptographic executions, we can make a differentiation among symmetric and awry figures. Symmetric figures serve for the most part for message uprightness checks, substance verification, and encryption, while deviated figures also give key-administration points of interest and nonrepudiation. Hilter kilter figures are computationally undeniably additionally requesting, in both equipment and programming. The presentation hole on obliged gadgets, for example, 8-piece microcontrollers is colossal. For instance, an upgraded lopsided calculation, for example, ECC performs 100–1,000 times more gradually than a standard symmetric figure, for example, the AES calculation, which associates with an a few sets of-greatness higher force utilization [25]. Symmetric-key cryptographic calculations utilize a similar key for encryption of a plain book and unscrambling of a message. The encryption key speaks to a mutual mystery between the gatherings that are associated with the safe correspondence.

9.3.1.1   Symmetric-Key LWC Algorithms

- The Tiny Encryption Algorithm (TEA) is a square figure famous for its effortlessness of depiction and execution, normally a couple of lines of code [26]. TEA works on two 32-piece unsigned whole numbers (could be gotten from a 64-piece information square) and uses a 128-piece key. TEA depends just on number juggling procedure on 32-piece words and uses just expansion, XORing, and movements. For IoT gadgets with little memory impressions, TEA is entirely appropriate since its calculation utilizes countless emphases, instead of a confused program, so as to maintain a strategic distance from preset tables and long arrangement times. TEA characterizes a straightforward and short figure that doesn't depend on preset tables or precomputations, consequently saving money on memory assets.

- The Scalable Encryption Algorithm (SEA) is focused for little installed applications [27]. The structure expressly represents a domain with constrained preparing assets and throughput necessities. A plan rule of SEA is adaptability: the plaintext size n, key size n, and processor (or word) size b are structure parameters, with the main requirement that n is a various of 6b; thus, the calculation is meant as SEAn;b. The principle weakness is that SEAn;b exchanges space for time and this may not be insignificant on gadgets with constrained computational force.

- PRESENT is a ultra-lightweight square figure calculation dependent on a Substitution-Permutation Network (SPN) [28]. PRESENT has been intended to be amazingly minimal and effective in equipment. It works on 64-piece squares and with keys of either 80 or 128 bits. It is for use in circumstances where low-power utilization and high chip productivity are wanted, hence making it exceptionally compelling for obliged situations.

- The HIGh security and light weigHT (HIGHT) [29] encryption calculation is a summed up Festal coordinate with a square size of 64 bits, 128-piece keys, and 32 rounds. HIGHT was structured with an eye on low-asset equipment execution. HIGHT utilizes basic activities, for example, XORing, expansion mod 28, and bitwise revolution.

9.3.1.2 Asymmetric LWC Algorithms

Open key (hilter kilter) cryptography requires the utilization of an open key and a private key. Open keys can be related with the personality of a hub by including them into an open declaration, marked by a Certification Authority (CA) that can be mentioned to confirm the testament. Open key cryptography requires the huge exertion of sending a PKI. Additionally, awry cryptography requires higher preparing and long keys (at any rate 1024 bits for RSA [30] to be utilized. Elective open key cryptographic plans, for example, ECC [31], might require shorter keys to be utilized so as to accomplish a similar security than RSA keys. Be that as it may, on account of these reasons, symmetric cryptography is favored as far as handling speed, computational exertion, and size of transmitted messages. Open key can be utilized to arrangement symmetric keys to be utilized in resulting correspondences. Lightweight cryptography calculations are appropriate for conditions that don't have stringent security necessities and where the requirements on accessible equipment and force spending plan can't be loose.

9.3.1.3 Key Agreement, Distribution, and Bootstrapping

A system for key dissemination and the executives must be set up when security components must be embraced. Unbalanced (open key) cryptographic calculations are generally utilized in key understanding conventions. In any case, different components that don't include the reception of awry cryptography have been proposed, to address the difficulties of asset compelled gadgets. A polynomial-based key predistribution convention has been characterized [32] and applied to Wireless Sensor Networks in Ref. [33]. A potential elective key understanding convention is SPINS [34], which is a security engineering explicitly intended for sensor systems. In SPINS, every sensor hub imparts a mystery key to a base station, which is utilized as a confided in outsider to set up another key, with no need of open key cryptography. The creators of Ref. [35] present three proficient arbitrary key predistribution plans for taking care of the security-bootstrapping issue in asset obliged sensor organizes, every one of which speaks to an alternate tradeoff in the structure space of irregular key conventions.

9.3.1.4   Security Bootstrapping

The key understanding conventions necessitate that some kind of qualifications, for example, symmetric keys, declarations, and open private key sets are preconfigured on the hubs, so the key understanding method can happen. Bootstrapping alludes to the grouping of assignments that should be executed before the system can interwork, requiring the right arrangement at all layers of the OSI model from connect layer to application layer. It tends to be seen as a procedure of making a security space from a lot of beforehand unassociated IoT gadgets. Current IoT models are completely incorporated much of the time, with the goal that a focal gathering handles all the security connections in an authoritative area. In the ZigBee standard, this substance is the trust community. Current recommendations for 6LoWPAN/Core distinguish the 6LoWPAN Border Router (6LBR) in that capacity an element. A unified engineering takes into consideration focal administration of gadgets and key affiliations. The impediment is that there is a solitary purpose of disappointment; a decentralized methodology will permit making specially appointed security areas that probably won't require a brought together online administration substance and will permit subsets of hubs to work in an independent way. The specially appointed security areas can be synchronized to incorporated element later, taking into consideration both unified and appropriated the executives.

9.4   Privacy in IoT Networks

This segment examines the protection angles and systems pertinent to IoT. The shrewd, associated items will connect with the two people and other savvy protests by giving, preparing, and conveying a wide range of data and signs. These items and their interchanges with the earth convey with them a hazard to protection and data spillage. Human services applications speak to the most exceptional utilization of IoT. The absence of certainty with respect to security brings about diminished selection among clients and is accordingly one of the driving components in the achievement of IoT. The universal selection of the remote mode for trading information may present new issue regarding security infringement. Actually, remote channel expands the danger of infringement because of the remote access capacities, which possibly open the framework to listening in and concealing assaults.

IoT gadgets and applications include a layer of multifaceted nature over the conventional issue of security over the Internet, for instance because of age of recognizable qualities and properties of people. IoT gadgets in human services present a significant worry, since these gadgets and applications normally create enormous volumes of information on singular patients through ceaseless checking of essential parameters. Right now, is critical to delink the characters of the gadget from that of the person, through components, for example, information anonymization. Information anonymization is the procedure of either encoding or expelling by and by recognizable data from informational indexes, so the originator of the information stays mysterious. Like the previous conversation of the OAuth convention, advanced shadows empower the person's items to follow up for their sake, putting away only a virtual personality that contains data about their parameters. Personality the board in IoT may offer new chances to expand security by joining differing confirmation techniques for people and machines. For instance, bio-recognizable proof joined with an article inside the individual system could be utilized to open an entryway.

9.4.1 Secure Data Aggregation

Homomorphic encryption is a type of encryption that permits explicit sorts of calculations to be executed on figure messages and get a scrambled outcome that is the figure content of the aftereffect of activities performed on the plain content. Applying the standard encryption strategies displays a situation: If the information is put away decoded, it can uncover touchy data to the capacity/database specialist organization. Then again, in the event that it is encoded, it is inconceivable for the supplier to work on it. On the off chance that information are scrambled, at that point nothing even a basic checking question (for instance, the quantity of records or documents that contain a specific catchphrase) would ordinarily require downloading and decoding the whole database content. A homomorphic encryption permits a client to control without expecting to decode it first. A case of homomorphic encryption is the RSA calculation. Different instances of homomorphic encryption plans are the ECC encryption, the ElGamal cryptosystem [36], and the Pailler cryptosystem [37]. Homomorphic encryption has a great deal of significance to IoT systems, since security can be protected at all phases of the correspondence, particularly without the requirement for middle of the road hubs to decode the data. For instance, a great deal of preparing and capacity can be wiped out at middle of the road hubs by information total with activities, for example, aggregates and midpoints. This thusly brings about lower power utilization, which is significant for compelled conditions. In any case, note that this kind of homomorphic cryptosystems is more process escalated and needs longer keys to accomplish a practically identical security level than run of the mill symmetric-key calculations.

Typically, secure data aggregation mechanisms require nodes to perform the following operations:

- at the transmitting node, prior to transmission, data are encrypted with some cryptographic function E
- at the receiving node, all received data packets are decrypted with the inverse cryptographic function $D = E^{-1}$ to retrieve the original data;
- data are aggregated with an aggregation function;
- prior to retransmission, aggregated data are encrypted through E and relayed to the next hop.

9.4.2   Enigma

MIT Researchers, Guy Zyskind and Oz Nathan, have as of late reported a task named Enigma that makes a significant theoretical advance toward this Holy Grail of a completely homomorphic encryption convention [38] proposed a shared system, empowering various gatherings to mutually store and run calculations on information while keeping the information totally private. Riddle's computational model depends on a profoundly advanced form of secure multiparty calculation, ensured by an obvious mystery sharing plan. For capacity, it utilizes a changed circulated hash table for holding mystery shared information. An outer square chain is used as the controller of the system, oversees get to control, personalities, and fills in as a carefully designed log of occasions. Security stores and expenses boost activity, rightness, and reasonableness of the framework. Like Bitcoin, Enigma evacuates the requirement for a confided in outsider, empowering self-ruling control of individual information. Just because, clients can impart their information to cryptographic certifications with respect to their security.

The average use instance of Enigma would be for collaborations among clinics and human services suppliers who store scrambled patient information according to HIPAA guidelines. Research associations and pharmaceutical organizations would profit by access to these information for clinical examination. For instance, a medical clinic can scramble its information and store it in the cloud, where conceivably different colleges, pharma organizations, and insurance agencies could get to it with consent from the starting emergency clinic. With the use of Enigma, note that there is no requirement for the beginning emergency clinic to initially unscramble and anonymize the information, it just needs to approve the outsider for get to.

9.4.3   Zero Knowledge Protocols

Zero-information conventions permit distinguishing proof, key trade and other fundamental cryptographic activities to be executed without releasing any mystery data during the discussion and with littler computational necessities than utilizing similar open key conventions. In this way Zero-information conventions appear to be alluring particularly with regards to IoT systems, particularly for certain applications like savvy cards. Zero-information conventions have been professed to have lighter computational necessities than, for instance, open key conventions. The standard case is that zero-information conventions can accomplish similar outcomes than open key conventions with one to two sets of extent less (1/10, 1/100) processing power. An average execution may require 20–30 measured increases (with full-length bit strings) that can be advanced to 10–20 with precalculation. This is a lot quicker than RSA. The memory prerequisites appear to be about equivalent: to have high security with zero-information conventions, we need long keys and numbers, so in memory terms, the necessities may not be altogether different [39].

9.4.4   Privacy in Beacons

Reference point in remote innovation is the idea of broadcasting little snippets of data. The data might be anything, running from encompassing information to essential signs, for example, internal heat level, circulatory strain, heartbeat, and breathing rate or microlocation information, for example, resource following. In view of the specific situation, the transmitted information possibly static or dynamic and change after some time. The Bluetooth signal opens another universe of conceivable outcomes for area mindfulness, and innumerable open doors for brilliant applications. Reference points are getting one of the key empowering influences of the IoT. One sort of guide is a low vitality Bluetooth transmitter or beneficiary. The force proficiency of Bluetooth Smart makes it ideal for gadgets expecting to run off a minor battery for extensive stretches. The upside of Bluetooth Smart is its similarity to work with an application on the cell phone or tablet you effectively possess. A significant use instance of signals is to acquire setting explicit perceptions and rehashed estimations after some time. Most information gathered from reference points are related in time, which may make genuine dangers information security and client protection.

Security and protection issues explicit to signals and time arrangement information transmitted from them are rising regions of research intrigue. There are the two points of interest and burdens of security dependent on the trouble of a fundamental calculation issue and data theoretic security, which depends on absence of data content. A progressively fundamental proportion of the data theoretic security is the intrinsic data accessible for misuse by an enemy, autonomous of how the foe abuses it or surely any expected computational impediments of the foe. In Ref. [40], another proportion of data theoretic measure, for example, restrictive entropy is demonstrated to be appropriate for assessing the security of bothered true time-arrangement information, contrasted and other existing measures.

A great part of the exploration and investigation of security issues in omnipresent registering frameworks is appropriate to the IoT. Building up significant personality, utilizing confided in correspondence ways, and securing logical data is all imperative to guarantee the assurance of client protection right now [41] have investigated unknown correspondence methods and the utilization of pen names ensure client protection while likewise dealing with measurements to survey client secrecy. Their work adopts a novel strategy by concealing personality from the applications that use it so as to all the more likely secure the client expending those administrations.

In their work on Decentralized Trust Management, [42] propose new advances that empower the bootstrapping of trust, and in this manner, the figuring of trust measurements that are more qualified to versatile, impromptu systems. Their model exhibits the innate issues with setting up trust in specially appointed systems like those in the IoT where new sensors, administrations, and clients are continually acquainted and asked with share information.

At last, applications in the IoT, which will be empowered by an omnipresent processing and interchanges foundation, will give subtle access to significant logical data in accordance with clients and their condition. Unmistakably, the effective arrangement of such applications will rely upon our capacity to verify them and the relevant information that they share.

One case of touchy relevant data is area. At the point when area mindful frameworks track clients naturally, a gigantic measure of possibly delicate data is created and made accessible. Security of area data is about both controlling access to the data and giving the suitable degree of granularity to individual requestors. The Location Services Handbook [43] investigates an assortment of area detecting advances for cell systems and the inclusion quality and security insurances that accompany each.

9.5   Summary and Conclusions

The IoT brings to the fore issues on security that were viewed as less effective on the World Wide Web. For instance, individuals have been sharing individual profile data on Social media destinations, for example, Facebook, and this thus empowers the plan of action of these applications through focused promoting in lieu of memberships. This setting has implied that the protection issues are to a great extent disregarded. In any case, the keen IoT gadgets uncover considerably more delicate data, and give substantially less degree to this kind of business model as it is to a great extent back-end information. Consequently clients are probably going to be both powerless and touchy to security concerns. These difficulties make it complex to operationalize IoT in a safe manner, while completely safeguarding protection. There are various promising methodologies that are being examined to understand for every part of the protection issues, and there is still some separation to go before we can see creation prepared business usage that are institutionalized and generally received.

References

1. Bonetto, R., Bui, N., Lakkundi, V., Olivereau, A., Serbanati, A., Rossi, M., Secure communication for smart IoT objects: Protocol stacks, use cases and practical examples, in: *IEEE International Symposium on a World of Wireless, Mobile and Multimedia Networks (WoWMoM)*, San Francisco, pp. 1–7, 2012.
2. Chan, H., Perrig, A., Song, D., Random key predistribution schemes for sensor networks, in: *Proceedings of the IEEE Symposium on Security and Privacy*, Oakland, pp. 197–213, 2003.
3. Cirani, S., Ferrari, G., Veltri, L., Enforcing security mechanisms in the IP-based Internet of Things: An algorithmic overview. *Algorithms*, 6, 2, 197–226, 2013.
4. Cirani, S., Picone, M., Gonizzi, P., Veltri, L., Ferrari, G., IoT-OAS: An OAuth-based authorization service architecture for secure services in IoT scenarios. *IEEE Sens. J.*, 15, 2, 1224–1234, 2015.
5. Eisenbarth, T. and Kumar, S., A survey of lightweight-cryptography implementations. *IEEE Des. Test Comput.*, 24, 6, 522–533, 2007.
6. El Gamal, T., A public key cryptosystem and a signature scheme based on discrete logarithms. *Advances in cryptology. Proceedings of CRYPTO 84*, Santa Barbara, USA, pp. 10–18, 1984.
7. Green, J., IoT reference model. http://www.iotwf.com/resources/72, 2014.
8. Hardt, D., The OAuth 2.0 authorization framework. RFC 6749, RFC Editor, *Internet Engineering Task Force* 2–18, 2012.

9. Hunkeler, U., Truong, H.L., Stanford-Clark, A., Mqtt-s—A publish/subscribe protocol for wireless sensor networks, in: *IEEE COMSWARE*, S. Choi, J. Kurose, K. Ramamritham (Eds.), pp. 791–798, 2008.

10. Aboba, B., Blunk, L., Vollbrecht, J., Carlson, J., Levkowetz, H., Extensible Authentication Protocol (EAP). RFC 3748, RFC Editor, 2004.

11. Aronsson, H.A., Zero knowledge protocols and small systems. *Information Scurity and Privacy* http://www.tml.tkk.fi/Opinnot/Tik-110.501/1995/zero-knowledge.html, 5, 3, 18. 2015.

12. Beresford, A.R. and Stajano, F., Location privacy in pervasive computing. *IEEE Pervasive Comput.*, 2, 1, 46–55, 2003.

13. Blundo, C., De Santis, A., Herzberg, A., Kutten, S., Vaccaro, U., Yung, M., Perfectly-secure key distribution for dynamic conferences. *Inf. Comput.*, 146, 1, 471–486, 1998.

14. Bogdanov, A., Knudsen, L.R., Leander, G., Paar, C., Poschmann, A., Robshaw, M.J., Seurin, Y., Vikkelsoe, C., PRESENT: An ultra-lightweight block cipher. *Proceedings of 9th international workshop*, Vienna, Austria, pp. 450–466, 2007.

15. Forsberg, D., Ohba, Y., Patil, B., Tschofenig, H., Yegin, A., Protocol for carrying authentication for network access (PANA). RFC 5191, RFC Editor, 2008.

16. Frankel, S. and Krishnan, S., IP security (IPSec) and internet key exchange (like) document roadmap, RFC 6071, RFC Editor, 2011.

17. Hammer-Lahav, E., The OAuth 1.0 protocol, RFC 5849, RFC Editor, 2010.

18. Heer, T., Garcia-Morchon, O., Hummen, R., Keoh, S., Kumar, S., Wehrle, K., Security challenges in the IP-based Internet of Things. *Wirel. Pers. Commun.*, 61, 3, 527–542, 2011.

19. Hong, D., Sung, J., Hong, S., Lim, J., Lee, S., Koo, B.-S., Lee, C., Chang, D., Lee, J., Jeong, K. *et al.*, Hight: A new block cipher suitable for low-resource device, in: *Cryptographic hardware and embedded systems*, pp. 46–59, Springer, CHES, 2006.

20. Hui, J. and Thubert, P., Compression format for IPv6 datagrams over IEEE 802.15.4 based networks, RFC 6282, RFC Editor, 2011.

21. Karlof, C. and Wagner, D., Secure routing in wireless sensor networks: Attacks and countermeasures. *Ad Hoc Networks*, 1, 2, 293–315, 2003.

22. Koblitz, N., Elliptic curve cryptosystems. *Math. Comput.*, 48, 177, 203–209, 1987.

23. Ma, C.Y. and Yau, D.K., On information-theoretic measures for quantifying privacy protection of time-series data, in: *Proceedings of the Tenth ACM Symposium on Information, Computer and Communications Security*, ACM, New York, pp. 427–38, 2015.

24. Martin, E., Liu, L., Covington, M., Pesti, P., Weber, M., Chapter: 1 Positioning technology in location-based services, in: *Location based services handbook: applications, technologies, and security*, S.A. Ahson and M. Ilyas (Eds.), CRC Press, Boca Raton. 2010.

25. Montenegro, G., Kushalnagar, N., Hui, J., Culler, D., Transmission of IPv6 packets over IEEE 802.15.4 networks, RFC 4944, RFC Editor, 2007.

26. Moskowitz, R., Nikander, P., Jokela, P., Henderson, T., Host Identity Protocol, RFC 5201, RFC Editor, Verlag Berlin Heidelberg. 2008.

27. Paillier, P., Public-key cryptosystems based on composite degree residuosity classes, in: *Advances in Cryptology—EUROCRYPT'99*, pp. 223–38, Springer, Verlag Berlin Heidelberg, 1999.

28. Perrig, R., Szewczyk, J.D., Tygar, V., Wen, D.E., Culler, SPINS: Security protocols for sensor networks. *Wirel. Netw.*, 8, 5, 521–534, 2002.

29. Raza, S., Trabalza, D., Voigt, T., 6loWPAN compressed DTLS for CoAP, in: *Eighth IEEE Distributed Computing in Sensor Systems (DCOSS)*, Hangzhou, China, pp. 287–89, 2012.

30. Rescorla, E. and Modadugu, N., Datagram transport layer security version 1.2, RFC 6347, RFC Editor, 2012.

31. Standaert, F.-X., Piret, G., Gershenfeld, N., Quisquater, J.-J., SEA: A scalable encryption algorithm for small embedded applications, in: *Proceedings of 7th IFIP WG 8.8/11.2 international conference, CARDIS 2006*, Tarragona, Spain, pp. 222–236, 2006.

32. Zhao, M., Li, H., Wouhaybi, R., Walker, J., Lortz, V., Covington, M.J., Decentralized trust management for securing community networks. *Intel Technol. J.*, 13, 2, 148–169, 2009.

33. Zyskind, G., Nathan, O., Pentland, A., Enigma: Decentralized computation platform with guaranteed privacy, CoRR, abs/1506.03471, *Information Scurity and Privacy* 5.3, 18. 2015.

34. Kent, S. and Seo, K., Security architecture for the Internet protocol, RFC 4301, RFC Editor, 2005.

35. Kent, S., IP encapsulating security payload (ESP), RFC 4303, RFC Editor, 2005.

36. Kothmayr, T., Schmitt, C., Hu, W., Brunig, M., Carle, G., A DTLS based end-to-end security architecture for the Internet of Things with two-way authentication, in: *Thirty Seventh IEEE Conference on Local Computer Networks Workshops*, FL, pp. 956–63, 2012.

37. Liu, D., Ning, P., Li, R., Establishing pairwise keys in distributed sensor networks. *ACM Trans. Inf. Syst. Secur.*, 8, 1, 41–77, 2005.

38. Rivest, R.L., Shamir, A., Adleman, L., A method for obtaining digital signatures and public-key cryptosystems. *Commun. ACM*, 21, 2, 120–126, 1978.

39. Shelby, Z., Chakrabarti, S., Nordmark, E., Bormann, C., Neighbor discovery optimization for IPv6 over low-power wireless personal area networks (6loWPANs), RFC 6775, RFC Editor, *Information Scurity and Privacy* 2012.

40. Shelby, Z., Constrained restful environments (CoRE) link format, RFC 6690, RFC Editor, 5.3, 18. 2012.

41. Wallgren, L., Raza, S., Voigt, T., Routing attacks and countermeasures in the RPL-based Internet of Things. *Int. J. Distrib. Sens. Netw.*, 2013, 11, 2013.

42. Wheeler, D.J. and Needham, R.M., TEA, A tiny encryption algorithm, in: *Proceedings of fast software encryption, 2nd internation workshop*, vol. 1008, Leuven, Belgium, vol. 1008, pp. 363–66, 1995.

43. Winter, T., Thubert, P., Brandt, A., Hui, J., Kelsey, R., Levis, P., Pister, K., Struik, R., Vasseur, J., Alexander, R., RPL: IPv6 routing protocol for low-power and lossy networks, RFC 6550, RFC Editor, *Information Scurity and Privacy* 5.4, 152012.

10

Realization of Business Intelligence using Machine Learning

Mamata Rath

School of Management (IT), Birla Global University, Bhubaneswar, India

Abstract

Progressive organizations largely depend on Business Intelligence software to predict market situation and business analysis. Technologies that involve Business intelligence can support organizations with analyzing patterns that are continuously changing in a portion of the overall industry; changes in the conduct of clients and expending designs; inclinations of clients; capacities of organizations; and economic scenarios. Business intelligence is used to encourage examiners and directors in order to examine which alterations are better in correlation with the continuously evolving patterns. The advancement in the information distribution centre as a vault, expansion in the range of programming and hardware infrastructure, development in purifying information, and the advancement in web designs all unite to make a more extravagant business intelligence condition than was available already. This paper is an endeavour to display a structure for building a Business Intelligence framework. BI frameworks join operational and recorded information with organized and systematic instruments to display cost-effective and insistent data to business personnel and chiefs. BI targets to improve the convenience and data nature, and allow chiefs to indeed better understand the situation of their firm compared to their competitors. The current article justifies how machine learning approaches play a greater role to achieve Business Intelligence in large commercial organizations.

Keywords: Business intelligence, machine learning, IoT, computer security, data analytics, artificial intelligence, cloud computing, data warehouse

Email: mamata.rath200@gmail.com

Parul Gandhi, Surbhi Bhatia, Abhishek Kumar, Mohammad Alojail and Pramod Singh Rathore (eds.) *Internet of Things in Business Transformation: Developing an Engineering and Business Strategy for Industry 5.0*, (169–184) © 2021 Scrivener Publishing LLC

10.1 Introduction

While the world of business is rapidly evolving and the business firms are winding up increasingly extra perplexing to make it progressively trouble-some for directors to have far-reaching understanding of business scenarios. Elements such as globalization acquisitions and mergers, deregulation, mechanical and rivalry advancement, have restricted firms to reconsider their tactics in business and many huge organizations have turned towards the strategies of BI (Business Intelligence) in order to enable themselves to understand and manage business procedures to add to upper hand. Business Intelligence [1] is principally adopted to improve the expediency and data nature, and allow chiefs to better comprehend the situation of their firm when compared to their competitors [2].

Innovations and applications of Business Intelligence assist organizations by analyzing varying patterns in correlation to the overall industry; changes in the conduct of client and expenditure on designs; the inclination of the client; abilities of the organization; and financial situations. It is used to encourage administrators work out which modifications can better react to varying patterns. It developed as a design for investigating collected information to enable basic leadership units to enable development in widespread knowledge of tasks of an association, and consequently help to figure out better business tactics and choices.

ML (Machine Learning) is an element of a promising AI (Artificial Intelligence) knowledge that has been adopted extensively over the years in a growing number of fields and branches in order to automate the problem solving and figuring out complex decision strategies [34, 36]. ML is a form of data analysis that enables the computers to learn from the data in order to gather experiences and knowledge about the data to solve real-world problems. ANN (Artificial Neural Network) is the most popular method in ML [35, 40] which is stimulated by the human brain's biological neural network and works on the principle of human learning aspects. Some other techniques are case-based reasoning, NLP, genetic algorithms, inductive learning, etc.

10.2 Business Intelligence and Machine Learning Technology

Machine learning is an emerging techical and programming methpode to train computers intelligently to enhance their performance criterion depending on application type using example data or sometimes past experience. Machine learning is the branch of computer science that aims at how to explicitly program computers to improve computational performance at solving problems based off of previous experiences. Machine learning algorithms have been considered to be of great importance in solving real-world problems of various practical domains [37, 38]. There are many intelligent frameworks developed using ML techniques for decision-making systems in various fields including biomedical applications such as heart disease diagnosis in a clinical environment. The investigators evaluated and examined research works related to heart disease DSS (Decision Support System) published in PubMed on 8th of June, 2015; the library of Cochrane and CINAHL. The data obtained from the 20 text articles (which met inclusion criteria) was grouped into the following branches; dataset formation methods, heart diseases, ML algorithms, ML-based DSS (Decision Support System, evaluation of outcome, types of comparators and clinical outcomes of the proposed DSS [39]. Twenty from a total of 331 studies finally fulfilled the inclusion criteria. Most of them are on ischemic heart diseases with the usage of ANN as the most common ML technique. ANN classifies myocardial perfusion scintigraphy with an accuracy of 87.5% and myocardial infarction with an accuracy of 97%. Classification of heart failures is done by CART with 87.6% accuracy.

On the other hand, neural network ensembles show 97.4% accuracy for classification of heart valves while support vector machine shows 95.6% accuracy for arrhythmia screening classification and logistic regression shows 72% accuracy for classifying acute coronary syndrome. Artificial immune recognition system outputs 92.5% accuracy for the classification of coronary artery disease. Multi-criteria decision analysis and Genetic algorithms output 91% accuracy for classifying the chest-pain patients [3]. Figure 10.1 demonstrates different applications of machine learning that include primary business applications. In various sectors of business, machine learning utilizes data analytic techniques to promote business and increase throughput.

Using Business Intelligence (BI) ideas, managers get big support to take the right decision in right time Business Intelligence enables people to make effective strategic business decisions by availing them with relevant, correct, accurate information when required. Business organizations use BI in order to examine business scenarios to achieve competitive advantage [4], and also regard such BI techniques as an important proponent of competition in some situations.

Major features of Business Intelligence module are data transparency, better performance, risk minimization, sustainable growth, increased efficiency and there is no additional IT resource. Figure 10.2 shows the basic feature of business intelligence [5].

Figure 10.1 Applications of Machine Learning.

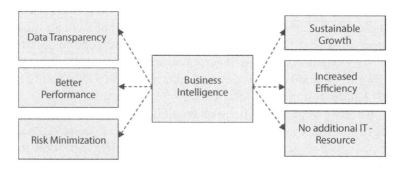

Figure 10.2 Basic features of Business Intelligence.

The rapidly evolving parameters of business, for example, deregulation, globalization, acquisitions and mergers, advancement in mechanical infrastructure, have constrained organizations to reexamine their techniques of business. In this scenario, Business Intelligence assumes a critical job in supporting the basic leadership procedure to increase aggressiveness, denoting a proficient connection within IT and business systems. Business Intelligence innovations are consistently growing and enhancing in order to work out increasingly more unpredictable business. BI is an empowering advancement that has developed incorporate DW (data warehouse), OLAP (online systematic preparing), and DM (data mining). Business Intelligence aims to enable individuals to gain better business choices by virtue of precise, recent and important data accessible to them when required [6]. Aggressive associations aggregate Business Intelligence techniques to survey condition in order to increase economic upper hand may see such intelligence as a significant center skill in a few examples.

10.3   Literature Study

To optimize natural methods of business rules and principles, Eckerson [7] mentioned in their research work that Natural language is utilized to speak to human considerations and for doing human activities. Business rules depicted by natural language are hard for machine to get it. With the end goal to tell machine the business rules, parts of business process, we have to make an interpretation of them into a language which machine can get it. Protest imperative language is one of those languages. A factual machine learning strategy has been introduced [8] to comprehend the natural business principles and after that make an interpretation of them into question requirement language. In this manner an interpretation calculation for business process displaying is likewise given. A real case, air freight stack arranging process is proposed by them to show the proficiency and power of the technique and the calculation. The outcome has demonstrated that this strategy and calculation advance business process displaying innovation and upgrade the productivity of programming designers in business process displaying. Business work process and their systematic operations using enhanced algorithm has been explained by research work of Kumar and Lim [9]. One such novel work has been proposed, which can deal with simultaneousness and repeat of the business procedure that are the limitations of different calculations. Besides work process demonstrating language named adaptable work process displaying language (FWF-NET) is advanced, which can show questionable and deficient business process data, so the business procedure mined by the calculation can undoubtedly be changed the FWF-NET. The model and analyses have demonstrated that the calculation mines business process viable, decreases the multifaceted nature in work process displaying and advancement, and assesses execution of existing work process show.

Currently, Artificial Intelligence (AI) and the very powerful machine learning (ML) concepts are being applied in the business activities. Lot of research work has been performed to focus on how they can support top level and middle level managers in business intelligence (BI). Also, currently there is much potential in systems that use natural language search to assist the management more rapidly to look into corporate information, execute analysis, and identify business plans. Basically the technology of machine learning and artificial intelligence are building up [10], yet it is extremely unpredictable to realize these models, incomplete subordinate must be ascertained and there is expansive deviation between fitted static parameter and genuine esteem and physical origination isn't clear. As per the hindrance above techniques, based on ideal parameter choice with matrix pursuit and cross approval, an ideal normal machine learning calculation (slightest squares bolster vector machine-LSSVM) strategy has been made arrangements for weakness break spread rate estimate. Confused and solid nonlinear weakness split spread rate bend was reproduced by system plan and compliance of LSSVM learning calculation and the upgraded SVM parameters were chosen by the strategy for system seeking and cross approval. Contrasted the blunders and yield estimation of the upgraded model and yield an incentive from nine parameters weakness split proliferation rate fitting model, LSSVM whose parameter was improved with cross approval had magnificent capacity of nonlinear displaying and speculation. It gave a straightforward and doable wise methodology for material weakness examination.

An emerging technology of machine learning are applied in most of the business applications, so change over to new concepts is a challenge for organisations at many levels. Given the confront, a resolution is needed. Fortunately, there is no need to start from beginning. Rather, there are different approaches in other areas of software that can be leveraged and adapted to the problem. Methodologies of machine learning and other tools can be borrowed from other areas of Information technology to help both compliance and business based decision making [11].

10.4   Business Analytics and Machine Learning

In machine learning approach, it is essential that the well-informed features can clarify the training set, as well as be utilized to anticipate concealed examples or future occasions. So as to look at the performance of learning, another dataset might be held for testing, called the test set or test data. For instance, before last, most decisive tests, the instructor may give understudies a few inquiries for work on (preparing set), and the manner in which he makes a decision about the performances of understudies is to look at them with another issue set (test set). So as to recognize the preparation set and the test set when they show up together.

Figure 10.3 illustrates Business Analytics Applications of Machine Learning. These include management of customer relationships, financial and marketing activities, supply chain management, human resource planning and to take pricing decisions. Business analytics deals with strategies related to profitability of business wih income of revenue and shareholder returns [12]. Business analytic methods understand the data and information intelligently and helps to generate informative reports for top level management.

Figure 10.4 depicts the scope of business analytics. There are three approaches in machine learning based business analytics. Descriptive

Figure 10.3 Business analytics applications of Machine Learning.

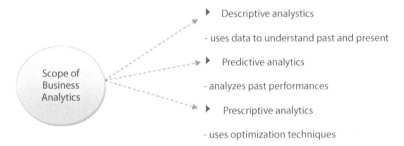

Figure 10.4 Scope of business analytics.

analysis uses business related data to understand past and present situation. Predictive analytics analyses the past performance and the presriptive analytics utilizes some optimization methods for improved performance. In a retail market down position, the Descriptive analytics approach examines the historical data for similar products (prices, units sold, advertising), the Predictive analytics approach predict sales based on price and the Prescriptive analytics strategy finds the best sets of pricing and advertising to maximize sales revenue [13].

Data source for business data analytics—Data are stored in relational database approach to be accessed intelligently for further analysis purpose. A sample view of data source is depicted in Figure 10.5 where data is available systematically in the form of fields and values in records.

Figure 10.6 demonstrates Decision Action Cycle in Business Intelligence. This cyclic approach is used for decision making at top level and middle level management in an organisation for taking some decisions. Before taking the final decision, at previous stages some level of knowledge is applied by coordination of humen members in the system such as managers, supervisors and employees [14].

Figure 10.7 shows type of decisions taken at different level in business intelligence systems. The operational level decisions are related to regular activities with short term effect which can be taken depending on work

▲	A	B	C	D	E	F	G	H
1	Sales Transactions: July 14							
2								
3	Cust ID	Region	Payment	Transaction Code	Source	Amount	Product	Time Of Day
4	10001	East	Paypal	93816545	Web	$20.19	DVD	22:19
5	10002	West	Credit	74083490	Web	$17.85	DVD	13:27
6	10003	North	Credit	64942368	Web	$23.98	DVD	14:27
7	10004	West	Paypal	70560957	Email	$23.51	Book	15:38
8	10005	South	Credit	35208817	Web	$15.33	Book	15:21
9	10006	West	Paypal	20978903	Email	$17.30	DVD	13:11
10	10007	East	Credit	80103311	Web	$177.72	Book	21:59
11	10008	West	Credit	14132683	Web	$21.76	Book	4:04
12	10009	West	Paypal	40128225	Web	$15.92	DVD	19:35
13	10010	South	Paypal	49073721	Web	$23.39	DVD	13:26

Figure 10.5 Sample data source of sales transaction for business analytics.

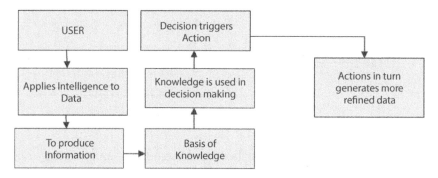

Figure 10.6 Decision action cycle in Business Intelligence.

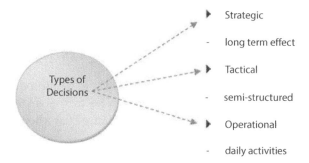

Figure 10.7 Decision types at different level.

assignments to lower level employees such as labors, operators and supervisors. The tactical decisions are semi-structured in nature and these are taken by middle-level of management for proper coordination in the departments [15]. Strategic decisions are long term effects that are unstructured in nature because they are not regular and important decisions are taken by top level management as per the demand of situation.

To take major business decisions for planning and controlling, experts using business intelligence tools process data from lower level to higher level in the following sequence. Data Source (lower level) → data warehouse → Data exploration (statistical analysis, Query, reports) → data mining → data presentation & visualization → Final decision making. At each level the business intelligence tools support the managers and top management to understand in better way as well as supports with technical guidance.

While the certainty of applying machine learning in data science and order issue is comprehended, there are some essential guidelines to guarantee its accessibility. These standards are known as the "no free lunch administers" and are characterized on both the dataset and the properties to learn. On the dataset, the no free lunch rules require the preparation set and the test set to originate from a similar circulation (same universal set). What's more, on the properties, the no free lunch rules request that the clients make suspicions on what property to realize and how to demonstrate the property [16].

10.5   IoT in Machine Learning

The fast development of the internet and its interfacing equipments makes the things associated with different technology in the whole world. In nowadays, the world is running on the Internet of Things (IoT), with the expanded correspondence capacity and best method for correspondence and transmission lines a large number of things are associated with the internet. The approach and unrest in brilliant sensor innovation draws in a considerable lot of the clients and the vast majority of the equipments are associated with the internet. Internet associated sensors and equipments produce exponential information. Purposely or unwittingly IoT is creating heaps of information. This information is critical in basic leadership framework, yet the issue is the way to isolate this information for the future investigation purposes. The Internet of Things (IoT) offers building groups an inventive method to gather information and watch the status of their items, administrations and hardware in the field. Machine supervision systems are utilized to gain from these information to make the gadget or thing savvy. For instance, utilizing the machine supervision to distinguish the irregularities in wearable and taking vital activities like calling specialist and rescue vehicle naturally when it essential. Table 10.1 illustrates details of domains associated with research in IoT [17].

With the various Internet of Things (IoT) equipments, the cloud-driven information handling neglects to meet the necessity of all IoT applications.

Table 10.1 Interdisciplinary domains associated with research in IoT.

Authors	Year	Domains associated with research in IoT
F. Ahamed, F. Farid	2018	data acquisition, decision support systems, diseases, electronic health records, health care, Internet of Things, supervision (artificial intelligence), patient treatment
A. Kumar, T. J. Lim	2019	firewalls, Internet of Things, invasive software, supervision (artificial intelligence)
R.R. Reddy, C. Mamatha, R.G. Reddy	2018	data handling, decision making, intelligent sensors, Internet, Internet of Things, supervision (artificial intelligence)
A.O. Aseeri, Y. Zhuang, M.S. Alkatheiri	2018	cryptography, Internet of Things, supervision (artificial intelligence), neural nets
J. Zhu, Y. Song, D. Jiang, H. Song	2018	cognitive radio, Internet of Things, supervision (artificial intelligence), scheduling
K. Gurulakshmi, A. Nesarani	2018	computer network security, Internet of Things, supervision (artificial intelligence), network servers, support vector machines
T. Park, W. Saad	2019	Internet of Things, supervision (artificial intelligence), resource allocation
W. Kang, D. Kim	2018	data compression, inference mechanisms, Internet, Internet of Things, supervision (artificial intelligence), quality of service
E. Anthi, L. Williams, P. Burnap	2018	computer network security, data privacy, Internet of Things, invasive software, supervision (artificial intelligence)
V.M. Suresh, R. Sidhu, P. Karkare, A. Patil, Z. Lei, A. Basu	2018	Internet of Things, supervision (artificial intelligence), low-power electronics, wide area networks
R.N. Anderson [18]	2017	supervision (artificial intelligence), natural gas technology, neural nets, oil technology, petroleum, petroleum industry support vector machines

(Continued)

Table 10.1 Interdisciplinary domains associated with research in IoT. (*Continued*)

Authors	Year	Domains associated with research in IoT
J. Hribar, L. DaSilva [19]	2019	Internet of Things, telecommunication power management
A. Ara, A. Ara [20]	2017	supervision (artificial intelligence), medical information systems, patient monitoring
J. Siryani, B. Tanju, T.J. Eveleigh [21]	2017	Bayes methods, belief networks, decision support systems, decision trees, Internet of Things, supervision (artificial intelligence), pattern classification, power engineering computing, power meters, smart meters, statistical analysis
J. Yu, S. Kwon, H. Kang, S. Kim, J. Bae, C. Pyo [22]	2018	data analysis, information retrieval, Internet of Things, meta data, semantic Web
Y. Chen, Z. Wang, A. Patil, A. Basu [23]	2019	CMOS integrated circuits, copy protection, current mirrors, Internet of Things, supervision (artificial intelligence), logic design, matrix algebra, multiplying circuits
F. Samie, L. Bauer, J. Henkel [24]	2019	cloud computing, Internet of Things, supervision (artificial intelligence)
Y. Sharaf-Dabbagh, W. Saad [25]	2017	cyber-physical systems, data privacy, Internet of Things, supervision (artificial intelligence), message authentication
A.C. Onal, O. Berat Sezer, M. Ozbayoglu, E. Dogdu [26]	2018	Big Data, Internet of Things, supervision (artificial intelligence), protocols
J. Tang, D. Sun, S. Liu, J. Gaudiot [27]	2017	Internet of Things, supervision (artificial intelligence)
E.V. Polyakov, M.S. Mazhanov, A.Y. Rolich [28]	2018	cloud computing, human computer interaction, Internet of Things, supervision (artificial intelligence), social networking
A. Roukounaki, S. Efremidis, J. Soldatos [29]	2019	computer network security, Internet of Things, supervision (artificial intelligence)

(Continued)

Table 10.1 Interdisciplinary domains associated with research in IoT. (*Continued*)

Authors	Year	Domains associated with research in IoT
F. Ganz, D. Puschmann, P. Barnaghi, F. Carrez [30]	2015	data mining, Internet of Things, supervision (artificial intelligence), semantic Web
A. Skjellum [31]	2016	computer network security, Internet of Things, internetworking, supervision (artificial intelligence), neural nets, radio networks
M. Mamdouh, M.A.I. Elrukhsi, A. Khattab [32]	2018	Internet of Things, supervision (artificial intelligence), security of data, wireless sensor networks

The restricted calculation and correspondence limit of the cloud require the edge figuring, i.e., beginning the IoT information handling at the edge and changing the associated equipments to insightful equipments. Machine supervision (ML) the key methods for data surmising, ought to stretch out to the cloud-to-things continuum as well. This paper audits the job of ML in IoT starting from the cloud to inserted equipments. Various uses of ML for application information handling and the board assignments are examined. The cutting edge uses of ML in IoT are arranged by their application space, input information type, misused ML systems, and where they have a place in the cloud-to-things continuum. The difficulties and research patterns toward effective ML on the IoT edge are talked about.

10.6   Conclusion

The quality of business information for an organization in today's world is not just a profit and loss choice but a bankruptcy or survival question. The benefits and advantages of business intelligence can never be denied by any organization. Recent studies show that in the near future a range of BI visual and analytics tools will be used by millions of people for the profit of the business. Organizations today are springing more benefits from Business Intelligence by spreading helpful data to various sorts of workforces, exploiting the utilization of current information assets. Business Intelligence has extended its limits to cover small, medium and big organizations. A range of analytical tools have probed into the market for the purpose of data analysis and to help make an informed decision. The fast evolution in the business atmosphere will upsurge the need for Business Intelligence. In this chapter, a detail discussion has been carried out about the importance of business intelligence in Organizations and how new approaches pertaining to machine learning can really make a difference in the business impact of the company.

References

1. Bochner, P. and Vaughan, J., BI today: One version of the truth. *Application Development Trends*, 11, 9, 18–24, 2004.
2. Mamata, R. and Pati, B. Appraisal of Soft Computing Methods in Collaboration With Smart City Applications and Wireless Network. Sensor Technology: Concepts, Methodologies, Tools, and Applications. IGI Global, 1273-1285, 2020.
3. Clark, T.D., Jones, M.C., Armstrong, C.P., The Dynamic Structure of Management Support Systems: Theory Development, Research, Focus, and Direction. *MIS Q.*, 31, 3, 579–615, 2007.
4. Cui, Z., Damiani, E., Leida, M., Benefits of Ontologies in Real-Time Data Access. *Digital EcoSystems and Technologies Conference, 2007. DEST '07. Inaugural IEEE-IES*, pp. 392–397, 21–23, 2007.
5. Schneider, D., Machine learning predicts home prices. *IEEE Spectr.*, 56, 1, 42–43, 2019.
6. Valter, P., Lindgren, P., Prasad, R., The consequences of artificial intelligence and deep learning in a world of persuasive business models. *IEEE Aerosp. Electron. Syst. Mag.*, 33, 5–6, 80–88, 2018.
7. Eckerson, W.W., Research Q&A: Performance Management Strategies. *Bus. Intell. J.*, 14, 1, 24–27, 2009.
8. Ahamed, F. and Farid, F., Applying Internet of Things and Machine-Supervision for Personalized Healthcare: Issues and Challenges. *2018 International Conference on Machine Supervision and Data Engineering (iCMLDE)*, pp. 19–21, 2018.
9. Kumar, A. and Lim, T.J., EDIMA: Early Detection of IoT Malware Network Activity Using Machine Supervision Techniques. *2019 IEEE 5th World Forum on Internet of Things (WF-IoT)*, pp. 289–294, 2019.
10. Reddy, R., Mamatha, C., Reddy, R.G., A Review on Machine Supervision Trends, Application and Challenges in Internet of Things. *2018 International Conference on Advances in Computing, Communications and Informatics (ICACCI)*, pp. 2389–2397, 2018.
11. Aseeri, A.O., Zhuang, Y., Alkatheiri, M.S., A Machine Supervision-Based Security Vulnerability Study on XOR PUFs for Resource-Constraint Internet of Things. *2018 IEEE International Congress on Internet of Things (ICIOT)*, pp. 49–56, 2018.

12. Zhu, J., Song, Y., Jiang, D., Song, H., A New Deep-Q-Supervision-Based Transmission Scheduling Mechanism for the Cognitive Internet of Things. *IEEE Internet Things J.*, 5, 4, 2375–2385, 2327–4662, 2372–2541, 2018.

13. Gurulakshmi, K. and Nesarani, A., Analysis of IoT Bots Against DDOS Attack Using Machine Supervision Algorithm. *2018 2nd International Conference on Trends in Electronics and Informatics (ICOEI)*, pp. 1052–1057, 2018.

14. Park, T. and Saad, W., Distributed Supervision for Low Latency Machine Type Communication in a Massive Internet of Things. *IEEE Internet Things J.*, 6, 3, 5562–5576, 2327–4662, 2372–2541, 2019.

15. Kang, W. and Kim, D., Poster Abstract: DeepRT: A Predictable Deep Supervision Inference Framework for IoT Devices. *2018 IEEE/ACM Third International Conference on Internet-of-Things Design and Implementation (IoTDI)*, pp. 279–280, 2018.

16. Anthi, E., Williams, L., Burnap, P., Pulse: An adaptive intrusion detection for the Internet of Things. *Living in the Internet of Things: Cybersecurity of the IoT—2018*, pp. 1–4, 2018.

17. Suresh, V.M., Sidhu, R., Karkare, P., Patil, A., Lei, Z., Basu, A., Powering the IoT through embedded machine supervision and LoRa. *2018 IEEE 4th World Forum on Internet of Things (WF-IoT)*, pp. 349–354, 2018.

18. Anderson, R.N., Petroleum Analytics Supervision Machine' for optimizing the Internet of Things of today's digital oil field-to-refinery petroleum system. *2017 IEEE International Conference on Big Data (Big Data)*, pp. 4542–4545, 2017.

19. Hribar, J. and DaSilva, L., Utilising Correlated Information to Improve the Sustainability of Internet of Things Devices. *2019 IEEE 5th World Forum on Internet of Things (WF-IoT)*, pp. 805–808, 2019.

20. Ara, A. and Ara, A., Case study: Integrating IoT, streaming analytics and machine supervision to improve intelligent diabetes management system. *2017 International Conference on Energy, Communication, Data Analytics and Soft Computing (ICECDS)*, pp. 3179–3182, 2017.

21. Siryani, J., Tanju, B., Eveleigh, T.J., A Machine Supervision Decision-Support System Improves the Internet of Things' Smart Meter Operations. *IEEE Internet Things J.*, 4, 4, 1056–1066, 2327–4662, 2372–2541, 2017.

22. Yu, J., Kwon, S., Kang, H., Kim, S., Bae, J., Pyo, C., A Framework on Semantic Thing Retrieval Method in IoT and IoE Environment. *2018 International Conference on Platform Technology and Service (PlatCon)*, pp. 1–6, 2018.

23. Chen, Y., Wang, Z., Patil, A., Basu, A., A Current Mirror Cross Bar Based 2.86-TOPS/W Machine Learner and PUF with <2.5% BER in 65nm CMOS for IoT Application. *2019 IEEE International Symposium on Circuits and Systems (ISCAS)*, pp. 1–4, 2158–1525, 2019.

24. Samie, F., Bauer, L., Henkel, J., From Cloud Down to Things: An Overview of Machine Supervision in Internet of Things. *IEEE Internet Things J.*, 6, 3, 4921–4934, 2327–4662, 2372–2541, 2019.

25. Sharaf-Dabbagh, Y. and Saad, W., Demo Abstract: Cyber-Physical Fingerprinting for Internet of Things Authentication. *2017 IEEE/ACM Second*

International Conference on Internet-of-Things Design and Implementation (IoTDI), pp. 301–302, 2017.

26. Onal, A.C., Berat Sezer, O., Ozbayoglu, M., Dogdu, E., MIS-IoT: Modular Intelligent Server Based Internet of Things Framework with Big Data and Machine Supervision. *2018 IEEE International Conference on Big Data (Big Data)*, pp. 2270–2279, 2018.

27. Tang, J., Sun, D., Liu, S., Gaudiot, J., Enabling Deep Supervision on IoT Devices. *Computer*, 50, 10, 92–96, 0018–9162, 1558–0814, 2017.

28. Polyakov, E.V., Mazhanov, M.S., Rolich, A.Y., Voskov, L.S., Kachalova, M.V., Polyakov, S.V., Investigation and development of the intelligent voice assistant for the Internet of Things using machine supervision. *2018 Moscow Workshop on Electronic and Networking Technologies (MWENT)*, pp. 1–5, 2018.

29. Roukounaki, A., Efremidis, S., Soldatos, J., Neises, J., Walloschke, T., Kefalakis, N., Scalable and Configurable End-to-End Collection and Analysis of IoT Security Data: Towards End-to-End Security in IoT Systems. *2019 Global IoT Summit (GIoTS)*, pp. 1–6, 2019.

30. Ganz, F., Puschmann, D., Barnaghi, P., Carrez, F., A Practical Evaluation of Information Processing and Abstraction Techniques for the Internet of Things. *IEEE Internet Things J.*, 2, 4, 340–354, 2327–4662, 2372–2541, 2015.

31. Canedo, J. and Skjellum, A., Using machine supervision to secure IoT systems. *2016 14th Annual Conference on Privacy, Security and Trust (PST)*, pp. 219–222, 2016.

32. Mamdouh, M., Elrukhsi, M.A.I., Khattab, A., Securing the Internet of Things and Wireless Sensor Networks via Machine Supervision: A Survey. *2018 International Conference on Computer and Applications (ICCA)*, pp. 215–218, 2018.

33. Feng, C., Wu, S., Liu, N., A user-centric machine learning framework for cyber security operations center. *IEEE International Conference on Intelligence and Security Informatics(ISI)*, Beijing, pp. 173–175, 2017.

34. Bulbul, H.I. and Unsal, Ö., Comparison of Classification Techniques used in Machine Learning as Applied on Vocational Guidance Data. *2011 10th International Conference on Machine Learning and Applications and Workshops*, Honolulu, HI, pp. 298–301, 2011.

35. Hoffman, T., 9 Hottest Skills for '09. *Computer World*, 1, 26–27, 2009.

36. Zhao, Li, Li, F., Statistical Machine Learning in Natural Language Understanding: Object Constraint Language Translator for Business Process. *2008 IEEE International Symposium on Knowledge Acquisition and Modeling Workshop*, Wuhan, pp. 1056–1059, 2008.

37. Liautaud, B. and Hammond, M., *e-Business Intelligence turning information into knowledge into profit*, McGraw Hill, New York, 2000.

38. Kobayashi, M. and Terano, T., Learning agents in a business simulator. *Proceedings 2003 IEEE International Symposium on Computational Intelligence in Robotics and Automation. Computational Intelligence in*

Robotics and Automation for the New Millennium (Cat. No.03EX694), Kobe, Japan, vol. 3, pp. 1323–1327, 2003.

39. Michalewicz, Z., Schmidt, M., Michalewicz, M., Chiriac, C., *Adaptive Business Intelligence*, Springer-Verlag, Berlin, Heidelberg, 2007.

40. Sharma, R. and Srinath, P., Business Intelligence using Machine Learning and Data Mining techniques—An analysis. *2018 Second International Conference on Electronics, Communication and Aerospace Technology (ICECA)*, Coimbatore, pp. 1473–1478, 2018.

11

Current Trends and Future Scope for the Internet of Things

Iram Abrar*, Zahrah Ayub and Faheem Masoodi

*Department of Computer Science, University of Kashmir,
Hazratbal, Srinagar, Jammu & Kashmir, India*

Abstract

Internet of things (IoT) is an emerging technology that is influencing every aspect of modern-day life. The idea is to provide a common platform irrespective of the underlying technologies, wherein the data from multiple devices can be integrated. This data is processed/analyzed, and is then used for increasing the level of automation, thereby improving the efficiency of the system. IoTs play a vital role in better decision making by facilitating the pooling of resources, and, at the same time, help us save a significant amount of time by delegating the job to multiple resources. The main aim of IoT is to provide better services to the users, thereby, improving the quality of life, and the idea of integrating IoT with other emerging technologies like AI, Block-chains and Cloud Computing can lead to the development of systems that are more robust, intelligent, secure and powerful. Already, a number of fields have been identified wherein the use of IoT has made a colossal impact. This chapter gives a brief overview of IoT and its applications in the field of healthcare, smart homes, agriculture, robotics, and industries.

Keywords: IoT, sensor, RFID, security, robotics

11.1 Introduction

The advancement of technologies has led to new ways of handling the machines. One such technology is the Internet of things (IoT) [1], which refers to the connection of devices to the internet. It can sense, accumulate [2],

Corresponding author: iram.abrar12@gmail.com

Parul Gandhi, Surbhi Bhatia, Abhishek Kumar, Mohammad Alojail and Pramod Singh Rathore (eds.)
Internet of Things in Business Transformation: Developing an Engineering and Business Strategy for
Industry 5.0, (185–210) © 2021 Scrivener Publishing LLC

and transfer data without any human intervention, thereby considerably reducing the human error and enable information access from anywhere and at any point of time. The ability of IoTs to sense the environment is due to the presence of sensors and actuators [3], which gives IoTs the ability to emit, accept, and process the signal. Sensors receive an analog signal from the environment and then convert these signals into digital streams, which are then processed depending on the specific requirement. This integration of the sensor-actuator framework forms the basis of IoT around which a smart environment is built. The data that needs more processing is forwarded to the cloud-based systems or physical data centers. This enormous amount of data after processing is useful and, thus, can be used for making our lives easier and safer. Moreover, the communication between the connected devices which are connected to a network is improved, thereby saving time.

IoTs have the capability of connecting various devices and enable them to share information by communicating with one another. It should also enable different heterogeneous devices that are based on different hardware platforms and networks to interact with one another. IoTs are dynamic in nature; thus, they have the capability to change their state based on the current situation, and hence, they can react to it in real-time. Since a large number of devices are connected with one another in IoTs, a considerable amount of data is generated by them. Thus, it becomes critical for IoTs to be able to manage such an enormous amount of data for proper functioning. Even though there are a number of advantages of using IoT, it is important to ensure that the safety of the data is maintained. As the data in IoTs is present on the network and is vulnerable to attacks by intruders, specific measures must be incorporated in order to ensure that the data is secured. This includes securing the network, end-points, and data present on the network.

Since security remains one of the critical factors in IoTs [4], IoTs must have the following properties:

> Confidentiality: Since the data collected by the sensor nodes is present on the network, it is essential to ensure that any unauthorized entity does not access the data [5], and hence, the confidentiality of data is maintained.
> Integrity: The data should not be modified during its transmission i.e., the data should be received as sensed by the sensor nodes for proper decision making [6].
> Authentication: It is vital to ensure that the data is received from a genuine source and not from an unauthorized entity.

For the same, the entities which are involved in communication must be authenticated through digital signatures.

> Availability and fault tolerance: The services should be available to authentic users without any interruption, and the system should be able to handle faults on its own so that the functionality of the system is not hampered.

> Data freshness: Every time the sensor nodes must send a new data frame to the processing system based on the real-time monitoring of a situation so that the replay of messages is prevented.

> Non-repudiation: The sensor nodes involved in the transmission of the data cannot, at any stage, deny their involvement in it.

> Authorization: Only authorized nodes must be able to transmit or receive the data in the network so that the confidentiality of the user's data is maintained [7].

> Self-healing: In case of a node failure, the remaining system should be robust enough to handle the situation on its own, so that the system, on the whole, is able to function correctly.

The rapid development of IoT has impacted several scientific and engineering domains. IoT offers several solutions for reforming existing industrial systems, such as transportation and manufacturing systems. For example, they can be used for creating intelligent systems for transportation authorities, treatment of waste products in waste energy plants, and making warning signals for mining disaster management. In industries, many devices are connected using IoT, which are synchronized through software, and enable machine-to-machine operations with a very minimal human intervention. IoTs have also improved the industry system, including integrated chips, electronic components, equipment, software, integrated systems, and telecom operators. Industry 4.0 and Industrial Internet of thing (IIoT) technologies provide a number of software solutions in many fields, particularly in industrial automation and manufacturing systems. Besides, there are several applications of IoT, which can be categorized as healthcare, agriculture, industrial automation, smart cities, and robotics [8]. Some of these applications of IoTs have been discussed in detail in this chapter. In the future, IoTs are expected to use different technologies for connecting physical objects, thereby supporting effective decision making [9].

11.2   IoT in Healthcare

An IoT-based healthcare system refers to the integration of sensor technology with IoT that can be used to monitor the patients. An IoT-based healthcare system has the capability of monitoring the patients and provide them with valuable suggestions in order to treat them. For example, a company, Body media, manufactured a wearable monitoring system, and their device showed good accuracy and reliability. Also, Google in 2008 developed a personalized healthcare system that enabled Google users to share their health records, but the project was stopped in 2011. This system provided a platform for Google users so that they could share their health records. The information provided by the users was then analyzed according to which they were informed about their health condition.

Specific other requirements for smart healthcare system include smart devices and smart nurse management systems. For example, smartphones can be used to drive the internet of things. A number of healthcare applications specifically designed for smartphones are available, which can be used to provide information about the health of the patient. Smartphones can be used to effectively monitor several parameters such as heart rate, level of oxygen in the blood, stress levels with the help of various hardware and software applications. For example, a smartphone note 8 from Samsung has inbuilt hardware that enables the user to determine the heart rate, oxygen saturation, stress levels, etc. Furthermore, a software application 'Samsung Health' keeps track of the steps taken by the user, track of other physical activities, and calories consumed by the user. The system, as such, provides information about the overall health of the user. Besides, real-time monitoring, smartphones are also cost-efficient. This smart healthcare system can be used in homes, communities, as well as worldwide, depending upon the requirements.

In healthcare, personalized monitoring is essential. The concept of self-awareness and big data can be combined using IoT-based system for this purpose [10]. The big data is used to obtain information about the situation in order to aware the patient. This self-awareness can be used to improve the behavior of the system depending upon the situation. In personalized monitoring, different parameters can be prioritized for different patients depending upon their needs [11]. For example, in the case of patients suffering from heart disease, monitoring the heart rate is extremely vital. Some of the applications of IoT in the healthcare system are mentioned below.

Diabetes, which is a metabolic disorder, is characterized by high blood glucose levels and results in severe morbidities, including death. The primary aim of the healthcare provider is to keep the levels of blood sugar in check as it tends to fluctuate very rapidly. It is of prime importance that the levels of glucose are continuously monitored so that the doses/frequency of the medication can be changed accordingly. An IoT-based healthcare system includes devices such as blood glucose monitor (which can be used to monitor the sugar level of patients with diabetes), a mobile phone or a computer/processor can be used to store and process the information so that a decision can be made in real-time, which in turn can enhance the quality of system which uses an IPV6 protocol to connect the patient and the healthcare system [12].

Similarly, the electrical activity of the heart can be measured by electrocardiography that can record the heart rate and rhythm. It is used for the diagnosis of some heart problems such as multifaceted arrhythmias, myocardial ischemia [13]. An IoT-based ECG system can be used in real-time to provide the best possible information about the heart conditions of the patient. Recently, several kinds of research have been done in this field [14–17]. For real-time monitoring of the heart rate, an IoT-based ECG system that consists of a wireless transmitter and wireless receiving processors can be used [18]. This system is used to monitor the heart rate of the patients in order to detect abnormal heart rates and, as such, can provide life-saving advice to the patients. So, it can be used as a quick diagnostic tool by the health care provider.

Likewise, in patients with altered blood pressure, an IoT-based BP monitoring system has a lot of potential, and can be used in real-time. For example, an IoT-based BP apparatus which consists of a communication module, a health post, and a health center can be used to monitor the BP of the patient.

To monitor the blood oxygen level, pulse oximetry is used. An IoT-based pulse oximetry can be used to aid medical healthcare applications, and several such devices are being developed. These devices are used to monitor the health conditions of the patient over an IoT network. For example, a pulse oximeter, namely, wrist OX2 device uses Bluetooth for connectivity between the device and the patient [19].

In the case of patients suffering from diseases such as asthma, tuberculosis, and lung cancer, it is essential to monitor their breathing patterns. For the same purpose, specific IoT-based sensors can be used. A thermistor is one such example that makes use of variations in the temperature to analyze the breathing pattern of the patients suffering from respiratory problems [20]. Another such device that can be used is a stretch sensor which works on the principle of tensile force for measuring respiratory rate [21].

Similarly, medical accidents such as heart attack, brain hemorrhage, stroke are likely to occur suddenly, particularly in elderly people. Thus, it is essential to detect such situations on time so that medical aid can be provided to them. For this purpose, IoT devices can be employed in which the sensor-based technology can be used to monitor the older adults in order to detect the possibility of such situations. Also, even when such a situation occurs, the collected data can be transmitted via a sensor to the medical experts for proper advice.

Other technologies, such as wireless sensor networks, can also be used by these devices to monitor health.

In the rehabilitation system, IoTs can play a critical role as they have the ability to improve the health conditions of physically impaired or specially-abled people. An IoT-based rehabilitation system has a lot of potential for real-time interaction with specially-abled patients and can be used to tackle problems associated with aging as well. They can also be used to aid patients suffering from depression and other mental health problems. Some of their applications are- an integrated application system for prisons [22], rehabilitation center, which is used to train patients suffering from hemiplegic [23], and a language-training system for children who have autism [24]. Using IoT, fully automated wheelchairs have been developed for the specially-abled people [25]. In these wheelchairs, various sensors are integrated to suffice the requirements of the patients. For example, the IoT department of Intel developed a smart wheelchair that has the ability to monitor the person sitting in the chair beside, gathering the information about its surroundings. Another such example is a smart IoT-based wheelchair that uses peer-to-peer (P2P) technology in order to control the vibration of the chair and for detection of the user's location.

IoT can be used to provide a solution for Parkinson's disease [26, 27], which is a neurological disorder in which a person tends to forget things (common in older adults). People suffering from this disease can use IoT devices to keep a reminder of their appointments. A common symptom of this disease is the freezing of gait, which causes a temporary memory loss. One of the proposed methods suggests that the IoT-based sensors can be used to monitor gait, and then an anomaly detection scheme can be used to extract the features which can be used to remind patients of certain events.

Malnutrition refers to the deficiency of nutrients or the lack of a proper diet. This is one of the common problems that need to be addressed. Recent research works have revealed that the rate of malnutrition is more common in older adults that can lead to many diseases such as cardiovascular and osteoporosis in them. This problem can be tackled with the help of a nutrition monitoring system, which is used to check whether the nutritional requirements of a person are met or not. A number of IoT-based nutrition monitoring systems have been proposed to check the well-being of older adults. ChefMyself is one such example that uses a cloud-based connection to monitor the nutritional requirements of older adults [28].

Similarly, DIET4Elders is another device which provides daily life services for older adults using a three layer system [29]. Here the data is first captured, then it's analyzed to obtain information, and finally, the medical experts give their advice. Furthermore, Ebutton is a wearable device based on IoT used to monitor the diet with the help of a visual sensor that is installed on the user's chest [30, 31]. Besides these, several other devices, such as medicine reminders and object location indicators, are also used to provide services to them.

A number of applications of IoT in healthcare from different perspectives have been explored. Using this technology, the health of the patients can be analyzed at regular intervals. IoTs provide an effective solution to many existing problems in healthcare as they can be used to monitor and nurse the patients in real-time and result in better diagnosis of various diseases.

11.3   IoT in Agriculture

With the ever-increasing population of the world, the arable land is shrinking fast, and as such, in the modern era, the importance of productivity in agriculture has assumed immense importance. The issues and challenges faced by the agricultural industries in terms of producing high quality and cost-effective crops can be tackled to a certain extent with the help of IoTs. Sensors can be installed at several places on a farm so that the parameters such as temperature, humidity, soil, and water content are analyzed at regular intervals in a timely manner. For example, a wireless sensor network (WSN) based IoT are used to monitor the quality of the soil and water content present in it. Several other sensors, such as climate sensors, ground sensors, radiation sensors, weather stations, are used in agricultural-based systems. Monitoring the environmental condition is also vital for early warning of floods and droughts. This information sensed by the sensors is then extracted by the central node and is transmitted via a network to the cloud for storage. This information can be accessed by a number of users based on which they can make an appropriate decision. The users can use their electronic devices such as mobile phones and computers to log in to the cloud storage to extract the data collected by the sensors. The advantage of using such a system is that productivity can be increased manifolds as the manual interaction in the farm-related activities can be minimized. Also, as no human intervention is required, the work can be carried out smoothly without any hassle. So, using IoTs, time can be saved as the personal inspection of the farm is no longer required. Besides, some limitations in terms of pest control, irrigation can also be managed. So, IoTs can play an essential role in agriculture as the productivity of the crops can be increased by analyzing the growth pattern of plants and their nutritional requirements. Furthermore, artificial intelligence, robotics, data mining, etc. can be used to control the environmental conditions on which the productivity of crops depends. Some of the applications of IoT in agriculture are discussed below.

Soil plays an important role as far as agriculture is concerned as it is through the soil plants obtain all the vital nutrients. With the help of sensors, it is possible to monitor the soil quality, and accordingly, specific measures can be taken into consideration in order to avoid its degradation. IoT-based devices can be used to monitor soil in terms of its texture, acidification, ability to retain water, nutrition level, and so on. For example, company Agrocares developed a "lab in a box" with the help of which large soil samples can be tested without having any lab experience. Remote sensors can also be used to obtain information about the water content present in the soil. For the same, the soil moisture and ocean salinity (SMOS) satellite was launched, which can be used to obtain soil water-deficient index. Apart from this, a number of other devices, such as image-based spectroradiometer sensors can be employed for analyzing the quality of the soil [32].

Only three percent of the water present on the earth is freshwater, among which 0.5% of the water lies above the ground [33]. For agricultural purposes, about 70% of this accessible water is used. Due to these facts, it is essential to conserve water and use it efficiently. The methodologies used in agriculture for irrigation should be replaced with IoT-based technologies so that the wastage of water can be reduced as it is an essential resource to sustain life on earth. For example, the water stress index can be used in order to reduce the wastage of water through irrigation. This index value is calculated on the basis of air temperature and crop canopy at various intervals. Several sensors can be installed in the field to calculate these parameters. This collected information is then transmitted to the processing centers where softwares are used for its analysis. Apart from sensors, weather data, and satellite image information can also be used to calculate this indexed value [34, 35]. Furthermore, IoT can be used to determine the duration and time of irrigation and can be used to automate the process of irrigation, which will not only lead to less manual intervention but will also lead to conservation of the resource and better plant growth.

Fertilizers are used to enhance the productivity of crops by providing them with essential nutrients. It is essential to use a proper quantity of manure. Since using them in less amount can lead to a deficiency of nutrients in the crops, and their excessive use can degrade the quality of the soil. IoT-based technologies can be used to calculate the normalized difference vegetation index with the help of which nutritional requirements of the crops can be analyzed. According to which an adequate quantity of fertilizers can be provided to them. Moreover, technologies such as global positioning system (GPS) accuracy [36], geo-mapping [37], variable rate technology [38, 39], and autonomous vehicles [40] can be employed for smart fertigation. Besides these, IoTs can also be used to enhance the process of fertigation and chemigation, which are considered as important agricultural practices [41].

Apart from this, image sensor based IoTs can be used to provide security for monitoring the crop growth with the help of cameras. In these systems, various image processing algorithms are used. Optimal sensors can also be used to provide information about crop reflection or temperature sensing [42–44]. Moreover, the environment and agriculture play a vital role in livestock. IoT can be used to optimize the performance of livestock by monitoring animals, their climate, and their feeding patterns. For this purpose, wireless sensor networks are employed to track their behavior.

It is vital to protect the crops from pests and rodents in order to avoid financial losses. To avoid such losses, pesticides are used. Although using pesticides has proven to be beneficial to the grower, but at the same time, they are very harmful to humans, and can even cause severe damage to the environment. Several IoT-based devices like drones, wireless sensors can be used to identify the pests so that they could be slashed in order to avoid crop losses. Also, IoT-based traps can be used for capturing insects. Besides, remote sensing imagery can be used effectively in order to identify these pests and their place of origin and their final trajectory, as such precautionary measures can be taken well in time to minimize the potential damage.

It is important to monitor the yield of the crops before they are harvested as it plays a vital role in estimating productivity; besides, this information can be used by the farmers for better decision making. Crops are monitored in terms of their color, shape, size. Also, by analyzing the crop, the right time for their harvest can be predicted. For this purpose, IoTs can be used. Sensors technology can be employed for monitoring the crops, and collect information about them. These sensors are linked to an application on the phone, such as FarmRTX, which can then predict the best time to harvest the crops. Besides this, optical sensors can be installed in the farms in order to check whether the fruits and vegetables are shrinking or not, particularly in the summer season. Also, techniques like depth imaging and satellite images can be used to determine the right time for harvest by analyzing various maturity signs of the crops.

Food supply chain tracking is crucial as it entails significant decisions that are taken to ensure that the quality of food is maintained [45]. This has led to a growing interest in food supply chain traceability systems from both the producers' and consumers' side. IoTs have the potential to provide a better solution for the maintenance of the Food Supply Chain (FSC). For example, an IoT-based radio frequency identification technology (RFID) is commonly found in FSC, and they provide an optimized solution for it. Here tags that are actually the sensor are present in RFID can be used to track the agricultural products. An artificial intelligence-based IoT system can be used to organize the information of FSC in order to maximize the profit.

With the advent of modern technology, new forms of agriculture have been devised, which includes green houses, hydroponics, etc.

Greenhouse cultivation has played a significant role in agriculture for the cultivation of crops as it increases the productivity of the crops. It is one of the most successful methods for cultivation as the crops present in the greenhouse remain unaffected by the external environmental conditions. Now as the cultivation of crops requires a certain suitable environmental condition for their growth due to which it is necessary to monitor these conditions. An IoT-based cloud system can be employed for monitoring the conditions inside a greenhouse. Here sensors are used to collect the information about the surroundings, and then this information is transmitted to the cloud where it can be analyzed. According to this analysis of information, an appropriate decision is taken. For example, an IoT-based model has been proposed in which MicaZ nodes have been employed for analyzing the conditions inside the greenhouse in terms of temperature, humidity, etc. [46]. Also, in order to have a proper irrigation plan for the crops in a greenhouse, an application, namely, online precise irrigation scheduling for greenhouses (OpIRIS), has been developed [47]. Here the information obtained by the sensors is forwarded to the cloud centers that can adequately predict the water requirements of the crops, thereby, increasing their productivity. Apart from this, a combination of IoT and radio frequency identification can be used to automate the process of irrigation [48]. IoT can also be used for pest control in the greenhouse. Furthermore, several parameters that need to be controlled, particularly, the carbon dioxide present in the environment, can be maintained for the proper growth of plants. IoT-based sensors can be used to control the environmental conditions in greenhouse. For example, non-dispersive infrared carbon dioxide sensors are used to measure the level of carbon dioxide present inside these farms. IoT-based boxed Gascard has been developed, particularly for this environment where a pseudo dual-beam NDIR measurement system can be used for improving the stability of the crops. Besides, sensors can also be used for waste management inside these farms.

Similarly, hydroponics is a technique where plants are cultivated without soil. In this technique, all the essential nutrients are provided to the plants with the help of water. The nutrients are dissolved in the water, and plants are allowed to remain in this water so that the plants are not deprived of any nutrients. In such a system, it is important to ensure the quantity of nutrients in the solution is maintained, and for this purpose IoTs can be used. Sensor modules present in IoTs can be used for measuring the level of water and nutrients present in the solution. Such a system can provide an effective solution for the cultivation of crops besides reducing the dependence on land for their cultivation.

Besides involvement in direct farming, IoT can be used to generate better breeds of the plants so that productivity can be maximized, ensuring pest and disease resistance. With the advancement of molecular and genetic tools, phenotyping came into existence. It is based on crop engineering and links plant genomics with its ecophysiology and agronomy. Phenotyping is used to analyze the characteristics of the plants that are responsible for their growth, quantity, and quality [49]. IoT-based technology can be incorporated with phenotyping in order to provide a better solution to the farmers. For example, CropQuant, which is used to analyze the characteristics of the crops, is an integration of IoTs and phenotyping [50]. It is used in digital agriculture and crop breeding. Here the sensors are used to monitor the characteristics of the crops. This collected information based on algorithms and machine learning techniques can be used to establish the relation between the crops and their environment. Accordingly, a more feasible environment can be provided to the crops for their better development.

Using IoT, smart farming practices can be adopted so that the productivity of the crops is increased in order to meet the increasing demands of food. IoTs have revolutionized agricultural practices in terms of their quality, quantity, irrigation, pest control, and much more. Moreover, it enables real-time monitoring of crops so that adequate measures can be taken in real-time based on which crop yield can be improved.

11.4   IoT in Industries

In industries, several devices are connected using IoTs and synchronized through softwares which enable the machine to machine operations with minimal human intervention, thereby increasing the level of automation. IoT offers several solutions for reforming existing industrial systems, such as transportation systems and manufacturing systems. The sensor-based technology of IoTs enable the devices and machines present in the industries to communicate with one another in real-time based on which the entire performance of the system can be enhanced. Several IoT-based industrial platforms like Predix, MindSphere [51], and Sentience cloud platforms are available, which are used to optimize industries by increasing the level of automation in them. For example, in the automobile industry, IoTs can be used for creating an intelligent transportation system, in which the transportation authorities will be able to keep track of each vehicle's current location, monitor its movement, and possible road traffic. IoTs have also improved the industrial system, including chips, electronic components, equipment, softwares, integrated systems, and telecom operators. Besides, the number of accidents at mining sites is reduced using IoT technologies, which can sense the mining disaster, and then generate signals in order to make early warnings. Industry 4.0 [52] and Industrial Internet of thing (IIoT) technologies provide several software solutions in many fields particularly in industrial automation and manufacturing systems, for example, they can be used in waste energy plant for the treatment of waste products. Some of the applications of IoT in industries are discussed below.

In the aviation industry, it is important to ensure that only the approved parts of an aircraft that have met the specific requirements are used in the manufacture/repair of the aircraft in order to ensure that the system is safe. It is a time-consuming task since each part needs to be adequately checked and there is a high chance of error caused by humans. IoT can provide better solutions to this problem. For example, electronic pedigrees can be used to store important information about the aircraft parts. These pedigrees are stored on RFID tags that are associated with a particular piece of an aircraft. Accordingly, based on the value of pedigree, the aircraft part can be authenticated, and this way, the safety of the system can be ensured [53].

Similarly, in smart vehicles, the processing power is increased with the help of advanced sensors installed in them. Besides, these sensors have the capability of monitoring the tire pressure, pollution level caused by the vehicles, thereby, providing better services to the customers. IoT-based radio frequency identification technology can be used for real-time monitoring of the vehicles, and in this way, they can be appropriately maintained. Furthermore, with the help of IoT, sensors can be used to enable the vehicle to vehicle communication with the help of which a smart transport system can be built.

IoT can be used to enhance the security in the transportation industry as it can be used for fare and toll collection, screening of passengers, monitoring the goods carried to and from a country. IoT-based systems can be installed in the airports, railways, etc. for tracking the passenger's luggage, and also, they can be used to keep a check on excessive luggage according to which the passengers can be charged. Besides, using wireless sensor technology, smart transport system can be built to avoid unnecessary traffic jams.

Usage of IoTs in the pharmaceutical industry [54, 55] can provide unprecedented benefits such as smart labels that can be associated with medicines that can be used to track them during their supply and avoid misuse of these drugs. Certain medicines should be stored in a specific environment. For example, most of the injections need cold temperature for their storage; IoT-based sensor technology can be used to ensure that these conditions are not violated, and even if they are, in that case, the drugs can be discarded as they no longer remain feasible for consumption. Also, intelligent medical cabinets can be built using IoTs for the storage of the drugs. Besides their storage, they can also inform the patients when to take medicines, the dosage of the medicine and their expiry dates. Statistics have also revealed that about 3.9% of sales are lost due to the absence of drugs in medical stores. So, retailers and chemists can use IoT-based shelves where drugs will be equipped with RFID technology. This way a more manageable system can be formed and also, the chemists will be aware of the shortage of a particular drug well on time, and thus, financial losses can be avoided.

As natural resources are scarce and costly to produce/manufacture, IoT and wireless technologies can be used to provide an effective solution for the reuse of things so that the resources are utilized in a better way. Radiofrequency identification devices can be used to identify the reusable electronic parts in cell phones, computers, and batteries in order to minimize e-wastes. Moreover, with the advancement in technology, companies are able to identify these reusable components efficiently, and new devices are developed using these components for better resource management.

In the traditional industrial system, the management of resources such as equipment and machine was difficult, but with the advent of IIoT, resource management is much more sophisticated and organized, thereby offering better services. The applications of IoT in industries (IIoT) have been discussed above. The industrial internet of thing has been revolutionized by incorporating a number of existing technologies such as artificial intelligence, cloud, and big data.

11.5 IoT-Based Smart Cities

With the help of IoT, smart homes having smart appliances, smart lighting control, and fire detection system can be built. The sensors present in smart devices can sense the data that is transmitted to the central controller through which the user can control the devices present at their homes. The concept of smart homes can further be extended to form smart communities [56]. In smart communities, smart homes are connected through a neighbor area network. There are a number of advantages of having a smart community such as a common city camera can be installed in the locality to report specific undesirable incidents to the police. Besides, smart communities can be used for proper management of resources, healthcare-related problems, pollution control, etc. A number of smart communities can further be combined to form a smart city. These cities are built using IoTs and information and communication technology (ICT) in such a way that they are capable of intelligently responding to several activities such as daily livelihood activities, public safety, and commercial activities, etc. The main goal of smart cities is to optimize the use of resources for the betterment of society and its people thereby, reducing energy consumption. Using this technology, the performance of the system is enhanced and thus, better quality of service is provided to the users. Moreover, with the advancement in technologies such as artificial intelligence, smart cities are becoming smarter. IoTs can be employed to transform houses, offices, factories, and towns into automatic and self-controlled systems which often operate without any human intervention. Some of the applications of IoT-based smart cities are discussed below [57].

A proper water management system equipped with sensors can be used to ensure that an appropriate supply of quality water is maintained, and the faults such as leakage are addressed. Moreover, it is essential to conserve rainwater so that, during the scarcity of water due to droughts or no rainfall, the problem of water can be resolved. This can be done by preserving rainwater in tanks where ultrasonic sensors can be used to check the water level. During adverse situations, IoT-based devices can be used to manage irrigation besides conserving water. Also, ultrasonic range finder based sensors can be used to gather information about the groundwater level in order to predict floods, and accordingly, alerts can be generated to aware the people of such situations before they occur [58].

In smart cities, energy consumption can be reduced by using smart homes where smart, IoT-based devices are used. For example, the light sensors sense the intensity of the light, and accordingly, the lights are dimmed during the daytime; heating and cooling devices will operate only in the presence of residents otherwise will automatically turn off to conserve electricity/gas.

Energy is also used in the form of public lighting, transportation, traffic lights, control cameras, heating and cooling of buildings. IoT-based sensors can be used for monitoring the energy used by these devices. The information collected by these devices can be analyzed, and consequently, priorities can be set in order to make efficient use of energy. According to a study, about 45% of energy can be saved by adopting smart lightning control systems [59]. Street lights need to be optimized in order to conserve energy, and this can be done by controlling the intensity of the lights [60]. For example, during the daytime, there is no need for a lightning system, whereas at night, it is essential to have a proper lighting system. Accordingly, the intensity of light should be high during the night to visualize things, and sensors present in the IoT devices can be used to control the intensity of the street lights based on time of the day. Moreover, this sensor technology can be used to detect faults in them and thereby help in timely repairs and avoid any inconvenience to the citizens.

An entire smart city can be monitored continuously with the help of smart devices, and there is a high chance of a threat to the data which is being monitored. In order to prevent any undesirable access to this data, which can be used for criminal activities, it is essential to have a secure system. IoT-based surveillance systems can be used to detect unusual events, and accordingly, alarms can be generated in order to inform the concerned authorities [61].

Devices using IoT-based technology can be used to optimize the food choices based on their availability. In smart cities, the concept of smart restaurants can be used that are connected to the network. The customers can view the menu on their smart device according to which an order can be placed. Also, smart devices can be used to deliver food to their respective customers. In this way, both time, as well as the energy, can be saved.

Management and proper disposal of waste is essential for a healthy environment. IoT can be used in this domain to provide an effective and cost-efficient solution. For example, IoT-based smart waste containers can be used, which are both capable of determining the level of the load as well as can be used to determine which route should be followed by the collector truck. In this way, an optimized solution to the waste management system can be provided thereby, reducing the cost [62]. Besides, when the garbage is dumped, IoT-based smart waste containers in combination with software can be used for their proper recycling. Environmental pollution can also be monitored and kept under check in the smart cities with the help of IoT devices [63]. This data can then be transmitted to the residents, and accordingly, the patients suffering from diseases related to pollution will be notified about the pollution level based on which they can adopt specific measures for the betterment of their health. Also, IoTs can be used to keep a check on the air quality. Sensors can be deployed across various cities in order to monitor the level of pollution present in the air. Besides this, the presence of other harmful gases such as carbon dioxide, carbon monoxide can also be detected. Furthermore, it is also important to keep a check on the level of noise as unnecessary noise can lead to specific problems, especially for the patients suffering from hearing disorders. Using IoT, smart sound detection systems can be used to keep a check on the level of noise in a particular area. Sensors can also be used to keep a check on the performance of the vehicles; thereby, servicing of the vehicles can be done on proper time and, thus, can be used to control pollution.

In smart cities, IoT-based sensor technology can be used to analyze the weather conditions such as temperature, humidity, rain in order to notify the residents beforehand, and they can adopt specific measures to minimize damage and increase human survivability.

In smart cities, traffic congestion can be avoided to a certain extent by using IoT based technologies. For example, traffic on the road can be monitored with the help of a global positioning system (GPS) installed on the smart vehicles that have the sensing ability [64]. Arrival and departure time of vehicles can be traced in smart parking using vehicular traffic information that can be used by the citizens to provide information about their arrival time. According to this, the allocation of parking slots can be done in a way that parking areas can accommodate a maximum number of vehicles [65]. Apart from saving time, there will be less congestion using smart parking. Furthermore, technologies like radio frequency identification or near field communication can be used by specially-abled people for the reservation of parking slots and in this way, better services can be offered to them.

Historic places can be preserved by continuously monitoring them in order to identify the impact of external entities on them. IoT-based devices can be used in order to analyze the condition of these buildings. The sensors present in the IoT devices can be used to check the level of stress, pollution level, and the impact of an environmental condition such as acid rain on these buildings [66]. All this gathered information can be stored in a database which can be accessible by the citizens so that they can come forward and help in their preservation. Furthermore, the advantage of using these devices is that the human effort is reduced as the need for structural testing is no longer required. Besides this, IoT-based sensor technology can also be employed to reduce the number of accidents caused due to the collapse of bridges, and for this purpose, it is essential to analyze their condition in real-time. A system formed by the integration of wireless technology and water level sensors can be used to analyze the status of the bridges. Moreover, in adverse situations such as earthquakes, the wireless sensors can send a message to the management authority according to which specific preventive measures can be adopted in order to avoid accidents.

A smart city is an emerging concept using which several heterogeneous devices can be connected with one another so as to optimize resource utilization. They offer better connectivity to the residents in real-time as the level of automation is increased as compared to that of traditional systems. In the future, the concept of smart cities can be implemented in villages to create smart communities for improving their quality of life as well as offering better services to them.

11.6 IoT in Robotics

The integration of IoT with robotics is referred to as IRoT (Internet of Robotic Things), wherein the intelligent devices monitor events from a variety of sources. This intelligence can then be used to determine the best possible action, according to which they are able to control the objects in the real world. In IRoT, IoT-based sensor technology and data analytics are integrated so that the awareness capabilities of the robots are enhanced. Due to this, the robots are able to make a decision in real-time, depending upon the specific situation. Furthermore, IRoT makes use of technologies like cloud computing and cloud storage for resource sharing and enabling interoperability among robotics things. In this way, the existing technology can be used to pave ways for their development, and besides this, they are cost-efficient as they take benefits from the current technology, and thus, the maintenance overhead is also reduced [67]. IoT aided modern robots can be used in the rescue management system, military applications, industrial plants, and, healthcare. For example, in industries, IoT technologies will enable interaction among different robots, a smart object which can be directly integrated into machinery thus, paving the way towards the development of some other services and applications. Some of the uses of IoTs in robotics are mentioned below.

In the field of medicine, robots can play a significant role by providing services to the patients in terms of nursing the patients or assisting the doctors during the course of treatment. In this regard, rehabilitation robotics is an active area of research in which they are used to enhance the recovery process of the patients. They can also be employed to assist the patients suffering from locomotion diseases. For example, the ACT system is used in the case of stroke survivors to measure the abnormal joint torque [68]. Recently, BioMotionBot [69] has been used to analyze the movements of the patients in a rehabilitation center and also can be employed to provide services to specially-abled and elderly people so that they can live an independent life. Robots are designed in such a way that they can be used in real-time and for real-life scenarios. So, it's essential to take users' perspective into account for the better performance of the robots. Today, robots are combined with artificial intelligence in order to assist the patients. But as technology is evolving, there is a need to switch to a better platform that can be presented in the form of IoTs. For example, in an ICU, if an emergency arises, the robots can be used to effectively handle such situations in order to prevent any criticality. Besides, these robots can also be used in hospitals to assist surgeries.

In industries, a set of machines work together to attain a common goal that can be used to manufacture a particular product. It is crucial to ensure that the power and temperature requirements, brakes, lubrication in machines are maintained so that they can function correctly. IoT can be used in industries to monitor the performance of the machines and ensure that they are functioning correctly. Also, the wireless sensor network (WSN) can be used in smart buildings for surveillance and energy control. Human-friendly robots can be used in industries and are able to adapt to various situations depending upon the need. This is due to the fact that robots can work in places where human can't such as inside a furnace or with harmful chemicals as it can be dangerous for humans to work in these places.

In military applications, IoTs can be employed to detect intrusion and hazardous chemicals with the help of sensors such as infrared, photoelectric, and image sensors. They can be used to detect mines, snipers, explosives in sensitive areas. In recent times, a Military-IoT (MIOT) has been proposed that has the ability to collect the information from its surroundings. This information is collected with the help of sensors, and the information is then shared among various military objects using the sensing layer. This layer is vulnerable to attacks and can be exploited by the attackers to get hold of confidential information. So, it's essential to secure this layer so that there is no breach of information. For this purpose, robots can be used.

Rescue operations are meant to save the lives of people trapped in certain undesirable situations such as person trapped in a building on fire or earthquakes, etc. During such circumstances, it is important that the entire place is properly analyzed and for this purpose, an enormous amount of data is to be collected. Wireless sensor networks can be used to collect this information in a minimum possible time [70]. In WSN, sensor nodes are used to gather the information, and then this information is forwarded to the control centers. By analyzing this information, the control center takes an appropriate decision for the betterment of the situation. IoT can also be used to indicate earthquake emergencies so that the damage and loss can be controlled to a specific limit by taking certain preventive measures [71]. In such situations, the data is collected by IoT devices based on which a proper decision can be made for post-earthquake reconstruction. Robots, namely rescue robots, are used for rescue operations. For example, they can be used in many situations, such as mining accidents, urban disasters, hostage kidnapping, and explosions. But since these teleoperated robots can face a number of challenges in real-time, there is a need to switch to fully autonomous robots. Fully autonomous robots have the capability of independent decision making, which makes them useful in real-time for undesirable situations, for which IoT technology can provide aid. In IoT-based robots, the actions of the robots are coordinated based on the information sensed by the IoT devices, and in this way, the system becomes more effective.

With the advancement of technology, IoT and robotics have been integrated to form IRoT so that better services can be offered to the users. IRoT allows robots to connect with one another so that they can share the information in real-time. So far IRoT has been implemented in a number of areas which have been discussed above and in the future, there is a scope of improvement in terms of connectivity and security.

11.7   Conclusion and Future Scope

The rationale behind the use of IoT is to improve the quality of life through both, automation and augmentation. It is capable of integrating a number of heterogeneous things with existing technologies, such as artificial intelligence and cloud computing, in a novel way, thereby offering better services to the users. One of the prime attraction of IoT usage is that it helps its users in better decision making with minimal human intervention and feasibility in terms of time and money. This is due to the fact that using smart sensor based devices, objects can be accessed from anywhere and at any time. The various applications of IoT have been discussed in the field of healthcare, smart cities, robotics, agriculture and industries.

Although IoT has several applications and offers many benefits to people, there are still some challenges that need to be addressed. In the case of IoTs, there should be functional internet connectivity as the devices are always connected to the network. Besides, the sensors and actuators must be functioning properly so that they are able to sense and react to the environmental conditions in real-time. Moreover, the data present on the network must be secured so that the privacy of the user's data is not hampered. Also, some protection mechanisms should be incorporated in order to ensure that there are no loopholes in the network, thereby preventing intrusive activities. Since interoperability among various devices in IoT remains a challenge, therefore, in the future, with the advancement in technology, this problem can be worked upon so that the heterogeneous network can work properly in a systematic manner. Emerging techniques like cloud computing, fog/edge computing, data mining can be integrated with the internet of things to improve user's experience and resilience of the services in case of failures.

References

1. Gubbi, J., Buyya, R., Marusic, S., Palaniswami, M., Internet of things (IoT): A vision, architectural elements and future directions. *Future Gener. Comput. Syst.*, 29, 1645–1660, 2013.
2. Bhuvaneswari, V. and Porkodi, R., The internet of things (IoT) applications and communication enabling technology standards: An overview, in: *International Conference on Intelligent Computing Applications*, IEEE, 2014.
3. Madakam, S., Ramaswamy, R., Tripathi, S., Internet of things (IoT): A literature review. *J. Comput. Commun.*, 3, 164–173, 2015.
4. Masoodi, F., Alam, S., Siddiqui, S.T., Security and privacy threats, attacks and countermeasures in Internet of Things. *Int. J. Netw. Secur. Appl.* (IJNSA), 11, 67–77, 2019.
5. Miorandi, D., Sicari, S., Pellegrini, F.D., Chlamtac, I., Internet of things: Vision, applications and research challenges. *Ad Hoc Networks*, 10, 1497–1516, 2012.
6. Rost, M. and Bock, K., Privacy by design and the new protection goals. *European privacy seal, EuroPriSe*, DuD, Germany, pp. 1–9, 2011. http://www.datenschutzgeschichte.de/pub/privacy/BockRost_PbD_DPG_en_v1f.pdf (Accessed: February 18, 2020).
7. Patel, K.K. and Patel, S.M., Internet of things—IOT: Definition, characteristics, architecture, enabling technologies, application & future challenges. *Int. J. Eng. Sci. Comput.* (IJESC), 6, 6122–6131, 2016.

8. Vermesan, O. and Friess, P., Internet of things From research and innovation to market deployment. *River Publishers Series in Communications*, 2014.

9. Domingo, M.C., An overview of the internet of things for people with disabilities. *J. Netw. Comput. Appl.*, 35, 584–596, 2012.

10. Agarwal, A., Miller, J., Eastep, J., Wentziaff, D., Kasture, H., Self-aware computing, *Technical report, AFRL-RI-RS-TR-2009-161*, Massachusetts Institute of Technology, USA, 2009.

11. Azimi, I., Rahmani,, A.M., Liljeberg, P., Tenhunen, H., Internet of things for remote elderly monitoring: A study from user-centered perspective. *J. Ambient Intell. Hum. Comput.*, 8, 273–289, 2017.

12. Istepanian, R.S.H., Hu, S., Philip, N.Y., Sungoor, A., The potential of internet of m-health things "m-IoT: For non-invasive glucose level sensing, in: *Proceedings IEEE Engineering in Medicine and Biology Society*, IEEE, pp. 5264–5266, 2011.

13. Drew, B.J., Practice standards for electrocardiographic monitoring in hospital settings. *Circulation*, 110, 2721–2746, 2004.

14. Yang, G., A health-IoT platform based on the integration of intelligent packaging, unobtrusive bio-sensor, and intelligent medicine box. *IEEE Trans. Ind. Inf.*, 10, 2180–2191, 2014.

15. Jara, A.J., Zamora-Izquierdo, M.A., Skarmeta, A.F., Interconnection framework for mHealth and remote monitoring based on the Internet of Things. *IEEE J. Sel. Area. Comm.*, 31, 47–65, 2013

16. You, L., Liu, C., Tong, S., Community medical network (CMN): Architecture and implementation, in: *Proceedings Global Mobile Congress* (GMC), IEEE, pp. 1–6, 2011.

17. Agu, E., The smart phone as a medical device: Assessing enablers, benefits and challenges, in: *2013 Workshop on design challenge in mobile medical device systems*, IEEE, pp. 76–80, 2013.

18. M.L. Liu, L. Tao, Z. Yan, Internet of things-based electrocardiogram monitoring system, Chinese patent 102764118 A, 2012.

19. Larson, E.C., Goel, M., Boriello, G., Heltshe, S., Rosenfeld, M., Patel, S.N., SpiroSmart: Using a microphone to measure lung function on a mobile phone, in: *Proceedings ACM International Conference of Ubiquitous Computing*, pp. 280–289, 2012.

20. Milici, S., Lorenzo, J., Lazaro, A., Villarino, R., Girbau, D., Wireless breathing sensor based on wearable modulated frequency selective surface. *IEEE Sens. J.*, 17, 1285–1292, 2017.

21. Mahbub, I., Pullano, S.A., Wang, H., Islam, S.K., Fiorillo, A.S., To, G., Mahfouz, M.R., A low-power wireless piezoelectric sensor-based respiration monitoring system realized in CMOS process. *IEEE Sens. J.*, 17, 1858–1864, 2017.

22. D.Y. Lin, Integrated internet of things application system for prison, Chinese Patent 102867236A, 2013.

23. Z. Guangnan and L. Penghui, IoT (Internet of Things) control system facing rehabilitation training of hemiplegic patients, Chinese patent 202587045U, 2012.

24. Y. Yue-Hong, F. Wu, F.Y. Jie, L. Jian, X. Chao, Z. Yi, Remote medical rehabilitation system in smart city, Chinese Patent 103488880A, 2014.

25. Islam, S.M.R., Kwak, D., Kabir, M.H., Hossain, M., Kwak, K., The internet of things for health care: A comprehensive survey. *IEEE Access*, 3, 678–708, 2015.

26. Pasluosta, C.F., Gassner, H., Winkler, J., Klucken, J., Eskofier, B.M., An emerging era in the management of Parkinson's disease: Wearable technologies and the internet of things. *IEEE J. Biomed. Health Inform.*, 19, 1873–1881, 2015.

27. Russmann, A.S.H., Wider, C., Burkhard, P.R., Vingerhoets, F.J.G., Aminian, K., Quantification of tremor and bradykinesia in Parkinson's disease using a novel ambulatory monitoring system. *IEEE Trans. Biomed. Eng.*, 54, 313–322, 2007.

28. Lattanzio, F., Abbatecola, A.M., Bevilacqua, R., Chiatti, C., Corsonello, A., Rossi, L., Bustacchini, S., Bernabei, R., Advanced technology care innovation for older people in Italy: Necessity and opportunity to promote health and wellbeing. *J. Am. Med. Dir. Assoc.*, 15, 457–466, 2014.

29. Sanchez, J., Sanchez, V., Salomie, I., Taweel, A., Charvill, J., Araujo, M., Dynamic nutrition behaviour awareness system for the elders, in: *Proceedings of the 5th AAL Forum: Impacting Individuals, Society and Economic Growth*, pp. 123–126, 2013.

30. Sun, M., Burke, L.-E., Mao, Z.-H., Chen, Y., Chen, H.-C., Bai, Y., Li, Y., Li, C., Jia, W., eButton: A wearable computer for health monitoring and personal assistance, in: *Proceedings 51 st Design Automation Conference*, pp. 1–6, 2014.

31. Bai, Y., Li, C., Yue, Y., Jia, W., Li, J., Mao, Z.-H., Sun, M., Designing a wearable computer for lifestyle evaluation, in: *38th annual northeast bioengineering conference*, IEEE, pp. 93–94, 2012.

32. Vagen, T.-G., Winowiecki, L.A., Tondoh, J.E., Desta, L.T., Gumbricht, T., Mapping of soil properties and land degradation risk in Africa using MODIS reflectance. *Geoderma*, 263, 216–225, 2016.

33. Water facts—Worldwide water supply. Bureau of reclamation, 2019. https://www.usbr.gov/mp/arwec/water-facts-ww-water-sup.html (Accessed: February 18, 2020).

34. Benincasa, P., Antognelli, S., Brunetti, L., Fabbri, C., Natale, A., Sartoretti, V., Vizzari, M., Reliability of NDVI derived by high resolution satellite and UAV compared to in-field methods for the evaluation of early crop n status and grain yield in wheat. *Exp. Agric.*, 54, 604–622, 2018.

35. Liu, H., Wang, X., Bing-kun, J., Study on NDVI optimization of corn variable fertilizer applicator. *Agric. Eng.*, 56, 193–202.10, 2018.

36. Shi, J., Yuan, X., Cai, Y., GPS real-time precise point positioning for aerial triangulation. *GPS Solut.*, 21, 405–414, 2017.

37. Suradhaniwar, S., Kar, S., Nandan, R., Raj, R., Jagarlapudi, A., Geo-ICDTs: Principles and applications in agriculture, in: *Geospatial technologies in land*

resources mapping, monitoring and management. Geotechnologies and the Environment, Springer, vol. 21, G. Reddy and S. Singh (Eds.), pp. 75–99, 2018.

38. Colaco, A.F. and Molin, J.P., Variable rate fertilization in citrus: A long term study. *Precis. Agric.*, 18, 169–191, 2017.

39. Bruno, B., Benjamin, D., Davide, C., Andrea, P., Francesco, M., Luigi, S. Environmental and economic benefits of variable rate nitrogen fertilization in a nitrate vulnerable zone. *Sci. Total Environ.*, 545–546, 227–235, 2016.

40. Khan, N., Medlock, G., Graves, S., Anwar, S., GPS guided autonomous navigation of a small agricultural robot with automated fertilizing system, *SAE Technical Paper*, 2018.

41. Ayaz, M., Ammad-Uddin, M., Sharif, Z., Mansour, A., Aggoune, E.-H.M., Internet-of-Things (IoT) based smart agriculture: Towards making the fields talk. *IEEE Access*, 7, 129551–129583, 2019.

42. Fisher, D.K. and Kebede, H., A low-cost microcontroller based system to monitor crop temperature and water status. *Comput. Electron. Agric.*, 74, 168–173, 2010.

43. Moshou, D., Bravo, C., Oberti, R., West, J.S., Ramon, H., Vougioukas, S., Intelligent multi-sensor system for the detection and treatment of fungal diseases in arable crops. *Biosyst. Eng.*, 108, 311–321, 2011.

44. O'Shaughnessy, S.A. and Evett, S.R., Developing wireless sensor networks for monitoring crop canopy temperature using a moving sprinkler system as a platform. *Appl. Eng. Agric.*, 26, 331–341, 2010.

45. Kodana, R., Parmarb, P., Pathania, S., Internet of things for food sector: Status quo and projected potential. *Food Rev. Int.*, 36, 1–17, 2019. https://doi.org/10.1080/87559129.2019.1657442.

46. Akkaş, M.A. and Sokullu, R., An IoT-based greenhouse monitoring system with Micaz motes. *Procedia Comput. Sci.*, 113, 603–608, 2017.

47. Katsoulas, N., Bartzanas, T., Kittas, C., Online professional irrigation scheduling system for greenhouse crops. *Acta Hortic.*, 1154, 221–228, 2017.

48. Tongke, F., Smart agriculture based on cloud computing and IOT. *J. Converg. Inf. Technol.*, 8, 26, 2013.

49. Tripodi, P., Massa, D., Venezia, A., Cardi, T., Sensing technologies for precision phenotyping in vegetable crops: Current status and future challenges. *Agronomy*, 8, 57, 2018.

50. Zhou, J., Reynolds, D., Websdale, D., Cornu, T.L., Gonzalez-Navarro, O., Lister, C., Orford, S., Laycock, S., Finlayson, G., Stitt, T., Clark, M.D., Bevan, M.W., Griffiths, S., CropQuant: An automated and scalable field phenotyping platform for crop monitoring and trait measurements to facilitate breeding and digital agriculture. *BioRxiv*, 1–41, 2017.

51. MindSphere: Enabling the world's industries to drive their digital transformations. Siemens: Ingenuity for Life, pp. 1–24, 2018. https://www.plm.automation.siemens.com/media/global/en/Siemens_MindSphere_Whitepaper_tcm27-9395.pdf. (Accessed: February 18, 2020).

52. Xu, L.D., Xu, E.L., Li, L., Industry 4.0: State of the art and future trends. *Int. J. Prod. Res.*, 56, 2941–2962, 2018.
53. Bandyopadhyay, D. and Sen, J., Internet of things: Applications and challenges in technology and standardization. *Wireless Pers. Commun.*, 58, 49–69, 2011.
54. Sun, C., Application of RFID technology for logistics on internet of things. *AASRI Procedia*, 1, 106–111, 2012.
55. Ngai, E.W.T., Moon, K.K., Riggins, F.J., Yi, C.Y., RFID research: An academic literature review (1995–2005) and future research directions. *Int. J. Prod. Econ.*, 112, 510–520, 2008.
56. Anastasia, S., The concept of 'smart cities' towards community development. *Netw. Commun. Stud., Netcom*, 26, 375–388, 2012.
57. Zanella, A., Bui, N., Castellani, A.P., Vangelista, L., Zorzi, M., Internet of things for smart cities. *IEEE Internet Things J.*, 1, 22–32, 2014.
58. Alder, L., The urban internet of things: Surveying innovations across city systems, 2015. https://datasmart.ash.harvard.edu/news/article/the-urban-internet-ofthings-727 (Accessed: February 18, 2020).
59. Martirano, L., A smart lighting control to save energy, in: *Proceedings of the 6th IEEE International Conference on Intelligent Data Acquisition and Advanced Computing Systems*, pp. 132–138, 2011.
60. Gharaibeh, A., Salahuddin, M.A., Hussini, S.J., Khreishah, A., Khalil, I., Guizani, M., Al-Fuqaha, A., Smart cities: A survey on data management, security, and enabling technologies. *IEEE Commun. Surv. Tutor.*, 19, 2456–2501, 2017.
61. Talari, S., Shafie-khah, M., Siano, P., Loia, V., Tommasetti, A., Catalao, J.P.S., A review of smart cities based on the internet of things concept. *Energies*, 10, 421, 2017.
62. Nuortio, T., Kytöjoki, J., Niska, H., Bräysy, O., Improved route planning and scheduling of waste collection and transport. *Expert Syst. Appl.*, 30, 223–232, 2006.
63. Venkateshwar, S.V. and Mohiddin, M., A survey on smart agricultural system using IoT. *Int. J. Eng. Res. Technol., ICPCN-2017*, 5, 1–6, 2017.
64. Li, X., Shu, W., Li, M., Huang, H.-Y., Luo, P.-E., Wu, M.-Y., Performance evaluation of vehicle-based mobile sensor networks for traffic monitoring. *IEEE T. Veh. Technol.*, 58, 1647–1653, 2009.
65. Lee, S., Yoon, D., Ghosh, A., Intelligent parking lot application using wireless sensor networks, in: *Proceeding International Symposium on Collaborative Technology Systems*, pp. 48–57, 2008.
66. Lynch, J.P. and Kenneth, J.L., A summary review of wireless sensors and sensor networks for structural health monitoring. *Shock Vib. Dig.*, 38, 91–130, 2006.
67. Ray, P.P., Internet of robotic things: Concept, technologies, and challenges. *IEEE Access*, 4, 9489–9500, 2016.
68. Ellis, M., Sukal-Moulton, T., Dewald, J.P.A., Impairment-based 3-D robotic intervention improves upper extremity work area in chronic stroke:

Targeting abnormal joint torque coupling with progressive shoulder abduction loading. *IEEE Trans. Rob.*, 25, 549–555, 2009.

69. Bartenbach, V., Sander, C., Pschl, M., Wilging, K., Nelius, T., Doll, F., Burger, W., Stockinger, C., Focke, A., Stein, T., The biomotionbot: A robotic device for applications in human motor learning and rehabilitation. *J. Neurosci. Methods*, 213, 282–297, 2013.

70. Saha, S. and Matsumoto, M., A framework for disaster management system and WSN protocol for rescue operation, in: *TENCON 2007—IEEE Region 10 Conference, IEEE*, pp. 1–4, 2007.

71. Chen, Z., Li, Z., Liu, Y., Li, J., Liu, Y., Quasi real-time evaluation system for seismic disaster based on internet of things, in: *2011 International conference on internet of things and 4th International conference on cyber, physical and social computing, IEEE*, pp. 520–524, 2011.

12

Challenges for Agile Autonomous Team in Business Organization

Gurmeet Kaur[1]*, Jyoti Pruthi[2] and Rachna Soni[3]

[1]Manav Rachna University, Faridabad, India
[2]Dept. of Computer Sciences, Manav Rachna University, Faridabad, India
[3]Dept. of Computer Sciences & Application, D.A.V. College For Girls,
Yamuna Nagar, India

Abstract

Framing self-organizing, cross–functional, autonomous, self-controlling out groups/teams in programming advancement is getting increasingly normal in numerous associations. Agile strategies are progressively utilized in huge development projects, with different group advancement groups to make business esteem by conveying working programming to clients at customary short time periods. Receiving the act of coordinated standards and self-governing agile group in fixed value groups when IT suppliers work with open clients, presents specialized, organization and social difficulties. The self-rule of the group was characterized by their opportunity to work in close collaboration with product owner and clients, to take possession to their procedures and experiences and to take obligations regarding their interface to different frameworks. At the point when self-organizing groups/teams need to cooperate, they should lose some degree of self-governance since work should be composed with different groups. Teams in enormous scale projects need to agree on different choices with partners, specialists, and administrators. The requirement for adjusting the work and the procedure to the remainder of the association diminish team selfsufficiency. Coordination by configuration is one technique to deal with this challenge. Research on autonomous team/group advancement has depicted that for a group to arrive at a gainful stage, it must be oversee difference and inner clashes proficiently. Most of contentions begin from team/group level factor and, in this way they ought to be dealt with on group level. Outside imperative like fixed extension and fixed

---

*Corresponding author: Grmtkaur02@gmail.com

Parul Gandhi, Surbhi Bhatia, Abhishek Kumar, Mohammad Alojail and Pramod Singh Rathore (eds.)
Internet of Things in Business Transformation: Developing an Engineering and Business Strategy for Industry 5.0, (211–230) © 2021 Scrivener Publishing LLC

value prompts the issue of absence of trust among team and director. Norms are the casual guidelines that help the team/group and manage colleague's conduct. This chapter portrays difficulties experienced in agile development comprising of self-governing autonomous group set up with resources from both IT and business advancement side of the organization.

Keywords: Autonomy, conflict, trust, coordination and communication

12.1 Introduction

Agile programming methods/strategies and procedures are progressively utilized in huge scale software improvement. As agile programming advancement is turning into a generally utilized methodology for programming improvement, organizations in the open space are progressively changing their advancement strategies to coordinate. The inspirations are many: customary traditional waterfall model development techniques have long delivery cycles while agile strategies urge to convey regularly and exploit quick input from clients to adjust the item, individuals in various jobs, for example, designers and product owner are progressively fulfilled when cooperating as a team, and the measure of work spent on non-productive activities, for example, coordination and handovers is diminished. An investigation dissecting essential presumptions with in huge scale agile advancement [1] presents such projects as having complex information limits inside them, just as an intuitive complexity and tight coupling with innovations and procedures outside the project. Agile programming improvement ordinarily includes various groups/teams which are liable for the advancement of various highlights of a solution, and frequently create frameworks that are critical to organizations or social orders. A key transition from small to enormous scale is that work across limits becomes at any rate as significant as work inside groups/teams.

12.2 Literature Review

Embracing agile methods for working and engaging self-governing, autonomous groups/teams in huge scale settings is getting progressively well known. At the point when self-sorting out groups need to cooperate; they should sacrifice some degree of self-rule [2]. Structure and programming should be facilitated with different groups/teams, and advancement endeavours are regularly part of a portfolio or a program. As indicated by Bass and Haxby [3], this implies, for instance, that self-sorting out groups must sacrifice some autonomy and creativity to arrive at accord on normal guidelines. Decreased creativity and autonomy could prompt lower team/group performance, yet the exhibition of a self-ruling group doesn't just rely upon the capability of the agile group itself; it likewise relies upon the authoritative setting gave by the management [3]. Likewise, most investigations report positive effects because of the strengthening of groups however some feature potential difficulties as difficulties in implementing self-organizing groups in specific settings or without sufficient administration and support [4]. With regards to enormous scale agile programming improvement settings, there is a requirement for additional exploration on the way toward structuring, supporting, and training independent agile groups to expand their performance. With the rise of agile improvement techniques, we have likewise observed a considerable research enthusiasm for group related subjects, for example, communication [5], coordination [6] and self-managing groups [7], to give some examples.

An advancement from traditional arrangement based development to agile advancement is dissected by Petersen and Wohlin [8], following a case with three huge subsystem parts designed by 116 people. There is a broad measure of literature on the advantages of full self-organizing groups. Agile improvement depends on cooperation, instead of individual job task that describes plan-driven advancement [9]. Self-governing groups animate inclusion and participation and an impact of this is expanded enthusiastic connection to the organization, bringing about more noteworthy inspiration and pledge to perform and desire for duty. Subsequently, representatives care increasingly about their work, which may prompt more prominent imagination and helping conduct, higher efficiency and administration quality [10]. Another investigation present how Ericsson utilized individuals of training to advance procedure improvement and information pass on in a huge improvement program with 40 groups [11]. A study presents chains of Scrum groups in the event of associations with 151, 33 and 6 groups [12]. Self-executives can likewise straightforwardly impact group adequacy since it brings basic leadership position to the degree of operational issues and uncertainties and, subsequently, speed up and exactness of critical thinking [13]. Further, Bass [14] explores technique fitting in enormous scale off shore improvement. Scheerer *et al.* [15] depict enormous extent agile advancement as a associative framework, and talk about hypothetically how strategy can be accomplished in this space [16] presents structural work, client inclusion and between group coordination in an enormous improvement program. Executions of huge scale agile improvement are regularly prompted by professional structures, most noticeably Large-Scale Scrum (LeSS) or Scaled Agile Framework (SAFe). The Large-Scale Scrum (LeSS) [17] model was prevalently conceived by Craig Larman and Bas Vodde to extent the first Scrum composition outside of individual Scrum groups. The Scaled Agile Framework (SAFe) [18] was made by Dean Leffingwell, situated to a limited extent on his encounters with the Nokia change [19]. The structure depends on the possibility of an undertaking model isolating a product advancement association into three sections: Program, Team, and Portfolio. While once in a while censured as excessively arbitrary, SAFe is the most applied expert system specifically conceived for agile techniques everywhere [20].

12.3 Types of Autonomy

Various sorts of self-rule incorporate self-sufficiency over item, individuals and planning choices. At another level, Moe *et al.* examine contrasts between singular independence, inward and outside self-autonomy [21]. Outer or external autonomy is characterized as the impact of the management and others outside the group in the group's activities. Inside or internal autonomy point out to how much all co-workers mutually share choice power, while singular self-autonomy alludes to the measure of opportunity and discretion an individual has in completing. Independence has some pre-conditions to be acknowledged, among them excess of abilities (since it influences the group's capacity to adjust to evolving circumstances), culture, (for example, group direction), sharing of data with the goal that all co-members have the information to impact choices, and the management support so as to make the correct condition for the groups. For instance, a contextual analysis of a computer game improvement studio presented in [22] talks about a circumstance where independence verifiable in agile project the executives brought about clash with the parent association and force chains of importance endured by and by inside and around the team.

12.3.1 Outside/External Autonomy

Ideally, in high trust associations, a group ought to be given an issue to solve, and afterward the arrangement ought to be exclusively the group's obligation. This reflects the convention of Mission Command, in which we "indicate the end state, its motivation, and the minimum potential constraints", and speaks to an establishment to make a high level of inside independence. In huge associations, groups are regularly obliged by a few elements. For our situation constraints were forced by enactment, security, all universal plan, programming engineering and legacy frameworks to name the most significant ones. Likewise, the groups expected to associate with different groups and assignment. This was taken care of by moving toward these groups face to face to understand conditions, and by effectively presenting the possibility of agile advancement in practice when working with different groups in the association.

12.3.2   Interior/Internal Autonomy

Teams need a common reason, the vital abilities, and shared trust among the co-members to create inside self-rule or autonomous. The mutual obligation and proprietorship to the product developed all through the task, making an establishment for the capacity of the groups to settle on their own choices about how to make the most ideal arrangements. Internal independence requires cross-functional and repetition of abilities; this additionally lessens the degree of individual self-rule in a group as co-members deal with the scheduling and execution of their own assignments. During the task time frame the groups increased a total arrangement of abilities to create, maintain, convey, monitor and support the applications they have assign regarding.

12.3.3   Singular Autonomy

The task was gathered with a group of individuals with the essential abilities, originating from both inside and outer sources. Components that most likely were definitive for this to happen were cautious determination of exceptionally motivate co-member based on their insight and unmistakable interest for agile technique notwithstanding their demonstrated role skills. Given the cross groups with an functional variety of abilities depending of one another, and the basic establishment in the agile attitude [23], a high level of individual self-autonomy was smothered from the earliest starting point.

12.3.4   Consistent Learning and Improvement Ensures Individual and Internal Autonomy

A close cooperation and face to face communication created great relation and domain for learning when trust increase among the team members.

It was observed that co-members were receiving new abilities from their group peers. This learning occurred in different settings; generally significant through the day by day work in the group, yet additionally through sorted out every other week reviews creating improvement activities and the groups turned out to be bit by bit increasingly strong and less subject to the people in the groups because of more co-members acting more than one job. The way to get this going is to make space for it, for example, dispense certain percent of each co-members ability to self-advancement.

12.4   Challenges for Autonomous Team

12.4.1   Planning

Planning is pivotal in enormous extent advancement [24] report on how Microsoft engineers organize, finding that strategy is for the most part centered around planning and highlights. They indicate that 'more correspondence and individual association for superior working to cause communications between groups to go all the more easily'. The most common example was Email, the most utilized instrument to monitor conditions on different groups, for engineers, analyzers and furthermore program chiefs. The study underlined that 'making and keeping up close to home connections between people on groups that arrange is demonstrated by numerous respondents as an approach to effectively work together with partners' and finally that 'respondents might want progressively productive and successful correspondence between groups to facilitate their everyday work burden'.

12.4.1.1   Planning Associate Teams

In 2001 Mathieu, Zaccaro and Marks created the term 'associative framework' to demonstrate at least two groups that interface straightforwardly and reliantly in light of ecological dangers toward the usage of aggregate objectives. A associative framework is excessively enormous and specific to effectively utilize direct common alteration among every single individual from the framework [25]. Associative framework limits are defined by estimation of the way that all groups inside the framework, while following distinctive essential objectives, share at any rate one regular middle objective; and in doing so display information, procedure and result interdependences with in any event one other group in the framework [26]. The term coordination has been utilized for various events. Produced by the generating the impractically of the various dentition's [27], analyzed existing literature and prescribed the 'Big Five' in cooperation working. The Big Five in cooperation working comprises of five parts which are found in practically all collaboration scientific categorizations: group authority, versatility, reinforcement conduct, common execution observing, and group direction.

12.4.1.2   Closed-Loop Communication

It is something beyond creating and sending messages; it additionally has to do with making a mutual significance [28]. Correspondence is the basic trade of data & information through closed loop correspondence includes an input circle: Was the data gotten and interpreted effectively. This additional input circle is basic for effective correspondence 220 F.O. Bjørnson *et al.* inside different groups [29]. Confidence or Trust is described as the mutual conviction that groups will play out their jobs and secure the curiosity of their associates. Common trust is the group's belief in the character, respectability, quality and capacities of another group [30] or team. Trust directs the connection between group execution and different factors [31]. Trust is a pivotal group process, anyway it doesn't grow effectively across bunch limits [32].

12.4.2   Conflict

12.4.2.1   Inter-Personal Conflict

Traditionally, brain research scientist's partition clashes into the three kinds (connection, process, and assignment) in view of their substance. In any case, these types are not well-characterized and their connection to execution not completely understood [33]. In this way, a contention has nothing to do with raising one's voice of fighting, even if that is the down to earth translation of the word in certain languages. Data framework (IS) analysts have likewise led studies identified to clashes/disputes. In a study from 2001, [34] revealed that as the group had well-functioning clashes/disputes management, the inter-personal clashes/disputes consisting of difference, obstruction, and adverse feeling had less of an effect on the project results [35]. Besides, an investigation by [36] demonstrated that relational clash was unfavourably associated with the agile group methods iterative Development and Customer Access. Concurrently, these referenced investigations farther reason the requirement for actual compromise in agile based teams/groups.

12.4.2.2 Intra-Group Struggle

Interpersonal clash shows itself regularly a dual link. A work-or relationship linked clash should be orally communicated by one individual at the time and regularly coordinated to other person. Nonetheless, this doesn't imply that the contention is segregated to the individual s communicating it [37]. Relational clashes are believed to be between two groups, be it in people, teams or countries [38]. Intra-group clashes, we contend requirement of a structure to be overseen at advance in time, since clashes are common to rise, and here and there seriously after some time [39]. Accordingly, groups are helped by talking about early clashes persistently before they become contaminated and individual.

12.4.2.3 Heightened Inter-Personal Conflict

This section describes content from various books on clash or disagreement management, to deliver tips for how to handle around clashes/disputes. There is a decent variety of circumstances that conceivably can prompt relational group clashes/disputes. For instance contending needs, disputing over rare resources, false impressions, vague circumstances, various perspectives on service or divisions, various qualities, standards or understandings, correspondence issues, rivalry/competition, authoritative change, and stress [40]. Having high passionate knowledge is an exceptionally helpful for fruitful clash management. The following is a list of regular mistakes that are common to activate forceful or reluctant reactions in clashes/disputes situations [41]:

- One viewpoint—to see the issue just from your point of view.
- Weak correspondence—to quit tuning in/consideration.
- Only paired choices—think "right or wrong"; there's just a single way, and that is my direction.
- Similar predisposition—it's not simply he solid issue that is the problem, it's the individual.
- Expanding data—introduce new data not common to the next gathering.
- Manipulation—with holding data, talks behind individuals' backs.
- Disabling intentionally—Finding individual faulty areas and assaulting.
- Neglecting civil principles—Stop making proper acquaintance, overlook, and prohibit from mailing records. On the

off chance that effectively staying away from the previously mentioned missteps, and rather perceiving others' points of view and mentioning to one's very own job in the contention, trigger considerably more readiness to discover pleasing arrangements.

- Define the issue as a thin, normal and explicit issue.
- Describe your emotions associated with the issue (tragic, furious, baffled, disregarded and so forth).
- Exchange intentions to your positions, what's behind your various perspectives? What should be satisfied? Tune in to every others' points of view.
- Identify conceivable outcomes for shared advantage by giving numerous potential arrangements, and picked one admirably [42]. A more clear bit by bit convention may be the accompanying:
- A: These days (What's the current circumstance? These are the thing that We/I/they do today)
- B: Expected final product (This is the manner by which I need it. I/we/they ought to do like this).
- C: Barriers (Why X rather of Y?).
- C1: Do we think regarding the hindrances?
- C2: Are the hindrances conceivable to expel?
- C3: Can we expel the impediments?
- C4: Do we need to expel the impediments?
- D: Activity (Advice/modification) [43].

It is critical to perceive that various methodologies are required relying upon how contaminated the contentions are. One important involvement when clashes are increasingly entangled is to utilize as negotiator between [44]. In the agile programming improvement setting, the procedure facilitator (i.e., the Scrum Master in Scrum) would be perfect to take on such a job when required also indicated that Scrum Master s frequently oversee groups in practical manner.

12.4.3   Trust

Agile techniques with centre around straightforwardness and feedback loop are appropriate to create trust. Reflective sessions, for example, reviews utilized in accomplish and presented in both SAFe and LeSS will probably effect the measure of trust. Practices, ancient rarities and jobs encourage and quick strategy, yet another influential factor barely gets consideration: the human. For instance, literature on trust expresses to us that it doesn't grow effectively across group limits and that it influences the measure of correspondence [44]. Trust is basic in large scale improvement and is trying to create. Remotely the agile acts of constant delivery appear to create trust.

The practices, for example, basic work spaces and collective lunch likewise made a type of personality and revived contact, expanded the degree of the trust between teams. The measure of open and casual correspondence and basic leadership has been demonstrated to be markers of how confidence or trust creates [45]. Furthermore, trust literature delivers that trust creates if there is increasingly relational contact [46]. There is an adverse connection between group size and inter personal relational. This connection between group size and confidence or trust may clarify why the agile techniques appear to exceed in littler associations contrasted with bigger ones. Nonetheless, connections inside groups and the setting around groups are not static. Consequently the static idea of the useful models doesn't line up with the truth of how relations create in associative frameworks.

12.4.4 Standards/Norms

The commitment of standards will empower more information driven experimental research around there so as to improve programming forms. Group standards are considered as collective desires for how to act in the group [47]. Standards have the ability to somewhat clarify human conduct by communicating our inspiration for doing certain activities [48]. Standards are regularizing as in the partner an incentive to specific examples of conduct. Standards there by separate among satisfactory and unsatisfactory practices of individuals in a group [49]. Moreover, standards are an essential component of a group's structure and comprise a significant medium for colleagues and co-workers' recognition with the group. At the point when co-workers distinguish themselves with a group they will all the more effectively execute to group objectives [49, 50]. One of the most significant attributes of group standards is that they don't exist on the off chance that they are not imparted to others [51]. Standards may advance effective and adaptive conduct since individuals feel constrained to act in manners that are reliable with the standards. Standards improve group forms since they make it workable for individuals to depend on specific things being done and different things not being done. An ongoing report at Google found that a few standards, for instance the standard that teams talk generally a similar knowledge, could raise the group's aggregate knowledge, while different standards could end the group [52]. An investigation by

Teh *et al.* proposed that group standards can be acclimated to advance certain practices in programming teams [53]. In that specific study, team standards were adjusted utilizing task preparing, whereby co-worker would finish a pilot task under direct direction to set up latest standards. Agile strategies require a move from order and control the executive to leader and cooperation [54]. McHugh [55] found that standards influence conduct in agile groups and contend that since conventional administrative procedure are frequently decreased in agile teams/groups, group standards might be significantly a greater amount of significance than in conventional programming groups. Further, Sharp and Ryan [56] contend that a product group, so as to enhance self-overseeing, require modifying the working standards inside the group, just as in the more extensive condition. While creating productive standards are significant in co-found programming groups, it is much increasingly significant in dispersed programming groups. Nerur *et al.* [57] noticed that a urgent component of essential group configuration was the foundation of a common arrangement of standards. They contend that essential group's asset from figuring out how to indicate external standards and roles desires to new individuals.

12.4.5   One to One/Injunctive Norms

Injunctive standards were the most straightforward kind of standard to distinguish on the grounds that the interviewees frequently communicated these as ways individuals should carry on. For instance, one designer in team1 depicted a standard of dressing for work: "We need to wear long jeans, and we can't wear shoes." In Teams 1 and 2 they had the standard that "the Product Owner (PO) isn't permitted to go to review assembly." A third model is that all groups had the one to one standard: "all members of teams have to be on time for assembly", and they attempted to neutralize the inclination to disregard this standard with solid approvals, for example, paying a fine. While discussing allotment of tasks, one engineer from Team 1 noted: "We have particular jobs so as to go inside and out in taking care of issues and to have the option to solve task quicker." The expected effort in this group was that co-worker picked tasks as indicated by specialization. This effort was emphatically sanctioned on the grounds that the team members accepted that it created/formed them increasingly beneficial. This standard recommends that the group organized role specialization at the expense of agile collaboration standards, for example, having assistances behaviour and information repetition [58]. Some other respondent in team 1 remarked on the self-rule level of the group: "The thing is the differences from now and the beginning of Scrum is that we have full structure rights. Already we didn't." The reference is here to the decidedly endorsed plan conduct, for example members of team are permitted to plan. Configuration is a piece of the work which decide course for the consequent coding. This is a standard that adds to group execution since it leads basic leadership power to the degree of functional issues.

12.4.6 Descriptive Norms

Descriptive norms or standards are worried about the conduct that for the most part happens, and these standards are prevalently situated in understood presumptions. Consequently, so as to recognize these standards, we needed to enhance the investigation of the meetings with observational information to distinguish the typical conduct of the team members. For instance, when exploring how the disprove graph was refreshed, one respondent in Team 3 asked: "In Team 4, the members of team report and the Scrum Master update it. We have inferred that we don't treat it so harshly as that. We do it without anyone else's help. Every last one of us has the responsibility to update it." This announcement recommends an example of conduct that is built up in the group. Nonetheless, we noticed that the members of team infrequently refreshed the disprove diagram. Consequently, the engaging standard in the group was to refresh the disprove graph infrequently, regardless of whether the team leader needed them to update it frequently. In Team 1, during arranging poker, the members of team who evaluated the most noteworthy or least number of hours needed to give a clarification of his or hers gauge. This had brought about a standard that most members of team attempted to evaluate a centre an incentive so as to abstain from making some noise and explain their merits to the others.

An additional case of an expressive standard in Team 1 was that it was alright to be available in group meetings without focusing, if the members of team said they had something progressively essential to do. For instance, some members of team coded during planning meetings. An outcome of this standard might be a limited common interpretation of the work and the group's objectives, which adversely influences group achievement.

12.4.7 Concurrent Norms

Injunctive norms/standards may coincide in the equivalent personal conduct standard. A case of an injunctive and clear standard acting all the while is the accompanying explanation from a designer: "When I have an issue, I request help quickly; I don't attempt to sit for a considerable length of time attempting to solve the issue myself." We frequently observe that co-workers approached each other for help, either by heading off to an individual sitting close by or by distributing the issue in the day by day stand-up meeting. The conduct of looking for and giving help from one another was emphatically authorized in these groups (one to one standard). Simultaneously, it was what individuals generally did (detailed standard). Another, progressively perplexing case of concurrent standards is outlined by the accompanying explanation from a director: "Dwindle isn't excessively cruel on the Product owner PO, so the PO would consistently give him new assignments behind the Scrum Masters back. This is the manner by which Peter approaches stuff, so we can simply let him. It isn't generally off-base incidentally; he is simply doing his part to improve the item." It is objected (and henceforth a one to one norms/standard) to enable the PO to move toward co-worker directly without the Scrum Masters assent. All things considered, this regularly occurs (detail standard).

Groups experience a characteristic procedure of making standards to find an agreeable method to work. They attempt to work so that they boost the odds for progress and limit the odds for failure, and that they additionally expand the fulfilment of the co-workers and limit relational disturbances [59]. For instance, the group in general are satisfied when they do whatever it takes not to acquire assignment from the PO, and yet they acknowledge that some co-workers explain this kind of undertakings since it limits relational distress to let this individual state yes. By the by, we accept that the injunctive standard (co-workers should dismiss assignments from PO) emphatically affected group execution, while the acknowledgment of this being damaged (the engaging standard) adversely affected group achievement.

12.4.8   Mental Safety

There are numerous different components than cultures are likewise significant in clarifying standards for correspondence. Standards of how co-workers act towards one another are firmly identified with the idea of mental security, which is a feeling of confidence that the group won't humiliate, dismiss or rebuff somebody for making some noise [59]. The findings in an ongoing investigation of standards that expressed that productive software groups have standards that encourages.

12.4.9   Changing Norms

A limit with respect to finding out about standards and how to transform them is expected to upgrade group achievement. The consequences of this investigation demonstrate that it is significant that groups reflect on the two sorts of standards related with how they are working as a group, and how such standards develop. Standards are socially created through communications among co-workers. As an outcome, they are dynamic. An interesting part of standards is that conduct that is discovered effective can continuously be moved toward procedure, standard driven conduct [60].

By examining the working understanding in Team 2, the group attempted to build up their own standards for effective cooperation. Groups that can improve their very own work techniques regularly accomplish a more elevated level of independence than groups that don't make on such choices [61]. One method for changing standards in a cognizant way is by reflection. To empower reflection, agile techniques commonly set up some type of review meeting. In perception of review gatherings, we noticed a few instances of issues identified with group standards, for instance: (1) how would we be able to ensure individuals are prompt to preparing gatherings? (2) How would we be able to make colleagues organize the review gatherings when they are caught up with getting ready for the run demo? (3) Should we prohibit PCs from gatherings? Also, (4) How would we be able to ensure that the disprove chart is refreshed all the more regularly? By examining these issues, the group's reflected on unmistakable standards and attempted to build up injunctive standards that would in this manner be received as common. This shows customs and services, for example, day by day stand-up gatherings and review gatherings may strengthen adequate practices. Examining the group's own standards is a case of tribe based control. Regularly, the group will try to build up authorizations to maintain these injunctive standards [61]. Faction rule is a sort of rule that works when the conduct in a group is prompted by distributed qualities and standards.

12.5 Suggestions for Training

It is accept that this investigation has the accompanying principle suggestions for training.

12.5.1 Locate the Correct Kind of Space

Three methodologies are

1) A group is liable for an end-client item and put all segments identified with the product in one space or

2) Mapping a group to a hierarchical unit.
3) Components may have different non-practical necessities, for example some have an all day, every day SLA. For this case, it might be important to cluster segments with a similar assistance level understanding in a similar group discipline.

12.5.2   Adjust the Administration Limits Constantly

On the off chance that a group can't convey includes autonomously, it is fundamental to persistently change the administration limits in like manner. Professionals regularly refer to Conway's Law when utilizing this technique, proposing developing your group and hierarchical structure to advance your ideal design. This is additionally worried to as the "Backwards Conway move".

12.5.3   Execute API Forming and the Executives

The outside area API that different groups rely upon should be steady. Programming interface the board and Versioning of an API are crucial, implying that different groups can depend on the strength of outside controls and its segments. Programming interface the board along these lines need to incorporate properties, for example, well-recorded APIs, well-defined administration level understandings (SLAs), validation and approval and realizing who is utilizing the API so it can advance in a sheltered way.

12.6   Conclusion

This chapter describes numerous challenges for autonomous cross-functional teams for successfully developing products using agile procedures and practices in a domain otherwise based on traditional project governance strategies. The association and practices of the self-sufficient groups were portrayed, just as the conditions for this idea to work. Sociology look into on group improvement have over and again demonstrated that for a group to arrive at a gainful stage it needs to, in a proficient way, have the option to oversee inward clashes and differences. To build the product designing general information on the best way to deal with clashes/ disputes within a group, we additionally propose that software engineering education ought to incorporate exchange and clashes/disputes resolution techniques. In this chapter, we have try to attempt to give introductory plans to what viewpoints to consider in such preparing. For instance, we contend that a larger part of the contentions start from group related components and that they, in this way, ought to be overseen utilizing a group level methodology. Trust/confidence is basic in enormous scale advancement and more testing to create than in small scale situations. To help the client build trust in such projects, the following actions were suggested: please the client and stronger customer involvement and joint effort between the gatherings. The outcomes demonstrated that trust was impractical to accomplish when the client had exacting authority over project scope.

Communication is one of the major factors to handle for cross functional and autonomous team. Closed loop communication was created because of a mix of (1) visit input as endorsed by using agile techniques, (2) co-area on one platform, and (3) fitting of techniques to improve coordination, for example, the act of 'small demos'. Co-area and the agile acts of regular conveyance appear to create trust.

Another major challenge is to handle norms and standards that designed for self-organizing teams. Productive groups, where co-workers act in a communitarian way to accomplish project objectives, are significant for effective programming projects. In such groups, co-workers regularly display a solid feeling of responsibility to the group, and individuals are influenced by shared standards. So as to support productive co-workers practices, we recommend that groups consistently reflect on both their one to one standards (what is endorsed/disliked conduct) and distinct standards (what is ordinarily done). Our commitment can fill in as an underlying premise to control and coordinate research findings about standards in programming groups.

Later on, researcher should draw further on findings in the associative frameworks field to give better exhortation on how these viewpoints can be cultivated being developed strategies.

References

1. Version One (2017) 11th Annual State of Agile Report. http://stateofagile.versionone.com. Accessed 31 July 2017.
2. Barker, J.R., Tightening the iron cage: Concertive control in self-managing teams. *Adm. Sci. Q.*, 38, 408–437, 1993.
3. Bass, J.M. and Haxby, A., Tailoring product ownership in large-scale agile projects: Managing scale, distance, and governance. *IEEE Softw.*, 36, 2, 58–63, 2019.

4. Bass, J.M., How product owner teams scale agile methods to large distributed enterprises. *Empir. Softw. Eng.*, 20, 6, 1525–1557, 2015.

5. Begel, A., Nagappan, N., Poile, C., Layman, L., Coordination in large-scale software teams, in: *Proceedings of the 2009 ICSE Workshop on Cooperative and Human Aspects on Software Engineering*, IEEE Computer Society, pp. 1–7, 2009.

6. Benner, M.J. and Tushman, M.L., Exploitation, exploration, and process management: The productivity dilemma revisited. *Acad. Manag. Rev.*, 28, 238–256, 2003.

7. Moore, C.W., *The mediation process: Practical strategies for resolving conflict (3rd ed.)*, Jossey-ass, San Francisco, California, 2003.

8. Cialdini, R.B., Reno, R.R., Kallgren, C.A., A focus theory of normative conduct: Recycling the concept of norms to reduce littering in public places. *J. Pers. Soc. Psychol.*, 58, 1015–1026, 1990.

9. Cialdini, R.B. and Trost, M.R., Social influence: Social norms, conformity and compliance, in: *Handbook of Social Psychology*, pp. 151–193, McGraw-Hill, New York, 1998.

10. Costa, A.C., Roe, R.A., Taillieu, T., Trust within teams: The relation with performance effectiveness. *Eur. J. Work Organ. Psychol.*, 10, 3, 225–244, 2001.

11. Currall, S.C. and Judge, T.A., Measuring trust between organizational boundary role persons. *Organ. Behav. Hum. Decis. Process.*, 64, 2, 151–170, 1995.

12. Hodgson, D. and Briand, L., Controlling the Uncontrollable: 'Agile' Teams and Illusions of Autonomy in Creative Work. *Work Employ. Soc. J.*, 27, 2, 308–325, 2013.

13. Goleman, D., *Working with emotional intelligence*, Bantam Books, New York, 1998.

14. Davison, R. and Hollenbeck, J., Boundary spanning in the domain of multi-team systems, in: *Multiteam systems. An Organization Form for Dynamic and Complex Environments*, pp. 323–362, Routledge, NY, 2012.

15. Pruitt, D.G., Stability and sudden change in interpersonal and international affairs. *J. Conflict Resolut.*, 13, 1, 18–38, 1969.

16. Dingsøyr, T., Moe, N.B., Fægri, T.E., Seim, E.A.: Exploring software development at the very large-scale: a revelatory case study and research agenda for agile method adaptation. *Empirical Softw. Eng.* 23(1), 490–520, 2018.

17. Dirks, K.T., The effects of interpersonal trust on work group performance. *J. Appl. Psychol.*, 84, 3, 445, 1999.

18. Duhigg C. What Google learned from its quest to build the perfect team. *NY Times Mag.* 2016.

19. Earley, P.C. and Gibson, C.B., *Multinational Work Teams: A New Perspective*, Routledge, Mahwah, 2002.

20. Edmondson, A.C., Psychological safety and learning behavior in work teams. *Adm. Sci. Q.*, 44, 350–383, 1999.

21. Feldman, D.C., The development and enforcement of group norms. *Acad. Manag. Rev.*, 9, 47–53, 1984.

22. Hackman, J.R., The design of work teams, in: *Handbook of Organizational Behavior*, pp. 315–342, Prentice-Hall, Englewood Cliffs, 1987.

23. Barki, H., and Hartwick, J. Interpersonal conflict and its management in information systems development. *MIS Quarterly*, 25, 2 (2001), 195–228.

24. Hinsz, V.B. and Betts, K.R., Conflict multiteam situations, in: *Multiteam Systems: An Organization Form for Dynamic and Complex Environments*, pp. 289–322, 2012.

25. Hoda, R. and Noble, J., Becoming agile: A grounded theory of agile transitions in practice, in: *Proceedings of the 39th International Conference on Software Engineering, ICSE*, 2017.

26. Wall, J.A., Jr. and Callister, R.R., Conflict and its management. *J. Manage.*, 21, 3, 515–558, 1995.

27. Tata, J. and Prasad, S., Team Self-Management, Organizational Structure, and Judgments of Team Effectiveness. *J. Manag. Issues*, 16, 2, 248–265, 2004.

28. Beck, K. *et al.*, *Manifesto for Agile Software Development*, Agile Alliance, Retrieved 14 June 2010.

29. Keyton, J., Ford, D.J., Smith, F.L., Zacarro, S., Marks, M., DeChurch, L., Communication, collaboration, and identification as facilitators and constraints of multiteamsystems, in: *Multiteam Systems: An Organization Form for Dynamic and Complex Environments*, pp. 173–190, 2012.

30. Keyton, J., Ford, D.J., Smith, F.L., Zacarro, S., Marks, M., DeChurch, L., Communication, collaboration, and identification as facilitators and constraints of multiteamsystems, in: *Multiteam Systems: An Organization Form for Dynamic and Complex Environments*, pp. 173–190, 2012.

31. Kirsch, L.J., Ko, D.-G., Haney, M.H., Investigating the antecedents of team-based clan control: Adding social capital as a predictor. *Organ. Sci.*, 21, 469–489, 2010.

32. Behfar, K.J., Peterson, R.S., Mannix, E.A., Trochim, W.M.K., The critical role of conflict resolution in teams: A close look at the links between conflict type, conflict management strategies, and team outcomes. *J. Appl. Psychol.*, 93, 1, 170, 2008.

33. Laanti, M., Salo, O., Abrahamsson, P., Agile methods rapidly replacing traditional methods at Nokia: A survey of opinions on agile transformation. *Inf. Softw. Technol.*, 53, 3, 276–290, 2011.

34. Langfred, C.W., Work-group design and autonomy: A field study of the interaction between task interdependence and group autonomy. *Small Gr. Res.*, 31, 1, 54–70, 2000.

35. Larman, C. and Vodde, B., *Large-Scale Scrum: More with LeSS*, Addison-Wesley Professional, Boston, 2016.

36. Leffingwell, D., *SAFe 4.0 Reference Guide: Scaled Agile Framework for Lean Software and Systems Engineering*, Addison-Wesley Professional, Boston, Mass. 2016.

37. Levine, J.M. and Moreland, R.L., Progress in small group research. *Annu. Rev. Psychol.*, 41, 585–634, 1990.

38. Gren, L., The Links Between Agile Practices, Interpersonal Conflict, and Perceived Productivity, in: *Proceedings of the 21st International Conference on Evaluation and Assessment in Software Engineering*, ACM, pp. 292–297, 2017.

39. Fenton-O'Creevy, M., Employee Involvement and the Middle Manager: Evidence from a survey of organizations. *J. Organ. Behav.*, 19, 1, 67–84, 1998.

40. Mathieu, J., Marks, M.A., Zaccaro, S.J., Multi-team systems. *Int. Handb. Work Organ. Psychol.*, 2, 289–313, 2001.

41. Mayer, R.C., Davis, J.H., Schoorman, F.D., An integrative model of organizational trust. *Acad. Manag. Rev.*, 20, 3, 709–734, 1995.

42. McHugh, O., A study of clan control in agile software development teams. Ph.D. thesis. NUI Galway, 2011.

43. McIntyre, R.M. and Salas, E., Measuring and managing for team performance: emerging principles from complex environments, in: *Team Effectiveness and Decision Making in Organizations*, pp. 9–45, 1995.

44. Moe, N.B., Dingsøyr, T., Dybå, T., A teamwork model for understanding an agile team: A case study of a scrum project. *Inf. Softw. Technol.*, 52, 480–491, 2010.

45. Moe, N.B., Dingsøyr, T., Dybå, T., Overcoming barriers to self-management in software teams. *IEEE Softw.*, 26, 20–26, 2009.

46. Moe, N.B., Key challenges of improving agile teamwork, in: *XP 2013. LNBIP*, vol. 149, H. Baumeister and B. Weber (Eds.), pp. 76–90, Springer, Heidelberg, 2013.

47. Nerur, S., Mahapatra, R., Mangalaraj, G., Challenges of migrating to agile methodologies. *Commun. ACM*, 48, 72–78, 2005.

48. Moe, N.B., Dingsøyr, T., Dybå, T., Understanding Self-organizing Teams in Agile Software Development. *19th Australian Conference on Software Engineering (ASWEC 2008)*, IEEE Xplore, 2008.

49. Paasivaara, M. and Lassenius, C., Communities of practice in a large distributed agile software development organization—Case Ericsson. *Inf. Softw. Technol.*, 56, 12, 1556–1577, 2014.

50. Coleman, P.T., Deutsch, M., Marcus, E.C., *The Handbook of Conflict Resolution: Theory and Practice (3rd ed.)*, John Wiley & Sons, San Francisco, California, 2014.

51. Petersen, K. and Wohlin, C., The effect of moving from a plan-driven to an incremental software development approach with agile practices. *Empir. Softw. Eng.*, 15, 6, 654–693, 2010. ISI Document Delivery No.: 653OB Times Cited: 2 Cited Reference Count: 46 Petersen, Kai Wohlin, Claes. Springer, Dordrecht.

52. Pikkarainen, M., Haikara, J., Salo, O., Abrahamsson, P., Still, J., The impact of agile practices on communication in software development. *Empir. Softw. Eng.*, 13, 303–337, 2008.

53. Salas, E., Sims, D.E., Burke, C.S., Is there a big five in teamwork? *Small Gr. Res.*, 36, 5, 555–599, 2005.

54. Scheerer, A., Hildenbrand, T., Kude, T., Coordination in large-scale agile software development: A multiteam systems perspective, in: *2014 47th Hawaii International Conference on System Sciences*, IEEE, pp. 4780–4788, 2014.

55. Sharp, J.H. and Ryan, S.D., A preliminary conceptual model for exploring global agile teams, in: *XP 2008. LNBIP*, vol. 9, P. Abrahamsson, R. Baskerville, K. Conboy, B. Fitzgerald, L. Morgan, X. Wang (Eds.), pp. 147–160, Springer, Heidelberg, 2008.

56. Nerur, S., Mahapatra, R., Mangalaraj, G., Challenges of Migrating to Agile Methodologies. *Commun. ACM*, 48, 5, 72–78, 2005.

57. Teh, A., Baniassad, E., Van Rooy, D., Boughton, C., Social psychology and software teams: Establishing task-effective group norms. *IEEE Softw.*, 29, 53–58, 2012.

58. Terry, D.J. and Hogg, M.A., Group norms and the attitude–behavior relationship: A role for group identification. *Pers. Soc. Psychol. Bull.*, 22, 776–793, 1996.

59. Version One (2017) 11th Annual State of Agile Report. http://stateofagile. versionone.com. Accessed 31 July 2017

60. Vlietland, J. and van Vliet, H., Towards a governance framework for chains of scrum teams. *Inf. Softw. Technol.*, 57, 52–65, 2015.

61. Williams, M., In whom we trust: Group membership as an affective context for trust development. *Acad. Manag. Rev.*, 26, 3, 377–396, 2001.

13

Role of Big Data Analytics in Business Transformation

Riyaz Abdullah Sheikh[1]* and Nitin S. Goje[2]

[1]College of Business Administration, Jazan University, Jazan, Saudi Arabia
[2]IT Department, College of Science, Tishk International University, Erbil,
Kurdistan Region, Iraq

Abstract

In recent years, big data, business analytics, and a "smart" environment are the latest tools attracting great attention in influencing organizational decision making. These tools are helping the organizations in delivering meaningful data, and get answers based on value that will give them a competitive edge by improving their performance. Big data analytics (BDA) not only perform pattern analysis but also allows the prediction of future events automatically. With the support of artificial intelligence, it can transform organizations and generates new business opportunities. BDA also helps in generating value for the sustainable development and prosperity of societies. It comprises of cutting edge analytical tools, equipment, programming, and platforms to perform analysis and management of big data. It offers incredible help for settling on choices and taking activities dependent on smidgens of proof. Notwithstanding, there is a constrained comprehension of how companies need to transform to grasp this technological development, and the business move they involve which can incite organizations and cultural change.

This chapter contains an in-depth literature review focusing on the need for business transformation and the role of BDA. Five case studies were discussed, compared, and analyzed for successful BDA implementation. The chapter addresses the potential challenges for adopting BDA in businesses. It will provide a road-map for the businesses to leverage BDA for business value.

*Corresponding author: rasheikh@jazanu.edu.sa

Parul Gandhi, Surbhi Bhatia, Abhishek Kumar, Mohammad Alojail and Pramod Singh Rathore (eds.) *Internet of Things in Business Transformation: Developing an Engineering and Business Strategy for Industry 5.0*, (231–260) © 2021 Scrivener Publishing LLC

Keywords: Big data, big data analytics, business intelligence, business transformation, digital business transformation, smart technology

13.1 Introduction to Technology-Enabled Business Transformation

13.1.1 21st Century Business Challenges and Problems

The complexity of business environment is increasing day by day offering new opportunities on the one hand but poses serious challenges on the other.

The organizations must aware of today's turbulent business environment and must transform to counter the pressure and to harness the benefits of it. Globalization for instance, allows you to find new customers and suppliers worldwide. It means that you can reduce your production cost and by selling more, you can increase your profit. However, globalization brings tough competition as well. The other important factors include a frequent change in a customer demand, technology innovation, growing government regulations and deregulation, etc. In addition, the intensity of these factors increases with the time posing high pressure, tough competition and more [1].

Businesses are confronting diminished spending plan and intensified pressure from top administration to expand execution and benefit. In such pressure, administrators must react rapidly, advance and be dexterous. The administrators need to persistently take part during the process of decision making. The extant literature shows that the advancement in analytical tools leads to the improvement in the process of business decision making. The managers must aware of the latest technological solution for information management and apply it in the most frequent and important task of decision-making.

13.1.2 Needs for Business Transformation

Transformation is critical for the sustainable growth of any organization. The objective could be to increase the efficiency and ability of an organization to tackle the future challenges in much better way [2]. Business transformation involves high-level commitment from all levels of management. This is compelled by the situational, technological or internal factors in an organization. It affects all the sections of an organization. The long-term goal of a business transformation is always to improve the performance and efficiency of the overall business operations. It begins with aligning the organization's business model with its core competency and eliminating non-value generating activities around the newly designed value generation business model through technology.

13.1.3   Digital Transformation

In the 21st century, technology has been embraced as a transforming tool to improve firms' response to tackle tough competition and to improve the customer satisfaction. The technology-enabled or digital transformation is allowing organizations to improve their performance, increase their productivity and access new customers. The digital revolution is transforming the world in various aspects and changing the way we communicate, interact and consume products and services [3]. Research on digital transformation identified three major compelling factors for transformation. The primary factor is the business agility to adjust to outer changes productively and viably, second innovation to align business and information technology strategy, and global need for new ideas, and third to support for new business opportunities [4].

This digital transformation brings several benefits for the firm like:

1. Increase profitability
2. Reduce operating expenses
3. Improve customer experience
4. Facilitate internal processes integration
5. Open new market possibilities
6. Strengthen and enhance your brand.

Today, digital transformation does not an option for a company, but it has become a necessity to be successful. It allows businesses to be more agile and efficient. According to the study 'Walking the digital tight rope', published by Fujitsu, the companies that have embraced digitization have improved their efficiency by 39% [11]. According to McKinsey report, technology transformation at Lenovo after it has acquired IBM's PC operations has benefited in reducing the IT spending from 2.8 to 1.4% in a short span of two year. Another interesting statistic shown in Figure 13.1 depicts how investment in technology transformation has made a large financial impact over time [5].

	YEARS IT TOOK FOR DIGITAL TRANSFORMATION	STOCK PRICE GROWTH RATE
MICROSOFT	5 YEARS	258%
HASBRO	7 YEARS	203%
BEST BUY	7 YEARS	198%
HONEYWELL	3 YEARS	83%
NIKE	2 YEARS	69%
TARGET	8 YEARS	66%
HOME DEPOT	2 YEARS	59%

Figure 13.1 Digital transformation & growth rate (Forbes.com, 2019).

13.2 Introduction to Big Data, Big Data Analytics & Business Intelligence

In recent years, Big Data (BD), business analytics, and a "Smart" environment are the latest tools attracting great attention in driving organizational decision-making. These tools are helping the organizations in delivering meaningful data, and get value-driven answers that will give them a competitive edge by improving their performance [6].

13.2.1 What is Big Data?

As indicated by IBM, 90% of the world information accessible today has been made over the most recent few years [7]. This data originates from everywhere such as the multiple daily transactions, social media posts, or from the increasing number of sensors mounted on numerous objects (e.g., home appliances, mobile phones, cars, etc.). This enormous amount of data is called "Big Data". The expression "Big Data" signifies to the amazingly immense volumes of information created and accessible online in advanced digital ecosystems. The companies have started realizing the importance of the data they own and how to harness it to get a competitive edge. Big data and business analytics are additionally challenging existing methods of business and settled organizations [8]. According to Gartner, the term "Big Data" is defined as *"Big data is high-volume, -velocity and -variety informa-tion assets that demand cost-effective, innovative forms of information pro-cessing for enhanced insight and decision-making."* The traditional definition of Big Data revolves around three Vs: Volume, Velocity & Variety [9]. These are three defining properties or dimensions of Big Data. Moreover, Veracity, Variability, and Value Proposition are the other dimensions of Big Data defined and added later by the leading solution providers [10].

13.2.1.1   Dimensions of Big Data

Volume: It is the most certain and common attribute of Big Data. The 6 dimensions of Big Data are shown in Figure 13.2. Clickstreams, system logs, online searches, and transactions are among the sources that produce an extremely large volume of data on a continuous basis. The world data is estimated to reach 35 ZB by 2017 compared to 0.8 ZB in 2000 [11]. The

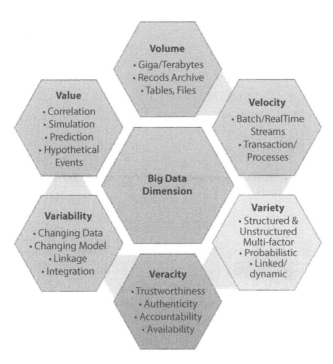

Figure 13.2 Dimensions of big data.

organizations are very much aware of the ever-developing information of various kinds and the potential difficulties and opportunities related with it.

For example:

- Analyze 500 millions of daily tweets into useful information to improve product sentiment analysis (business.twitter.com)
- Convert 350 billion yearly meter readings to more readily anticipate power utilization

Velocity: Velocity alludes to both the speed at which the data is produced and how quick it must be processed to make a value for the businesses. Some 900 million photos are uploaded on Facebook on each day, twitter receives 500 million tweets every day, more than 400,000 h of videos are uploaded on YouTube, and Google records more than 3.5 billion search daily [12]. Timing plays a vital role while handling Big Data. The value of the Big Data debases over the long haul, and in the long run gets useless.

For example:

- Inspect 500 million daily trade event for potential fraud detection
- Convert 500 million call detail record on regular schedule continuously to foresee client stir quicker

Variety: In Big Data, Variety alludes to the assortment of organized and unstructured data produced either by the people or by machines. Text documents, pictures, videos, and tweets are the most commonly added structured data while emails, voicemails, stock ticker data, audio recording are among the unstructured data which is equally important under Variety. It is evaluated that 80 to 85% of all ventures information is in an unstructured or semi-organized format. The decision-makers cannot ignore the value of such huge data. This data must be wisely utilized in the analysis process for improving business decision-making.

- Continuously monitor thousands of live video feeds from security camera to detect any point of interest
- Explore the ever-growing data comprising documents, images and videos to improve customer experience

Veracity: Big Data Veracity alludes to the adjustment to realities: quality, dependability or honesty of the data. One in three business leaders is susceptible to use generated information for decision-making. If you cannot trust information, you cannot expect others to act upon it. The expansion in the quantity of sources and an assortment of data represents a colossal challenge for setting up trust among the business leaders.

Variability: Variability in Big Data alludes to the conflicting pace at which enormous data is stacked into your database. For example, the big trending on social media, New Year celebration or White Friday offers. This peak data load activated by a day by day or regular occasions is very challenging to oversee particularly when the social media is included.

Value Proposition: Last yet apparently the most significant of every single Big Data qualities is the value proposition. Other qualities would be of no utilization in the event that you can't get business value from the data. This is the primary objective of your Big Data activity. Large value can be derived from Big Data that can helps you to understand better your customer, optimize the business processes, improve business performance and gain a competitive advantage [13].

13.2.2   Big Data Analytics

13.2.2.1   What is Big Data Analytics (BDA)?

Big Data Analytics (BDA) is the utilization of cutting edge analytical tools against enormous data-set. This big data could start from various sources, arrangement, and sizes from terabytes to zettabytes. It contains expanded data sets which incorporates organized, semi-organized, and unstructured data. This permits analyst, scientists, and business clients to settle on brisk and better choices by utilizing data that was before blocked off or unusable. The business heads can utilize machine learning, predictive analytics, data mining, and natural language processing to gain new business insights of knowledge from already undiscovered data sources uninhibitedly or together with the current companies database. Big data analytics permits pattern analysis, events prediction [14], bolster process automation through artificial intelligence, change organizations and make new kinds of business [15]. Most important, it creates value for the advancement of sustainable and prosperous social orders. It comprises of cutting edge analytical tools, programming, and platforms to perform big data analysis and management. It offers incredible help for decision making and taking activities dependent on data [16]. Be that as it may, there is a restricted understanding of how organizations need to transform to grasp this technological development which can prompt organizations and cultural transformation [17].

13.2.2.2　Why is Big Data Analytics Important?

BDA empowers businesses to tackle their data and use it to recognize new business openings. This will assist organizations with making more astute and snappier business moves, improved efficiency, higher benefits and more joyful clients [18]. A research completed in USA on an example of 50+ organizations uncovers that the business heads got values from the use of BDA as cost decrease, quick and improved decision making and propelling new and better products and services (see Figure 13.3) [19].

13.2.3　Business Intelligence (BI)

Business Intelligence is an umbrella term that associates tools, architecture, databases, and methods to import huge data streams and use them to produce significant insight for explicit business circumstances. BI's prime reason for existing is to empower intuitive access (some of the time progressively) to information to empower control of information, and to enable business pioneers and experts to perform suitable investigations. It incorporates set of procedures for data transformation, at that point to decisions, and lastly to actions.

In the present time, it's not possible for anyone to deny the significance from securing information in business. It is considered as the new oil for business. The business leaders can settle on important decisions simply

Figure 13.3 Big data analytics value.

Figure 13.4 Relationship between big data analytics & business intelligence.

in the wake of breaking down the data and these decisions will additionally assist organizations with sustaining and develop. Both BD and BI help to analyze the data and get useful insight into business decision-making. They are not same but they share the common goal and hence they need to be synchronized and are used together. Figure 13.4 depicts the relationship between BDA and BI (Analytics & Business Intelligence, n.d.).

Following are the advantages of Business Intelligence

- Improved decision-making
- Accurate & Timely analysis and reporting
- Improved data quality
- Reduced costs
- Increase income
- Improved performance

13.3 Big Data Analytics and its Role in Business Transformation

BDA is the use of statistical and analytical tools to huge data to address dynamic client request and to create and sustain a competitive edge. Big data is another yet an incredible asset for increasing financial and social qualities and is similarly significant like capital resources and human ability. As per a report distributed by PromtCloud in 2016, big data has developed from $6.8 billion to $32 billion industry in a limited span of three years. It is gauge by International Data Corp (IDC) that the enormous information market to develop at a yearly pace of 23.1% coming to $48.6 billion by 2019. The business leaders and analysts are grasping this extraordinary chance to benefit from big data gaining a competitive edge. Numerous organizations are accounted to spend 10% of their total IT spending on data just and are in the transformation mode to leverage big data analytics to control their decisions for better and improved business results.

On the contrary, many firms are experiencing immense pressure for the adoption of BDA as they don't want to lag behind in the competition. However, the ultimate success of BDA depends primarily on its ability in realizing the strategic business value of a firm which can provide them with a competitive edge. A survey reported by Gartner in 2016 reveals that even though there is huge ongoing investment in big data, there were signs of tapering. In excess of 60 percent of the big data projects extends by 2017 would fail to go past the phase of piloting and experimentation resulting in project closure. These worries forces businesses to reevaluate on their big data appropriation strategy and how this system will help them in value creation. It is challenging for firms to assess the actual value of big data and how the investment in big data can provide tangible business value. This is likewise named as "data monetization" and "data valuation". The data value can be comprehended by the mix of business knowledge created and the genuine utilization of it in business [20].

13.3.1   Big Data Analytics and Value Proposition

The achievement of big data analytics does not merely dependent on data asset, data acquisition, and experience in using analytic methods and tools for knowledge creation. Be that as it may, it to a great extent relies upon the capacity to utilize BDA to tackle the key business worth and keep the firms competitive. The business insight realized by the BDA can be utilized to generate valuable business insights in many areas like process improvement, innovation, customer retention, and improving the reputation and brand value of the firm. While embracing BDA as a strategic resource, the following questions should be posed to survey whether it can possibly produce strategic business value. The questions depend on the resource-based view of the firm following the classical VRIO framework (Value, Rarity, Imitability, and Organization) [21].

Value: What kind of business value insight can be obtained from BDA to outfit new business openings and/or to tackle the competition?

Rarity: How much rare is your big data content and analytical capacities? This incorporates the business' analytical information, human asset, skill, and involvement in cutting edge big data management and analysis tools.

Imitability: How much it is hard for your rival to impersonate the BDA capacities like yours? The BDA capacity is dependent upon an organization's

IT development, decision making culture and authority which make it interesting and hard to mirror.

Organization: To what degree your firm's strategy and culture bolster the appropriation of BDA abilities? The accomplishment of BDA strategy relies to a great extent upon the consideration of it in the company's long term strategy and the accessibility of supporting component to align business to this strategy. Such arrangement includes policies, procedures, processes, governance, and corporate culture to exploit data for competitiveness.

13.3.2   Strategic Business Value of BDA

The business insight generated by BDA could be beneficial at both functional and symbolic level. The functional value like market share, financial performance can be improved directly from adopting BDA, whereas symbolic value includes the firm's reputation, brand value, etc. At the strategic level, we can consider functional value as a fit among technology and organizational tasks while symbolic value a fit among technology and organization environment. It is shown in Figure 13.5.

The business partner may decipher the sign as worth improving and lift the stock price and the value of the organization. The investment in BDA, employee analytical skills, leadership, innovation and social media discourse are the signals for showing an increase in the symbolic value of a firm [22], whereas, the increase in functional value can be measured by its effect on organizational efficiency, coordination, and smart decision-making.

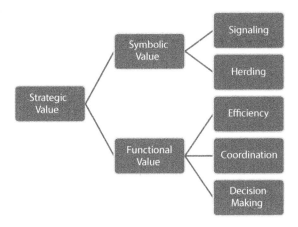

Figure 13.5 Strategic value of BDA.

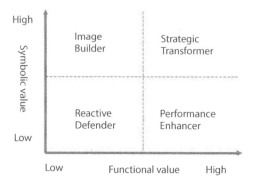

Figure 13.6 Strategic role of BDA.

The relationship between functional and symbolic strategic value helps us to better understand the role of BDA in strategic value creation. This is well represented in Figure 13.6 in the form of a matrix showing the strategic roles of BDA.

The BDA could be a key transformer for a firm if both functional value and symbolic value are high. This will assist the firm with improving both inner qualities and notoriety in the commercial center. At the point when just functional value is high, BDA can be a decent impetus for improved profitability. At the point when just symbolic value is foreseen as high, BDA selection might be an image builder helping firms to construct positive signs to stakeholders. On the off chance that both functional and symbolic values are low, the organizations may not look for BDA value however and embrace similarly a cautious strategy [23].

13.3.3 BDA Framework for Creating Business Value

Realization of strategic business value is the foremost concern for the firms while adopting BDA. There is a need of a comprehensive approach that can address not only how to build BDA but most importantly how to make use of it for value creation. It should address both tangible (e.g., Increased income or decreased expense) and intangible (e.g., Increased consumer loyalty or expanded brand value) business values [24]. In 2018, a new conceptual framework is proposed which is based on IT-Value Model [25] and change management concept. The framework includes two sets of processes: capability building capability building and capability realization [26]. It is shown in the following Figure 13.7.

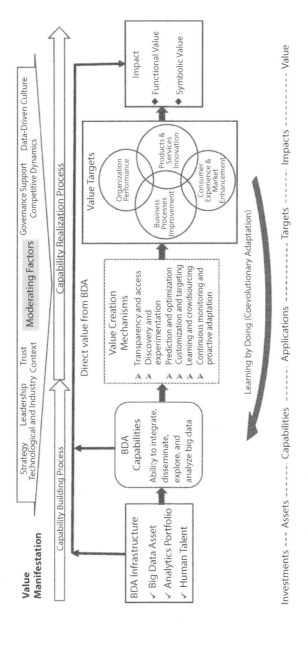

Figure 13.7 A conceptual framework for BDA adoption in business.

13.3.3.1   Building Big Data Analytics Capabilities

As shown in the framework, the first part includes processes for building BDA infrastructure and building BDA capability. BD assets, analytical portfolio and human talent are the three building blocks of BD infrastructure [27]. The firms need to invest in these three areas continuously as they are the primary source for business value realization. BD assets provides a set of tools for data collection, processing, integrating, sharing, and storage of data coming from varied sources like social media, clickstream, transaction, and external databases. Analytical portfolio includes a set of tools for processing BD assets and generates useful business insights. There are many applications of these business insights like financial risk modeling, customer sentiment analysis, fraud detection in banks, price and performance optimization, etc. Human talent is the most important asset which includes developers, programmers, analysts, and modelers. They play a pivotal role during strategy formulation and interpreting the BDA outcome for business value [28].

The new BDA capabilities must enable high velocity capture of very large volume and variety of data and generate business value through continuous discovery and analysis in real-time [29]. The BDA capability should include mechanism for descriptive analytics to answer what happen in the past, predictive analytics to develop a model for future prediction, and prescriptive analytics to design a recommendation system for best possible solutions. It should also include the capabilities to perform text analytics, audio-video analytics, geographic analytics, and social media analytics to fully exploit the benefits of BD infrastructure [30].

13.3.3.2   Realization of Big Data Analytics Capabilities

The second set of processes focuses on the realization of BDA capabilities to generate new, meaningful, and actionable insight. The volume of the data does not hold any importance if you are not able to generate new and meaningful value with it [31]. The goal is to help business leaders to refine business processes, accelerate innovation, drive optimization, better understand customer, improve product design, and improve business performance. The framework incorporates six components for portraying the connection between BDA capacities and value targets. These components are straightforwardness and simple access, revelation and experimentation, forecast and optimization, customization of products and services, learning and crowdsourcing, and monitor and adapt.

The framework ought to have the option to coordinate the perspectives and needs of stakeholders while characterizing the value targets. The model incorporates a component for creating helpful business incentive to improve performance, process improvement, products and services automation, and client experience. This will help firms not exclusively to increase functional value yet in addition improves firm's image through company's creative image, administration, showcase impact, and stakeholders' fulfillment [32].

Another significant thing to recall while building BDA ability is the organization's data driven outlook [33]. The firm ought to have a component to set up forms, administration structure, and group with included data aptitudes. The expression "active data governance" alludes to the general administration of the information from accessibility, ease of use, integrity, and security. The data administration group in a firm should have an overseeing body or committee, administration techniques, and an arrangement to execute and follow those strategies [34].

As appeared in the system, capability building and capacity realization happen through a progression of interconnected decisions that help authoritative learning. This learning takes into account co-evolutionary application (i.e., the reverse arrow) which resembles a feedback cycle. It shows the capacity of a firm to build and acknowledge future BDA abilities through experience, achievement, and failures [35].

13.4   Successful Real World Cases Leveraging BDA for Business Transformation

13.4.1   BDA in Retail: Walmart

In the retail industry, the opportunities for the adoption of BDA are enormous. It has been observed that companies investing in BDA for the last 5 years in their marketing and sales program yielded a Return on Investment (ROI) of 15–20%. The retail companies are using BDA to improve their operations especially marketing, store management, vending, supply chain, etc. [36]. It is important for the retailer to understand their customer and their preferences. The big data streams (sales, income, operations, stock, and so forth) are productively dissected continuously to separate helpful and already obscure client purchasing inclinations. This knowledge can be additionally used for market basket analysis to dispatch new plans/offers. This won't just improve the client experience yet in addition help the organization to expand sale and to decide sufficient stock level. The stakeholders in the retail business, in the present period, can leverage BDA for profit maximization and to avoid/reduce the customer shift from physical retail store to e-commerce websites.

Walmart is the world's biggest retail organization and the biggest organization by income, with more than 2 million partners enlisted, 245 million clients visiting 20,000 stores through 10 dynamic sites in 28 nations. The organization announced a daily sale of $36 million from more than 4,000 stores in the United State in particular. The organization oversees 2.5 PB of data from more than 1 million clients on an hourly premise. The organization has recognized the value of data analytics at this scale of operation very prior. Supermarket is a profoundly competitive industry offering a large number of items to a great many clients consistently. The competition doesn't just on the price yet in addition on customer care, vitality and convenience. It is challenging for the organizations to supply the correct items in the opportune spot and at the ideal time, so the ideal individuals can get them. To use the advantages of such tremendous information, Walmart sets up the world's biggest private cloud and analytical center "Data Cafe" in 2011. At Data Café, the data analysts can create helpful business insights by observing in excess of 200 streams of inside and outer data. It incorporates a lot of tools for modeling, manipulation and displaying 40 PB of the considerable number of sales transactions created each week progressively.

This allows the company to reduce the company's response time to tackle a problem situation from 2 to 3 weeks to 20 min only. It is vital for a firm to get quick access to insights to gain a competitive edge.

The Data café allows the analyst to set the threshold for various performance metrics. When there is a fall of any particular metrics, the system can automatically alert the relevant team so that they can find the solution fast. The company also developed a big data analytics solution is known as the Social Genome. The solution can investigate the consolidated public data from the web, online networking, and exclusive data like contact information and messages. With this tool, the company can reach out to the customer or friend of customer who has shown some interest in Walmart products and services that they may be interested in special discounts. The predictive analytics stage gained from Inkiru joined with machine learning helps the organization in focused marketing, fraud recognition and counteraction and stock administration. The value gain from the application of big data analytics can be measured by comparing the sale before and after leveraging BDA. The online sale of Walmart has increased significantly by 10–15% ($1 billion) from the previous year and at the same time substantial gain in the reputation of being the front runner of BDA.

13.4.2   BDA in Online Retail: Amazon

Amazon—an electronic trade organization established in 1994 is presently perceived as one of the world's biggest online retailer organization. The company started primarily with selling physical goods like books and now into virtual goods like e-books, streaming videos, and web services. The credit of this success mostly goes to the strategic use of pioneered technology "Recommendation Engine". The prediction system is designed to help the consumer to decide what he wants, when he wants it and offers the easy payment mechanism. For the last two decades, information overload is a big problem. The online retailers are putting numerous products and services available online to increase the probability of a sale. Organizations like Amazon and Walmart has prospered by adopting an "everything under one rooftop" supermarket model. The problem is, with this huge range of buying options, the customer becomes confused about what to buy and when to buy. To tackle this problem, Amazon has utilized Big Data accumulated from 152 million clients while they peruse the site to create and calibrate a recommendation framework. The framework depends on the hypothesis that the more they know about you, the almost certain they can anticipate what you need to purchase. After streamlining the big data, the system can persuade you to buy by offering a customized catalogue based on your need and choice. Amazon's recommendation system depends on collaborative filtering. This implies the system first forms an image of what your identity is and afterward offers you a redo list of products and services that individuals with similar profiles have bought. The organization accumulates information on all of its customers while they browse the site like what you purchase, search, your address and so forth. With this advantage, the company made a whopping sale of nearly $135 billion in 2016. The net income has increased to $2.4 billion in 2016 compared to $596 million in 2015. In addition, the organization's strategy in data-driven shopping and customer support has made them one of the top brand on the planet. Amazon likewise utilizes Big Data to monitor, track and make sure about its 1.5 billion items in retail locations spread around its 200 fulfillment bases around the world.

13.4.3   BDA in Social Media: Facebook

Facebook is the undefeated champion of social media network acquiring more than 60% of the total internet users [37]. The website allows its user to sign-up online for free and connects with friends, colleagues, and people they don't know. The users can share pictures, music, video, article and their thoughts and opinions with the people they like. They have more than 2.45 billion active users and more than 1.62 billion users visiting the website on a daily basis spending hours on scrolling through Facebook feeds. With such a massive audience, Facebook offers an easy and cheap marketing opportunity for small businesses. The company has registered more than 80 million small businesses around the world. The revenue model of Facebook is mostly dependent on selling the huge wealth of consumer data and by providing the advertising space for the businesses. In the US only, more than 86% of businesses are using Facebook for advertising generating a whopping revenue of above $10 billion.

Facebook's users create more than 2.5 million pieces of feeds each moment. This content along with Facebook generated database which includes business listings, films, music, books, and TV shows are continuously analyzed to find the clues for an advertiser. Facebook uses PHP and MySQL databases as an open-source technology for software development. The software engineers have developed HipHop for MySQL compiler to speed up the processing and to reduce the CPU load. The organization claims Hadoop's HBase platform for distributed storage management and Apache Hive for real-time data analytics.

Facebook is without a doubt the lord of web based life has changed the manner in which we communicate with one another on the web. This colossal measure of client information holds huge incentive to sponsors for target marketing. This is particularly very useful for small business with a limited budget. The data scientist at Facebook has developed tools based on Deep Learning like DeepText, DeepFace, Targeted Advertising, Flow and Torch platform for analyzing the data and generates useful insights for the company and advertisers (Marr, 2019). It is important for the company to gain and maintain the trust of its 2.45 billion active users. User data privacy, predator, cyberbullying, and content authentication are the major challenges for the company.

13.4.4   BDA in Manufacturing: Rolls-Royce

Rolls-Royce—a very innovative industry fabricate huge motors that are utilized by about 500 airline companies and in excess of 150 military forces around the globe. A solitary error in the plan or assembling of aircraft motor can cost billions and human life also. It is essential for the organization to have the option to screen the health of their products and recognize potential issues before they happen. The organization is utilizing big data to design more robust products, improve efficiency and to improve client experience. In this manner, design, manufacturing and after-sales support are the three significant regions where the organization is leveraging BDA (Rolls-royce.com).

Rolls-Royce prepares its engines and propulsion system with many sophisticated sensors that are equipped for recording each minor detail and report any adjustment in real-time to the decision-makers. The organization has set up a few operational assistance revolves far and wide where the engineers can monitor and analyze the data gathered by the sensors from their engines. This BDA capability causes the organization to improve the design process, lessen the cost, decline the product development time and improve the quality and performance of the products. The organization is in a position to give better client care by distinguishing the requirement for maintenance well in advance hence reducing any trouble/delay to the passengers due to maintenance.

13.4.5   BDA in Healthcare: Apixio

The potential for the application of BDA in healthcare is enormous. It incorporates enormous health data from gene expression, sequencing data, electronic health record, clinicians' notes, prescription, biomedical sensor data, online social media data, and so on [38]. In the last two decades, the pressure of adoption of BDA in the USA is increasing not only to reduce the health care expenses but also due to the rise in evidence-based medicine and patient care. It is estimated that the best possible adoption of BDA in the US health services area would make more than $300 billion in value each year. With the advancement in scientific medical knowledge, there is a pressure of rapid introduction of new drugs and treatment. Also, the increase in healthcare costs forces medical experts to embrace new information and deploy BDA to improve decision-making in personalized medicine and personal care.

Apixio—a California-based cognitive computing firm is revealing and making accessible clinical knowledge in order to improve decision making in the healthcare industry. The company is preparing enormous unstructured data originating from various sources in various arrangements and formats utilized by the doctors to draw valuable insights. The company first extracts the data and then turns it into information that can be analyzed. This is done by using OCR (optical character recognition) technology and machine learning algorithm based on NLP (natural language processing).

The company has launched its first product HCC Profiler aiming to insurance companies and healthcare delivery network which include hospitals and clinics. These organizations need too many details about each individual like what is the severity of their illness, what are the diseases being treated actively, what treatments are given, etc. With HCC profiler, it becomes easy to process 80% of the unstructured data and 20% of structured data and generate valuable insights for personalized medicine and personal care. The company is using non-relational database technology and distributed computing platform like Hadoop and Spark for big data infrastructure. Amazon Web Service (AWS) on cloud is used to perform all operations because of its robustness, healthcare privacy, security, and regulatory compliance.

The application of BDA in healthcare is still in its infant stage. There are many opportunities available for the researchers to apply DBA in healthcare. The valuable insight from DBA can help the hospitals in reducing the healthcare expenses, fast and efficient diagnosis, application of evidence-based medicine and patient care.

Table 13.1 shows a summary of the BDA infrastructure, capabilities, value creation mechanism used by the companies stated above:

Table 13.1 Summary of Case Studies [16].

Sr. no.	Company	Industry	BDA foundation	BDA capacity	Mechanism for value creation	Business benefits	Business effect
1	Walmart	Retail	Data Café; Hadoop Cluster Sales; Data Online; Clickstream social media data, etc.	Online analytics; Social Media Analytics; Predictive Analytics; Trend Analysis; Data Visualization; Market Basket Analysis	Discovery; Prediction; Monitoring; Customization; Optimization;	Increase in sales; Cost reduction; Improved Customer satisfaction; Improved performance	Functional (income) and Symbolic (brand image, leadership)
2	Amazon (Hewage et al., 2018)	Online Retail	Dynamo; S3; Data Warehouse	Models and real time; BDA	Customization; Prediction; Machine-Learning	Improved customer experience and loyalty	Functional (revenue) & Symbolic value (image building)
3	Facebook (Hewage et al., 2018)	Technology	DeepText; DeepFace; Targeted Advertising; Flow & Torch platform	Real-time BDA; Social Media Analytics; Predictive Analytics; Trend Analysis; Market Basket Analysis	Discovery; Prediction; Customization	Target Marketing; Improved Customer; experience & loyalty	Functional (revenue) & Symbolic value (reputation)

(Continued)

Table 13.1 Summary of Case Studies [16]. (*Continued*)

Sr. no.	Company	Industry	BDA foundation	BDA capacity	Mechanism for value creation	Business benefits	Business effect
4	Rolls-Royce	Manufacturing	VHF radio, SATCOM en route, and 3G/Wi-Fi at the gate; Private Cloud; IoT; Sensors	Real-time BDA; signature matching and novel anomalous behaviors; diagnosis and prognosis	Discovery; Prediction; Monitoring	Improved Operational efficiency; Cost Reduction; Improved customer experience	Functional (revenue) & Symbolic value (reputation)
5	Apixio	Healthcare	OCR (optical character recognition) technology; NLP (natural language processing) Hadoop and Spark Amazon Web Service (AWS)	HCC Profiler; Real-time BDA; Predictive Analytics; Prescriptive Analytics; Data Visualization	Discovery; personalized medicine; personal care	Reduced healthcare expenses; fast and efficient diagnosis; evidence-based medicine and patient care	Functional (operational efficiency) & Symbolic value (reputation)

13.5   BDA Capability Building Challenges

While building BDA, data management poses several challenges. It is shown in the following Figure 13.8.

13.5.1   Data Quality

It is observed that data recorded are often noisy, incomplete, or flawed. This poses a critical challenge for analyzing the data. Therefore, a thorough data cleaning and preprocessing are required for applying analytics. Another issue is the continued exponential growth of the data making it difficult for the companies to check the trustworthiness. The problem of veracity is considered as the most difficult challenge compared to volume, velocity and variety in BDA. The companies are encouraging their customers for surveys, reviews, and feedback can help them for product evolution, or innovations. In any case, 20–25% of these shopper surveys were phony. Accordingly, it is essential to clean and preprocess the data to expel commotion and irregularity from the data. The value of data analytics to a great extent relies upon the quality of the data.

After veracity, variety of data is the next big challenge while building BDA capabilities. The company receives heterogeneous data from multiple sources which make it highly difficult to integrate and perform a range of analytics to generate useful business insights in real-time. Consequently, it is significant for a firm to set up a robust data management system that can deal with an assortment of data, on-request investigation of data

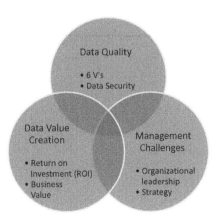

Figure 13.8 BDA capability building challenges.

continuously and produce business insights that can be utilized by the business decision makers.

Data Security is another big challenge while building data assets. It is important for the firms to anticipate any type of data breach and design the system to detect such breaches in real-time to minimize the negative consequences of it and design highly safe and robust data management systems.

The organizations can deploy three types of analytics capabilities including aspirational, experienced, and transformational. The aspirational analytics capability which is at the lowest focuses on operational efficiency and finds the ways for cost-cutting. Organizational analytics capabilities go beyond cost-cutting to design effective ways to collect, integrate and generate business insights for business optimization.

The most significant test while building BDA doesn't simply the technology yet how to assemble and keep up human capital and organizational culture that helps such an initiative. The organizations need to build up a group of exceptionally energetic individuals with sufficient BDA aptitudes to exploit the colossal capability of BDA.

13.5.2   Management Challenges

Management challenges include primarily the organizational leadership and strategy, can hinder the successful implementation of BDA. It is important for a company to have an active leadership align with strategic goals for success. They can all the more likely characterize achievement and approach the correct inquiries for it. Organization culture and administration are the other significant management challenges for making the correct condition for BDA success. Data and evidence-driven decision making culture and administration that shows accountability and responsibility for data are the two impetuses for business value creation through BDA. The successful implementation of BDA demands centralized governance of data collection and analysis enabling an organization to apply common standards, methods, tools, and protocols [39].

13.5.3   BDA Value Assessment

A survey of IT and business experts directed by Gartner in 2016 about return on investment (ROI) for big data investment uncovers that a huge portion (38–43%) of them didn't have a clue whether their ROI would be positive or negative [40]. Deciding and estimating the business value of

BDA is a major test for companies. The organizations should be cautious in deciding and measuring the ROI from BDA and breaking down the connection among BDA and business results. This requires the suitable mapping of data, analytics, and business procedures to the ideal business results and afterward measuring the effect on the accomplishment of the results [41].

13.6   Conclusion

In the current modern world, technology-enabled transformations have become a well-known means of improving business performance and customer experience. Big data, business analytics, IoT, and business intelligence are the latest tools attracting great attention for business transformation from business leaders. The digital revolution is transforming the world in various aspects and changing the way we communicate, interact and consume products and services. The organizations are compelled to transform for business agility, innovation, and brand value. From past research, it is proven that investment in technology transformation has yielded large financial gain over time.

BDA is the use of statistical and analytical tools to large data to address dynamic client demand and to create and sustain a competitive edge. It empowers firms to saddle their data and use it to recognize new business opportunities. This will assist organizations with making more astute and speedier business moves, improved execution, higher benefits, and more joyful customers. The business leaders have forecast that the big data market growth will be doubled by 2019. Many companies are making a huge investment in BDA and are in the transformation mode to leverage BDA to guide their decision-making for the better and improved business outcome. However, the success of big data analytics does not merely dependent on technology but, it largely depends on the ability to use BDA to tackle the key business strategic value and keep the firms competitive. The business decision makers need to evaluate the BDA potential to produce the business value before embracing it. This business insight should benefit the organization at both functional and symbolic levels.

The conceptual framework provides a detailed roadmap for business leaders for the adoption of BDA for value creation. The framework depicts two important phases from the capability building process to the realization process. The prior focuses on BDA infrastructure and capability building whereas the later targets on value creation mechanism. Six value creation mechanisms are shown in the framework to convert results into actions that can have a positive impact on decision-making, process improvement customer retention, or other targets. The successful implementation of BDA largely depends on the organizational leadership and data-driven culture in a firm. The firms are required to build processes, governance structure, and teams with added data skills. Several case studies of successful BDA implementations are discussed here covering different industrial sectors.

To conclude, BDA is a powerful tool for transforming a firm to achieve strategic business value. The organizations need to put resources into BDA foundation and analytics as well as on skilled analysts and strategic positioning to uncover new data-driven business openings.

References

1. Analytics & Business Intelligence, (n.d.), *Transform Data into Valuable Business Insights*, Global Data Strategy™. Available at: https://global-datastrategy.com/our-services/business-intelligence-bi-big-data-analytics/, [Accessed 10 Dec. 2019].
2. Ayres, R. and Williams, E., The digital economy: Where do we stand? *Technol. Forecast. Soc. Change*, 71, 4, 315–339, 2004.
3. Basu, K.K., The Leader's Role in Managing Change: Five Cases of Technology-Enabled Business Transformation. *Glob. Bus. Organ. Excell.*, 34, 3, 28–42, 2015.
4. Benes, R., *Are Marketers Leveraging Facebook?—eMarketer Trends, Forecasts & Statistics*, 2019, [online] eMarketer. Available at: https://www.emarketer.com/content/how-many-marketers-in-the-us-use facebook, [Accessed 2 Feb. 2020].
5. Business.twitter.com. (n.d.)., *Twitter for Business | Twitter tips, tools, and best practices*, [online] Available at: https://business.twitter.com/, [Accessed 4 Jan. 2020].
6. Chen, C. and Storey, Business Intelligence and Analytics: From Big Data to Big Impact. *MIS Q.*, 36, 4, 1165, 2012.
7. Costigan, S., Isaac Sacolick: Driving Digital: The Leader's Guide to Business Transformation Through Technology. *Publ. Res. Q.*, 34, 2, 310–311, 2018.
8. Davenport, T. and Dyché, J., *Big Data in Big Companies*, International Institute for Analytics [online] Sas.com. Available at: https://www.sas.com/content/dam/SAS/en_us/doc/whitepaper2/bigdata-bigcompanies-106461.pdf, [Accessed 1 Feb. 2020].
9. Fisher, D., DeLine, R., Czerwinski, M., Drucker, S., Interactions with big data analytics. *Interactions*, 19, 3, 50, 2012.
10. Forbes.com, *7 Examples Of How Digital Transformation Impacted Business Performance*, 2019, CMO Network [online] Available at: https://www.forbes.com/sites/blakemorgan/2019/07/21/7-examples-of-howdigital-transformation-impacted-business-performance/7bc0dbed51bb, [Accessed 18 Feb. 2020].

11. Fujitsu (n.d.), *Walking the digital tightrope—Fujitsu Global*, [online] Fujitsu. com. 2016. https://www.fujitsu.com/global/Images/br-fujitsu-digital-tightrope-report-em-en.pdf.

12. George, G., Haas, M.R., Pentland, A., Big data and management. *Acad. Manage. J.*, 57, 2, 321–326, 2014.

13. Grover, V., Chiang, R., Liang, T., Zhang, D., Creating Strategic Business Value from Big Data Analytics: A Research Framework. *J. Manage. Inf. Syst.*, 35, 2, 388–423, 2018.

14. Groves, P., Kayyali, B., Knott, D., Van Kuiken, S., *The "big data" revolution in healthcare: Accelerating value and innovation*, 2013, McKinsey & Company. https://www.ghdonline.org/uploads/Big_Data_Revolution_in_health_care_2013_McKinsey_Report.pdf, [Accessed on February 12, 2020].

15. Hare, J. and Heudecker, N., *Survey Analysis: Big Data Investments Begin Tapering in 2016*, 2016, [online] Gartner. Available at: https://www.gartner.com/en/documents/3446724, [Accessed 4 Feb. 2020].

16. Hewage, T., Halgamuge, M., Syed, A., Ekici, G., Review: Big Data Techniques of Google, Amazon, Facebook and Twitter. *J. Commun.*, 13, 2, 94–100, 2018.

17. IBM, *Big Data Analytics*, 2013, [online] Available at: https://www.ibm.com/analytics/hadoop/big-data-analytics, [Accessed 18 Dec. 2019].

18. InGRAM, *6 Big Data Use Cases in Retail*, 2017, [online] Imaginenext.ingram-micro.com. Available at: https://imaginenext.ingrammicro.com/data-center/6-big-data-use-cases-in-retail, [Accessed 7 Nov. 2019].

19. Kohli, R. and Grover, V., Business Value of IT: An Essay on Expanding Research Directions to Keep up with the Times. *J. Assoc. Inf. Syst.*, 9, 1, 23–39, 2008.

20. Kumar, R., A Framework for Assessing the Business Value of Information Technology Infrastructures. *J. Manage. Inf. Syst.*, 21, 2, 11–32, 2004.

21. Laney, D., *Application Delivery Strategies*. [online] Blogs.gartner.com, META Group Inc. 2001, Available at: https://blogs.gartner.com/doug-laney/files/2012/01/ad949-3D-Data-Management-Controlling-Data-Volume-Velocity-and-Variety.pdf, [Accessed 3 Jan. 2020].

22. Loebbecke, C. and Picot, A., Reflections on societal and business model transformation arising from digitization and big data analytics: A research agenda. *J. Strategic Inf. Syst.*, 24, 3, 149–157, 2015.

23. Manyika, J., Chui, M., Brown, B., Bughin, J., Dobbs, R., Roxburgh, C., Byers, A.H., *Big data: The next frontier for innovation, competition, and productivity*, McKinsey Global Institute, McKinsey & Company, 2011. Available at https://www.mck-insey.com/~/media/McKinsey/Business%20Functions/McKinsey%20Digital/Our%20Insights/Big%20data%20The%20next%20frontier%20for%20innova-tion/MGI_big_data_full_report.pdf, [Accessed 18 Dec. 2019]

24. Marr, B., *How Facebook Uses Data Analytics To Understand Your Posts And Recognize Your Face*, [online] Linkedin.com, 2019. Available at: https://www.linkedin.com/pulse/how-facebook-uses-data-analytics-understand-your-posts-bernard-marr/, [Accessed 18 Jan. 2020].

25. Marr, B., (n.d.), *How Much Data Do We Create Every Day? The Mind-Blowing Stats Everyone Should Read*, [online] Bernard Marr. & Company Available at: https://www.bernardmarr.com/default.asp?contentID=1438, [Accessed 25 Dec. 2019].

26. Mckinsey.com, *Creating Competitive advantage from big data in retail*, McKinsey & Company, 2017, [online] Available at: https://www.mckinsey.com/~/media/mckinsey/industries/retail/how%20we%20help%20clients/big%20data%20and%20advanced%20analytics/cmac%20creating%20competitive%20advantage%20from%20big%20data.ashx, [Accessed 1 Feb. 2020].

27. Mikalef, P., Pappas, I., Krogstie, J., Giannakos, M., Big data analytics capabilities: A systematic literature review and research agenda. *Inf. Syst. e-Bus. Manag.*, 16, 3, 547–578, 2017.

28. Mohsin, M., *TOP 10 Facebook Statistics You Need to Know in 2020 [Infographic]*, 2019, [online] Oberlo Inc. Available at: https://www.oberlo.com/blog/facebook-statistics, [Accessed 3 Feb. 2020].

29. Ng, A., *How artificial intelligence and data add value to businesses*, [online] McKinsey & Company, 2018. Available at: https://www.mckinsey.com/featured-insights/artificial-intelligence/how artificial-intelligence-and-data-add-value-to-businesses, [Accessed 13 Dec. 2019].

30. NOIE, *Productivity and organisational transformation: optimising investment in ICT. NOIE Canberra (Book, 2003).*

31. Park, E., Ramesh, B., Cao, L., Emotion in IT Investment Decision Making with A Real Options Perspective: The Intertwining of Cognition and Regret. *J. Manage. Inf. Syst.*, 33, 3, 652–683, 2016.

32. Qiao, Z., Zhang, X., Zhou, M., Wang, G.A., Fan, W., A domain oriented LDA model for mining product defects from online customer reviews, in: *50th Hawaii International Conference on Systems Sciences*, Waikoloa, Hawaii, pp. 1821–1830, 2017.

33. Rolls-royce.com. (n.d.), *Cutting edge medical technology and smart engine maintenance*, Rolls-Royce Heritage Trust [online] Available at: https://www.rolls-royce.com/media/our-stories/discover/2018/cutting-edge-medical-technology-and-smart-engine-maintenance.aspx, [Accessed 20 Jan. 2020].

34. Sharda, R., Delen, D., Turban, E., *Business intelligence and analytics*, Pearson Education Limited, New York, 2014.

35. Sheng, J., Amankwah-Amoah, J., Wang, X., Technology in the 21st century: New challenges and opportunities. *Technol. Forecast. Soc. Change*, 143, 321–335, 2019.

36. Soh, C. and Markus, M.L., How IT creates business value: A process theory synthesis, in: *International Conference on Information Systems*, ICIS 1995 Proceedings 4, Amsterdam, NL, pp. 29–41, 1995.

37. Statista, *Facebook audience worldwide 2020|Statista Inc. Germany*, 2019, [online] Available at: https://www.statista.com/statistics/490424/number-of-worldwide-facebook-users, [Accessed 10 Feb. 2020].

38. Verma, N. and Singh, J., An intelligent approach to Big Data analytics for sustainable retail environment using Apriori-MapReduce framework. *Ind. Manage. Data Syst.*, 117, 7, 1503–1520, 2017.

39. Vidgen, R., Shaw, S., Grant, D., Management challenges in creating value from business analytics. *Eur. J. Oper. Res.*, 261, 2, 626–639, 2017.

40. Wang, P., Chasing the Hottest IT: Effects of Information Technology Fashion on Organizations. *MIS Q.*, 34, 1, 63, 2010.

41. Wang, Y., Kung, L., Byrd, T.A., Big data analytics: understanding its capabilities and potential benefits for healthcare organizations. *Technol. Forecast. Soc. Change J.*, 126, 3–13, 2018.

14

Internet of Thing Trends

Sunny Preety* and Ibanga Kpereobong†

*Dept. of Computer Science Application, PDM University,
Bahadurgarh, Haryana, India*

Abstract

With the advent of the Internet of Things, things can be done quickly and it has made life more agreeable. In the Internet of Things, sensors and actuators are installed on physical objects which are combined by wired or remote innovation. Sensors get a contribution from clients and actuators covert the sensor's contribution to the machine frame and plan yield to include. The case of the Internet of things are wellness gadgets, keen vitality meters, lifx, and so forth. IoT patterns are exquisite and as a result, a major change will occur in the realm of innovation.

Keywords: IoTs trends, healthcare, environmental monitoring, pig, hive, H base, NoSql, self-ruling driving

14.1 Architecture of IoT

There are a couple of methodologies associated with the Internet of Things, even though it is considered a venture. It is important to note that the apparent intricacy of this concept cannot be compared to the potential outcome of problem-solving solutions it provides which are invaluable in our world today. A lot of IT solution providers make use of frameworks that incorporate this concept, for example, Vitality organizations now make use of arranged instruments to quantify sensations in turbines, provide information used for registering frameworks that dissect machines to help foresee how long they can function and when they will require maintenance. Fly motor manufacturers make use of sensors that take various readings such

---
**Corresponding author*: sunnypreety83@gmail.com
†*Corresponding author*: Kpereib01@gmail.com

Parul Gandhi, Surbhi Bhatia, Abhishek Kumar, Mohammad Alojail and Pramod Singh Rathore (eds.) *Internet of Things in Business Transformation: Developing an Engineering and Business Strategy for Industry 5.0*, (261–278) © 2021 Scrivener Publishing LLC

as compression, temperature, and different situations to improve efficiency. Bushel businesses use sensors to measure temperature such that if away or in travel temperature begins to rise, it will help speed up conveyances. This has a double-bit of leeway of expanding consumer loyalty while keeping away from item decay. Internet of Things has undeniably opened a great number of possibilities in many associations, some of which may not be recognized by IT pioneers.

The stages of IoT solution architecture are divided into four which have been described as follows:

- Stage 1—Sensor and Actuator layer: This is the first layer in the architecture and it is a physical layer. It involves an arranged networked instrument that includes remote sensors and actuators. Sensors are devices used to gather data from the environment while Actuators are devices that possess the ability to change the existing conditions of their environment.
- Stage 2—Internet Gateway Layers and Data Acquisition Systems: This involves the acquisition of information by sensors collection frameworks and its transformation of the data collected. The data collected is usually in analog form and it must be converted into its digital equivalent. The implementation of this stage is such that collection is done in real-time and the devices are designed with functionalities like data management, analysis, and security.
- Stage 3 involves the use of the Edge IT framework for analysis and pre-processing of information which is sent over to the cloud. It is directly linked to its previous stages as the data which is processed is gotten from above. The Edge framework is very vital because data collected may be so huge and could take up all network bandwidth so it helps to reduce the workload on central infrastructures.
- Stage 4 is the last which ensures the proper investigation of information and that is overseen and placed on the accustomed backend server framework. The state of the sensor/actuator reflects the area of activity innovation (OT) experts. Below is a well-illustrated diagram that describes the stages of IoT Architecture.

Rundown of Some Emerging IoT Trends

- Covering big information issue
- Data handling utilizing edge registering

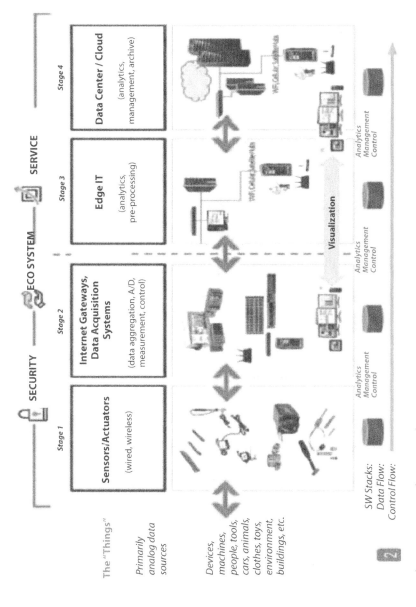

The 4 Stage IoT Solutions Architecture

SECURITY — ECO SYSTEM — SERVICE

Stage 1

The "Things"

Primarily analog data sources

Devices, machines, people, tools, cars, animals, clothes, toys, environment, buildings, etc.

Sensors/Actuators

(wired, wireless)

Stage 2

Internet Gateways, Data Acquisition Systems

(data aggregation, A/D, measurement, control)

Stage 3

Edge IT

(analytics, pre-processing)

Stage 4

Data Center / Cloud

(analytics, management, archive)

Analytics
Management
Control

Visualization

SW Stacks:
Data Flow:
Control Flow:

- High request for brilliant homes
- The dependency of human services on IoT
- Secure information by AI
- Secure IoT by Block chain
- IoT integration for brilliant urban areas
- Analytical maintenance lift-up by IoT
- Role of distributed computing in the eventual fate of IoT
- Awareness and training in IoT security

14.1.1 Covering Big Information Issue Using IoT

In any organization today, its take on data cannot be downplayed and it is very important to take properly examination on its processing and utilization. Big data as described by Gartner is defined "as high-volume, high-variety information assets that demand cost-effective, innovative forms of information processing that enable enhanced insight, decision making, and process automation". He also proposed that IoT is assessed to accelerate up to 26 billion associated gadgets by 2020 [1] when examining the associated gadgets world. Therefore, the four principles of big information to be watched are:

    i.   How to grow information volume?
    ii. How to grow the speed of information as information changes?
    iii. Increase the arrangement of information structures and types.
    iv. Information accuracy.

IoT is vital as it helps to manage the three V's of big data which are;

- Volume: This is the amount of data which is created in contrast to traditional data sources.
- Variety: This is the type of data created as they come from various sources and are created from different people and systems.
- Velocity: This is the speed at which data is generated.

14.1.2 Tools and Analytics of Big Data

There are a number of strategies and devices used in explaining numerous IoT information and challenges such as Big information, middleware, information combination methods, distributed computing, sensor web, and semantic. We also have systems and procedures that are understand IoT information handling and investigation issues in numerous ideas and the below figure demonstrates the Apache Hadoop Biological System.

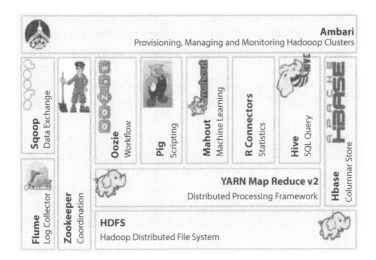

a) Apache Hadoop: It is a collection of open-source software framework which was developed by the Apache Software Foundation in 2006 which helps in storing data, provides processing power for handling huge jobs and handle virtual concurrent tasks or jobs. It is planned to complement information preparing through figuring hubs to hustle calculations and shroud inactivity. The two fundamental segments include the core which is known as Hadoop Distributed File System (HDFS) and the processor which is known as the Map Reduce motor.

b) Map Reduce Motor: It is a framework developed as a wide programming worldview that is used to process an enormous amount of data for distributed computers built on Java programming language. It incorporates two capacities, one is the Map which evaluates a set of data and converts them to another set of data and the Reduce which takes result from the Map and manipulates those data tuples into a smaller set of tuples. It is the latest advancement even though it is mainly used for calculation. To fully optimize the Map-Reduce, something must be implemented other than just calculation.

There must be an assortment of items or advances so it can deal with big information efficiently [2].

c) HBase: The structure of a Hadoop structure resembles the first arrangement of Big Table and the HBase is a framework in a distributed column-oriented database that is used to deliver random entrée when accessing a huge amount of structured data. The main function of the HBase is to provide exploit the fault tolerance observed in the Hadoop File System (HDFS). A segment of the HBase is vital to ensuring its main file is utilized and ensures it get back the lines. Users can store data either directly into HDFS or through HBase and they can read/write in HDFS randomly via HBase. The information gotten in HBase is also spared assets, key, esteem, where the subject in the non-key segments can be spoken to by qualities [3].

d) Hive: Hive is a framework that is considered to be a great data warehousing tool and it was developed on the Hadoop Distributed File System (HDFS). It is a great tool for analysis of big datasets and information, data encapsulation and ad-hoc queries. Users can interact with the platform via a web GUI and a Java Database Connectivity (JDBC) interface. The idea of the Map Reduce is such that it demands the capacity to compose work strategies. The framework was to be considered as an essential part of the Hadoop File System and perspectives located at the top that is the association for an information distribution center. The Hive platform doesn't treat applications and exchanges of the continuous that is accomplished on the web. The inspiration driving it is a confounded strategy [4].

e) Pig: It is another very important tool of the Hadoop ecosystem, which offers an extra database for greater productivity. The table in Pig is an assembly of tuples, where each field is worth several tuples. It has a procedural data flow language known as Pig Latin and it is mainly used for programming. The language offers all the fixed concepts of SQL, examples include joins, arrange, projection, and gathering. It also allows a higher extraction level when compared with the Map-Reduce system, as an inquiry in Pig Latin might be changed over into a succession of Map Reduce undertaking [5].

f) Mahout: It was developed as a sub-project of Apache's Lucene in 2008, and it is a framework that is open-source mostly used for developing accessible machine learning algorithms. The following machine language techniques are implemented such as:

    i.   Collaborative sifting

    ii. Clustering

    iii. Categorization/Classification [6].

g) NoSQL:

It is the abbreviation for Non SQL or Non-relational, it is a database that provides a mechanism for retrieval and storage of data usually used for non-social databases. Different sorts of NoSQL databases, which are key value pair report, section situated, and chart databases, that license software engineers to show the information reasonable to the structure of their pre-owned applications. Due to the development of the Internet ease of use and the openness of ease stockpiling, an enormous amount of organized, semi-organized and unstructured information are procured and put something aside for various sorts of uses. This information is normally meant to as Big information. Google, Facebook, Amazon, and a few different endeavors use NoSQLdatabases [7].

h) Big Table:

A Big Table advancement is started in 2004 and is presently utilized by a lot of Google applications, for example, Map Reduce. It is frequently utilized for delivering and changing information put away in Big Table, Google Reader, Google Maps, Google Book Search, Google Earth, Blogger.com, Google Code facilitating, Orkut, YouTube, and Gmail. Google's inspiration for developing its particular database contain versatility, and better control of execution highlights. Big Table is enlarged for information read forms by dispersed information stock piling the board model, which depends on section stockpiling to improve information recovering adequacy.

14.2   Dependency of Healthcare on IoT

IoT or the Internet of things has set another achievement in the computerized period through which, physical articles can speak with one another and work without human reliance. These articles are named as keen gadgets and can be constrained by an application introduced on your cell-phone or just by your voice order. IoT can be utilized in any cutting edge IoT supporting electronic gadgets. To make them IoT empowered, these items are inserted with a systems administration chip that will help in remote access and regulation [8]. The social insurance gadgets can be customized to react to pointers which can be outside elements like temperature, time, light and soon or inside markers that are sourced from other human services IoT gadgets. The extent of IoT in social insurance is very wide and is quickly turning into a piece of our regular life. The most significant use of IoT is its uses and advantages in human services. Constant observing of patients gets conceivable with the utilization of IoT human services gadgets in the emergency clinic or the utilization of shrewd clinical gadgets that will permit medicinal services people to screen patients remotely upgrading the degree of treatment that is given.

14.2.1   Improved Disease Management

IoT permits medicinal services gadgets for ongoing checking of patients which implies no information according to the state of the patient is missed. For instance, the pulse, circulatory strain, internal heat level and so forth. This encourages the best possible determination of the sickness. This will ensure that regardless of whether the specialist or the attendant isn't accessible with the patient, all that time his/her condition can be observed remotely through a clinical application. The IoT human services gadgets are likewise interconnected which implies that they can be modified to give prompt help at whatever point required [9].

The IoT human services gadgets can be set up with a higher and a lower esteem limit. In the event that any of the clinical gadgets enrolls a sequential worth cutoff, at that point it will naturally trigger another associated medicinal services gadget that will assist with balancing out the state of the patient. All the while it will likewise trigger a caution to the application in the cell phone of the specialist or nurture or the overseer. This will guarantee the consistent clinical help that is required in escalated units in medical clinics [10].

14.2.2   Remote Monitoring of Health

IoT empowered keen gadgets takes into consideration patients to be checked remotely too. Regardless of whether the patient isn't in the medical clinic the brilliant gadgets will gather consistent information. For instance, the pulse and temperature wearable is a little shrewd gadget that can be worn on the wrist that will assist with observing the heartbeat, circulatory strain and the internal heat level of the patient. The high and the low pointers can be set at specific levels which when arrived freely convey a caution to the application in the cell phone of the patient or parental figure and the patient can get the necessary clinical consideration immediately.

14.2.3   Connected Healthcare and Virtual Infrastructure

The information gathered by IoT empowered medicinal services gadgets are put away in the cloud, which makes its stockpiling and access simple for future reference or remote investigation. Additionally, in light of the fact that the information that is gathered by the keen gadgets continuously and can be gotten to from anyplace by the web it gets conceivable to give medicinal services remotely. This implies, regardless of whether an expert isn't situated close to the patient, he can in any case get the necessary help as his condition can be observed remotely and analyzed precisely. Right now, understanding need not be in the emergency clinic he can be at home and still get the human services that he needs because of the nearness of the virtual medical clinic by means of IoT medicinal services gadgets. IoT engaged gadgets can go far towards helping individuals in the territories where there are no appropriate emergency clinics and staff [11]. IoT gadgets help you enormously in medicinal services enterprises as well as improves different ventures also. For building IoT gadgets, you have to build up an IoT application for secure and reasonable utilization of the application by patients and specialists moreover. Remote access to medical clinic application can permit specialists and attendants to screen and analyze sicknesses to give essential and fundamental Social insurance that is required [12].

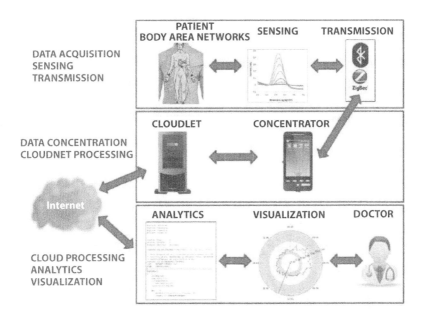

14.2.4   Accurate Data Collection and its Availability

The steady robotized observing of the patient takes into consideration precise information assortment without the chance of mistake. This upgrades the investigation of the patient's condition prompting appropriate finding and exact treatment. This information can be put away for future reference too. In the event that a specialist must allude to the case history of the patient he can get to it by means of the IoT cloud and have a superior comprehension of the patient's condition. It is appropriate in the event of crises too when prompt help is required, and there may not be sufficient opportunity to contact the family for past conditions and sensitivities. Access to the IoT information can give the information quickly improving the clinical consideration that the patient requires. IoT social insurance gadgets likewise help the specialists in tolerant diagramming which in any case would have taken hours to finish. Be that as it may, with new innovation, this should be possible inside hours with straightforward voice directions [13].

14.2.5   Drug Management

IoT has presented talking gadgets that will help patients to remember the drugs that they have to take. This upgrades the opportune conveyance of medications particularly to old individuals experiencing circulatory strain, diabetes, Alzheimer and so on [14].

14.2.6   Emergency

Remote checking of patients with the assistance of the IoT wearables has made it conceivable to keep an ongoing track of wellbeing conditions. Any sign that the patient will require prompt clinical consideration will caution the medical clinic or guardian, and the patient can be brought to the clinic so as to get crisis clinical consideration. This is certainly a lifeline as time is an enormous factor in giving the correct treatment to maintain a strategic distance from intricacies and lessen hazard [15].

14.3   High Demand of Smart Homes

These days, home computerization is assuming a critical job in our life. Home Automation let the client to control the home from their PC and dole out activities that ought to happen contingent upon time or other sensor readings, for example, light, temperature or sound from any gadget in the

Home Automation organize. It diminishes the human intercession in this manner utilizing the vitality productively and spares the time. The point of this innovation is to mechanize the machine around us which empowers us to control them and aides in notice us during basic circumstances. It encourages the correspondence between numerous true articles by working together with different advances. IoT includes improving system to capably gather and examine the information from different sensors and actuators at that point sends the information to the cell phone or a PC over a remote association. Building IoT has advanced basically over the most recent a long time since it has made another time in the realm of data and correspondence innovations. Security is a significant issue these days, as the conceivable outcomes of interruption are expanding step by step. Wellbeing from interruption, robbery, fire and spillage of combustible gas are the most significant necessities of home security framework for the individuals. Comprehensively, the expanding significance toward the need to counter security issues is foreseen to fuel up the interest development for brilliant and associated homes. The brilliant home framework requires a cell phone application or web-based interface as a UI, to cooperate with a computerized framework. The extent of this investigation incorporates an examination of the gadgets that can be constrained by switches, clocks, sensors, and remote controllers, aside from other control gadgets. Home computerization and brilliant homes are the two uncertain terms utilized in reference to a wide scope of answers for observing, controlling, and robotizing capacities in a home. The savvy home framework requires a cell phone application or online interface as a UI, to connect with a computerized framework. The extent of this investigation incorporates an examination of the gadgets that can be constrained by switches, clocks, sensors, and remote controllers, aside from other control gadgets [16].

Key Trends Include:

- The shrewd HVACR (warming, ventilation, cooling and refrigeration) frameworks are basic as for the ecological controls around the house. They involve savvy thermites, sensors, control valves, brilliant actuators, cooling frameworks, and keen room warmers, among different frameworks. Over the globe, attributable to the expanding government guidelines across created and creating nations, the majority of the new structures need more intelligent warming and cooling frameworks, in this manner enlarging the development of HVAC frameworks.

- However, current clients need items without impediment of HVAC frameworks, yet in addition request combination of different arrangements in a similar suite. This especially incorporates vitality the board. This pattern suggests that players in the market need to either actualize capacities that they recently viewed as out of their fragment or possibly give the likelihood to handily interface different items to the stage/biological system.
- The vitality investment funds thought process is for the most part tended to via robotized radiator controls. The interest for productive warming gear has prompted the expanding interest for robotized radiator controls, accordingly making it one of the most huge supporters of the worldwide HVAC hardware showcase. The warming gear gives the necessary warming condition in a financially savvy way [17].

14.3.1 Advantages of Home Automation System

Wi-Fi have become more and more used in typical in home systems organization. In home and constructing robotization frameworks, the utilization of remote inventions gives a few focal points that couldn't be expert utilizing a wired system in particular.

1. Reduced formation costs: First and outstanding, formation costs are altogether decreased since no cabling is major. Wired provisions require cabling, where material just as the expert laying of links is costly.
2. System adaptability and easy growth: Organizing a remote system is particularly positive when, because of new or changed fundamentals, development of the system is essential. As opposed to wired establishments, in which cabling augmentation is repetitive. This makes remote establishments an original speculation.
3. Esthetical advantages: Apart from covering a bigger territory, this ascribe assists with fulling esthetical prerequisites also. Models incorporate agent budings with all-glass engineering and chronicled budings where plan or studio reasons don't permit laying of links.
4. Integration of mobi gadgets: With remote systems, partner mobi gadgets, for example, PDAs and Smartphones with the

mechanization background becomes conceivable all over the place and whenever, as a gadget's precise physical area is never again essential for an connotation [18].

14.3.2   Smart City Implementation using IoT

The IoT idea use a few universal administrations to empower Smart City arrangements everywhere throughout the world. IoT presents new open doors, for example, the ability to screen and oversee gadgets remotely, examine and take activities dependent on the data got from different continuous traffic information streams. Therefore, IoT push acts are changing urban communities by upgrading frameworks, making progressively powerful and cost-proficient civil administrations, improving transportation benefits by diminishing street traffic clog, and improving residents' security. To accomplish the maximum capacity of IoT, brilliant city architects and suppliers perceive that urban areas must not offer a different keen city highlight, but instead convey versatile and make sure about IoT arrangements that incorporate effective IoT frameworks.

14.3.3   IoT Applications for Smart Cities

It is fascinating to consider the utilization of the IoT worldview to a urban setting. Surely, numerous national-level government broadly are presently considering and arranging how to embrace Information Communication Technology (ICT) arrangements in the administration of open administrations so as to acknowledge Smart City idea [19].

14.3.4   Fitness of Buildings

To appropriately keep up the verifiable structures of a city we have to: constantly screen the genuine states of each building and to distinguish the most influenced zones because of different outer specialists. The city contains numerous structures, which have various sizes and various ages. It is unique in relation to one city to another, at the same time, for the most part, a large portion of the structures are old, (for example, structures, dams, or extensions).

To evaluate the states of a configuration, uninvolved WSN can be inserted inside a solid structure, and intermittently impart a radio sign of reasonable plentifulness and stage trademark to educate about the configurations state.

14.4 Environmental Monitoring

WSN processes, investigate, and spread data gathered from various situations. The different parameter estimated by sensors is: level of water in lakes, streams, sewage. Gas fixation noticeable all around for urban communities, research facilities, and stores Soil mugginess and other characteristics. Inclination for static structures like spans, dams. Spot changes like for landslides. Lighting conditions either as a major aspect of consolidated detecting or standalone likes identify interruptions in dim places [20].

14.5 Waste Management

Squander the board turns into an expanding issue in urban living. It is identified with numerous viewpoints including financial and natural ones. One significant component in squander the executives is natural manageability. A significant advantage of worldwide IoT frameworks is that they furnish us with the capacity to gather information and, further assistance in improving viable administration for different issues. These days, the dump truck needs to get all trash jars in any event, when they are unfilled. By utilizing IoT gadgets inside the trash can, these gadgets will be associated with the figuring server utilizing one of LPWAN innovations. The registering server can gather the data and advance the best approach to trash assortment is performed by the waste vehicles.

14.6 Smart Parking

Right now, there is a remote sensor (or associated object) at each parking space. On the off chance that a vehicle leaves, or if a left vehicle leaves a parking space, the sensor at the leaving spot sends a warning to an administration server. By gathering information with respect to the leaving inlet inhabitance, the server can give leaving opening data to drivers through a perception plat-structures, for example, advanced mobile phones, vehicles' Human Machine Interfaces (HMIs) or ad loads up. These data will likewise empower the city board to apply fines if there should be an occurrence of stopping encouragements. Radio Frequency IDentification (RFID) innovation is robotized and can be exceptionally valuable to vehicle distinguishing proof frameworks. Vehicles are distinguished and parking garage expenses are gathered consequently through this framework. With respect to the equipment prerequisites, by using RFID per users, obstructions, parking area registration and registration controls can be accomplished. Right now, differentiation to work force controlled conventional parking area activities, an unmanned, robotized vehicle control and recognizable proof framework can be created as depicted in the improvement of Vehicle Ad Hoc Networks (VANETs) alongside the advances and wide arrangements of remote correspondence advances, many significant vehicle manufactories and media transmission businesses are progressively accommodating their autos with On Board Unit (OBU) specialized gadget. This permits various vehicles to speak with one another just as with the side of the road foundation. Along these lines, applications that give data on parking spot inhabitance or guide drivers to exhaust parking spots, are made conceivable through vehicular interchanges.

14.7   Routing System for Inner-City Bus Riders

UBN depends on an IoT engineering which utilizes a lot of conveyed delicate product and equipment parts that are firmly coordinated with the transport framework. The UBN framework sent in Madrid, Spain is com-presented of three key parts:

1. The system empowered inner-city transport framework with WiFi prepared transports.
2. The UBN route application for transport riders.
3. The transport swarm data server which gathers constant inhabitancies data from transports working on various courses in Madrid.

14.8   Self-Ruling Driving

In a keen city, independent driving innovations will be identical with sparing time for the client. The given innovation would assist speed with increasing the progression of traffic in an area and spare practically 60% of parking spot by leaving the vehicles closer to one another. As per Nissan-Renault, independent vehicles will liable to be promoted in 2020. These "programmed autos" will course self-governingly at around 30 to 50 km/h as the Renault Next Two-self-governing model of the French producer. In 2017, Volvo will explore different avenues regarding a hundred self-ruling vehicles driving in genuine rush hour gridlock situation on streets in London and a few Chinese urban communities. Through a blend of radar, cameras and ultra-sonic sensors situated around the vehicle, a self-governing vehicle can recognize abnormalities all around and trigger a ready that naturally enacts the crisis brakes to forestall mishaps or impacts. The Intelligence of Transport System could empower whole world to figure the best course continuously by associating diverse vehicle modes to spare time and lessen carbon outflows. Systems administration and transport issues for accomplishing brilliant urban areas. IoT will incorporate a colossal number of items that ought to be reach-capable. Moreover, each item will deliver content that can be recovered by any approved client paying little mind to his/her area. To accomplish this objective, compelling tending to approaches ought to be actualized. Presently, IPv4 is the most overwhelming convention. In any case, it is notable that the quantity of accessible IPv4 addresses is diminishing quickly and IPv4 will before long become deficient in giving new locations. In this manner, we have to utilize other tending to strategies.

IPv6 tending to speaks to the best option to IPV4. Numerous works that expect from incorporate IPV6 with 'IoT' have attempted as of late. For instance, 6LowPAN depicts how to actualize IPV6 convention in a WSN setting. Be that as it may, since RFID labels use identifiers instead of MAC addresses (as institutionalized by EPC worldwide it is important to display new arrangements so as to empower the tending to of RFID labels in IPV6 based systems.

References

1. Aggarwaal, C.C., Navin, Sheeth, A., The Internet Of Things: A Survey From The Data-Centric Perspective, in: *Managing And Mining Sensor Data*, pp. 384–428, 2013.
2. Blazhievsky, S., Introduction to Hadoop, MapReduce and HDFS for Big Data Applications. *SNIA Education,* 2013.
3. Silberstein, E., Residential Construction Academy HVAC, chapter 7, *Delmar Cengage Learning,* 2nd edition, pp. 158–184, 2011.
4. Handtte, S., Kortueem, G., Marón, P., *An Internet-of-Things Enabled Connected Navigation System for Urban Bus Riders,* 1–1, 2016.
5. Hossain, M., Shahjalal, Md, Nuri, N., Design of an IoT-Based autonomous vehicle with the aid of computer vision, 752–756, 2017.
6. Singh, K. and Kaur, R., Hadoop: Addressing Challenges Of Big Data, pp. 686–689, 2014.

7. Khana, A. and Anaand, R., IoT-Based Smart Parking System, *IJRTE* (IOT-Based Smart Parking Management System), 7, 374–378, 2016.

8. Obaidata, M.S., and Nicoplitidis, P., *Smart cities and homes: Key enabling technologies*, pp. 91–108, 2016.

9. Lamonaca, F., Carnì, D.L., Spagnuolo, V., Grimaldi, G., Bonavolontà, F., Liccardo, A., Moriello, R.S.L., and Colaprico, A., A New Measurement System to Boost the IoMT for the Blood Pressure Monitoring. In *2019 IEEE International Symposium on Measurements & Networking (M&N)*, pp. 1–6. IEEE, 2019.

10. Waste Management using Internet-of-Things (IoT). *IEEE*, 2518–2522, 2019.

11. Raju, L., Sobana, S. and Ram, G., A smart information system for public transportation using IoT. *IJRTER*, 3, 222–230, 2017.

12. Sastra, N.P. and Wiharta, D., Environmental monitoring as an IoT application in building smart campus of Universitas Udayana. *IoT-based smart security and home automation system*, 85–88, 2016.

13. Kodali, R.K., Jain, P., Bose, S., Boppana, L., IoT-based smart security and home automation system. *2016 International Conference on Computing, Communication and Automation (ICCCA)*, Noida, 2016, pp. 1286–1289, 2016.

14. Kodali, R., Swammy, G., Lakshmmi, B., An implementation of IoT for healthcare. *2015 IEEE Recent Advances in Intelligent Computational Systems (RAICS)*, Trivandrum, 2015, pp. 411–416, 2015.

15. Mishra, V. and Naaik, Mkp., Use of wireless devices and IoT in management of diabetes. Use of Wireless Devices And IOT in Management of Diabetes conference paper (*ETSTM-2017*) vol-3, 2017.

16. Park, K., Park, J., Lee, J., An IoT System for Remote Monitoring of Patients at Home. *Appl. Sci.*, 7, 260, 2017.

17. Nogueira, V. and Carnaz, G., An Overview of IoT and Healthcare, 2019, https://www.researchgate.net/publication/330933788_An_Overview_of_IoT_and_Healthcare

18. Di Mauroo, A., Di Narrdo, G., Venticiinque, S., An IoT System for Monitoring and Data Collection of Residential Water End-Use Consumption, IEEE, 2019, https://ieeexplore.ieee.org/document/8847120

19. Mamboou, E.N., Nlom, S. M., Swart, T. G., Ouahada, K., Ndjiongue, A. R., and Ferreira, H.C. Monitoring of the medication distribution and the refrigeration temperature in a pharmacy based on Internet of Things (IoT) technology, *2016 18th Mediterranean Electrotechnical Conference, IEEE (MELECON)*, Lemesos, 2016, pp. 1–5, 2016.

20. Rathore, M.M., Ahmmad, A., Paull, A., Wan, J., Zhang, D., Real-time Medical Emergency Response System: Exploiting IoT and Big Data for Public Health. *J. Med. Syst.*, 40, 10, 2016.

15

Internet of Things: Augmenting Business Growth

Trapty Agarwal*, Gurjot Singh, Shubham Pradhan and Vikash Verma

Maharishi University of Information Technology, School of Data Science, Noida, India

Abstract

IoT, Internet of Things, is a growing technology augmenting humans as well as today's business. Products are changing to smart products, which leads to the exponential growth in the business. IoT is a stepping-stone towards artificial intelligence, which further plays an important role in business growth. In this chapter, we will discuss the role of IoT in increasing business. We will also touch upon the IoT business architecture. The architecture is the base of any technology setup but it is also very important to know its workflow for a better understanding. This chapter will also throw some light on the IoT business workflow. Any concept is incomplete without the challenges it faces. It is essential to know about the short comes or the hurdles in pursuing IoT. A deep study on these challenges might lead to a new growth strategy and the future prospects of IoT in Business.

Keywords: IoT, digital business transformation, smart technology

15.1 Introduction

Internet of Things in simple terms is nothing but all the electronic devices connected through the Internet. IoT is a smart way to connect the people thereby connecting societies. IoT in turn connects consumers and thereby

---

**Corresponding author*: trapty@gmail.com

Parul Gandhi, Surbhi Bhatia, Abhishek Kumar, Mohammad Alojail and Pramod Singh Rathore (eds.) *Internet of Things in Business Transformation: Developing an Engineering and Business Strategy for Industry 5.0*, (279–292) © 2021 Scrivener Publishing LLC

connecting Business. IoT has become the most hyped and familiar word and technology that is augmenting the business growth [1].

There is a drastic change the catalyst in last four decades. The things were digitalized through this period.

Wristwatch in 80s

Wristwatch in 2020

Telephone in 80s

Mobile phone in 2020

The Wristwatch in the 80s was a simple mechanical watch. The trend has changed and simple mechanical watch has now converted to the IoT electronic watch. The watch gets you connected with all other electronic devices through internet. It is a smart watch, which also provides your health statistics. The mode of communication in the 80s was just used for telecommunication but the device has been updated to smart mobile phone. It is not only used for telecommunication but all sorts of communication purpose. It gets you connected with the society in all manners [2]. It connects you to the electronic devices at home. It connects with the health statistics of the whole family and many more features are there. In short, the world is in your hands. The data is being used through Internet.

The business is growing exponentially as everything in the world is connected and is in front of you at one click. The data is everywhere and is being collected, analyzed and used through internet.

15.2   Role of IoT in the Business Growth

Internet of Things (IoT) is the first step towards the Artificial Intelligence. It is the main ingredient of the business towards Artificial Intelligence [3].

| IoT | + | Data Science | = | Artificial Intelligence |

IoT when combined with the Data Analysis leads to the Artificial Intelligence. AI is the future.

15.2.1   Architecture of IoT

Much architecture is used in IoT worldwide. In this topic, we will be dealing with few basic architectures of IoT:

1. 3-layer architecture
2. 4-layer architecture
3. 5-layer architecture.

15.2.1.1   3-Layer Architecture

This architecture was introduced in the early stages of the research of IoT [4]. It consists of Application layer, Network layer and Perception layer.

Application layer: The delivery of services i.e. application specific services, is the main responsibility of the application layer. It takes care of all

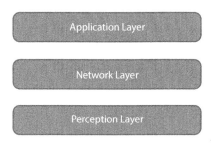

Figure 15.1 3-layer architecture of IoT [4].

the applications where Internet of Things can be deployed. For example: smart phones, smart televisions, smart health, etc.

Network layer: It consists of network devices, servers or other smart things. It is responsible for connecting these devices or objects. In other words, we can say that the network layer is used to transmit or process sensed data.

Perception layer: It is also called physical layer. Sensors are the main ingredient of this layer. These sensors are used for gathering data or information about the environment by sensing. It senses or identifies some physical objects in the environment.

15.2.1.2   4-Layer Architecture

3-Layer architecture is the basic architecture for IoT [4]. Researchers wanted more detail on the same. The research further gave rise to 4-layer architecture.

    i)   Sensors and actuators
    ii)   Internet gateways and Data Acquisition System
    iii)   Edge IT
    iv)   Data center and cloud

First Stage:
The first stage is similar to the Perception layer of the 3-layer architecture. The sensors sense the environmental data and then process it.

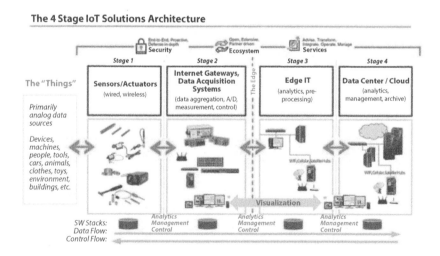

Figure 15.2 Layer IoT architecture [4].

Second Stage:
The second stage consists of Internet gateways, data acquisition systems, etc. This stage collects all data and optimizes the data for further transmission. This stage makes data digitalized and aggregated.

Third Stage:
The third stage is similar to the network layer of the 3-layer architecture. It connects all the IoT devices. The digitalized and aggregated data is distributed among IoT devices in this stage.

Fourth Stage:
The first stage deals with the Cloud computing and cloud storage of the data that will be further analyzed, processed and used.

15.2.1.3   5-Layer Architecture

The 5-layer architecture was the extension of 3-layer architecture. Two new layers are added: Business layer and Processing layer. The functions of application layer and perception layer remain the same as that of 3-layer architecture.

The transport layer is between perception layer and processing layer. Its role is to transfer data from perception layer to processing layer as well as from processing layer to perception layer. It is done through different networks like Bluetooth, 3G, 4G, wireless, etc. [5].

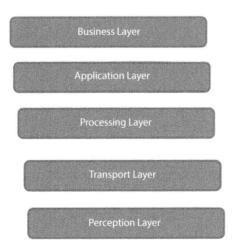

Figure 15.3 Layer architecture of IoT [5].

The processing layer lies in the middle of all the five layers of the architecture. It is used to store the data and analyze huge data for further processing. It is composed of cloud computing, different databases and big data processing models [6].

The business layer is the higher layer of the architecture. This layer deals with all the business processes required in IoT [6, 7]. It takes care of profit and business models.

15.2.2 Business Process

One of the important part of any business is its processes i.e. Business Processes. Service Level Agreements (SLAs), as per customer's requirement, need to be fulfilled. Key Performance Indicators (KPI) measures the efficiency and effectiveness of the business processes. The goal of any organization is meeting SLA and improving the KPI [8].

IoT is huge and enormous in terms of business opportunity and the volume of data created on daily basis. The data generated in a day is roughly 2.5 quintillion bytes. The data is so immense that this data deluge will continue to plague organizations during their transition from initial experimentation phase to full deployment of IoT applications [9]. The organizations try to capture the data, process the data and act on the immense volume of information generated continuously [10]. The rigid architectures and traditional data models are quickly becoming obsolete. These models are not able to handle the speed, agility and volume of this data along with new programming techniques like machine learning algorithms, which are very much required to drive IoT.

Workflow Management System (WMS) is a process that is used to manage data. WMS implements the business processes, which have human participation as well as automated tasks. The state of a business process is captured and the state transition is enabled when the trigger is received.

When a customer clicks the "Submit" button on a shopping cart to approve the items that are to be bought, the state of the shopping cart approval workflow will move from "Approve Cart" to the "Payment" window.

This is nothing but the IoT workflow where messages or triggers could be sent on IoT cloud infrastructure to change the state of workflow. The tracking of the states of various processes in any organization can easily managed by IoT workflows.

It is very important to keep the track of SLA and KPIs. KPIs represent the organizational goals whereas SLA is an agreement documented between the service provider and a customer. The KPI of a shopping mart could be the "average cost of a package delivery trip". The SLA of the same service provider could be "latest time of delivery of the package".

There are many advantages of IoT workflow. A few of them are listed below:

- It helps in business actions.
  IoT workflows provide a view of different states of the business process in real time and hence make it easier for the decision makers to take action or make any decision that is based on the available data.
- It provides a granular view.
  As compared to the traditional workflow, it gives a granular view as it is based on the low level IoT messages.
- It provides insight to make predictions.
  As data of different states of process are stored, it can be further mined and analyzed to make predictions. For example, all data of SLA violations can be analyzed and predictions can be made to avoid any further violations.
- It provides benefits in Business.
  The business will have all benefits as it leads to constant monitoring of SLAs and KPIs.

15.2.3   Business Models

There are different business models of IoT that can be used or are being used to increase the revenue, profit, market share and adaptability of the product [11].

Alexander Osterwalder is the author of the book "Business Model Generation: A handbook for Visionaries, Game Changers, and Challengers". According to him, a business model is defined as:

> "A business model describes the rationale of how an organization creates, delivers, and captures value."

This definition focuses on the role and responsibility of a manager who has to deliver products. The focus should be on the value of product. However, in today's IoT market, the product is associated with sensors and display of data on dashboard is known as "value". The business is not growing because value is not there in real sense.

The business model of IoT should focus on the capturing and delivering the value associated with the product. The business model should work on some unique characteristics that provide 24 * 7 service and connectivity with the customer thereby leading to differentiate and innovate value.

Model 1: Subscription Model
SaaS (Software as Service) is the model is used in subscription model. Instead of selling the product once, the customers are offered a

subscription model where they have to pay a fee to enjoy the continuous value of software.

Model 2: Asset-Sharing Model
All IoT products are different. To produce one product, expensive equipment is bought. However, the equipment is not utilized to its maximum capacity. Thus leading to less profit. Due to this concern, the model of asset-sharing was introduced. The common assets could be shared thus drastically reducing the manufacturing cost.

Model 3: Outcome-Based Model
Outcome-base model is a very innovative model. It gives an edge to innovation. According to this model, the customer needs to pay for the outcome of the product rather than the product. The payment needs to be done for the benefits of the product only. The company could be creative while working on this model.

Model 4: The Razor-Blade Model
In Razor-Blade model, the focus is on selling the product. Sometimes the product can be sold for less or may be free. This model is very lucrative for the products that require constant replacement or upgradation. It is very important that customers should never run out of consumables and they should be provided the products even if free. This model could be used to turn "normal" product to IoT product. The companies like HP connected printers and Brita's Infinity Water Pitcher are using this model. HP connect printers reorders the ink cartridge automatically.

15.3   Short Comes or Hurdles of IoT

IOT is growing rapidly and so are the problems related to it [12]. It is very important for us to understand them so that we can overcome them in the most efficient ways possible.

15.3.1   Security Issues

Over the years, IoT has grabbed a lot of attention due to its security issues. According to F-Secure, in 2019 Telnet alone attracted 760M attacks followed by UPnP with 611M attacks.

Growth of IoT will add a massive amount of new hubs to the systems and the web, which will only provide attackers with more systems to attack.

TOP TCP PORTS TARGETED

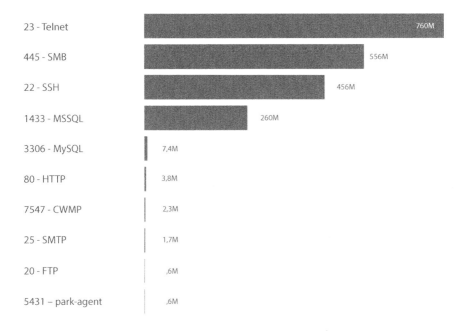

23 - Telnet	760M
445 - SMB	556M
22 - SSH	456M
1433 - MSSQL	260M
3306 - MySQL	7,4M
80 - HTTP	3,8M
7547 - CWMP	2,3M
25 - SMTP	1,7M
20 - FTP	,6M
5431 – park-agent	,6M

The malwares can affect infinite numbers of IoT devices like smart-home devices and closed-circuit cameras and deploy them against their own servers.

Studies show that the internet connected Cameras cause around 30% of the security concerns followed by 15% due to House Doors, 12% by cars, 10% by TVs, 6% by iron, 6% by heating systems, 6% by smoke systems, 5% by oven and 5% by lighting appliances.

Which object would you be most concerned about being connected to the Internet?
Besides cars all items mentioned below are home automation items

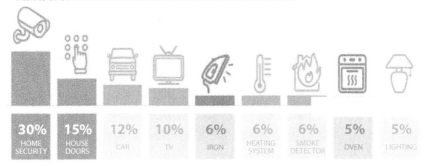

30%	15%	12%	10%	6%	6%	6%	5%	5%
HOME SECURITY	HOUSE DOORS	CAR	TV	IRON	HEATING SYSTEM	SMOKE DETECTOR	OVEN	LIGHTING

Source: MEF Global Consumer Trust Survey 2016

15.3.2   Size Miniaturization

As we are moving towards the wireless era; engineers are facing several challenges, like making smaller devices and package a radio transmitter into them. These devices also have to be user friendly, comfortable and efficient to use and these devices should also be unobtrusive to the environment so that they can serve the needs of the consumers [13].

Over the years, the industry has adopted many different approaches and helped in the advancement of silicon manufacturing processes. This has helped solve the space issue for IoT implementations. The Microprocessor (MCU) and Radio Frequency (RF) can be combined into system-on-chip (SoC) configurations, thereby making wireless microprocessors available. However, the trend towards SoCs still has the issues related to the functioning of the radio frequency transmitter—the antenna. The design of Antenna is generally left for a customer to work out. The customers may be guided or advised to choose ready-to-use wireless modules with an integrated antenna. The challenge is the space which is required for an antenna while designing small IoT equipment. The efficiency of the equipment also has to be kept intact while enabling reliable wireless connections.

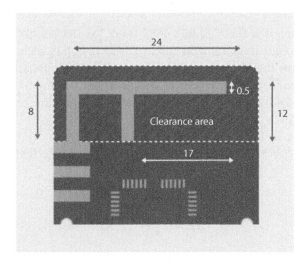

The printed PCB antennas are normally in the range of 25 mm × 15 mm, which is a significant size requirement, thereby making enormous IoT equipment.

15.3.3   Ethical Challenges

1. Author Identification: IoT devices collect large amounts of data. The traceability of the original author becomes very difficult. When the information about author is not known, it will become difficult to get his consent to use the collected data for further analyses or processing.
2. Private and Public Borderline: The IoT is so widely spread and constantly used that it has left no difference between private and public life. Private life will be virtually transparent.
3. Life Attacks: As IoT is increasing, the dependability (on the IoT network) of everyone in the world is also increasing. Any attack on IoT network or device will not stop only at data loss or any physical loss of the system. It will further continue to affect the life of people. This could be explained with an example of medical application. Any change in the patient's information, which is available on IoT medical application, may result in wrong medication, which can thereby affect the life of the patient.

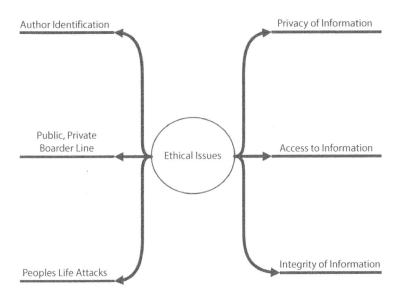

15.3.4   Legal Concerns

There will be a considerable amount of switches and routers that will be used to exchange data and information at a very fast rate but less expensive. It will be very challenging in near future to control, monitor and govern them. This arrangement will raise few legal questions that will need answers as soon as possible.

1. All IoT network and devices will be working on internet. What will happen when there will be issues (technical or legal) with the internet service? Who will be held responsible for the loss due to lack of internet service: application service provide, local or global internet service provider?
2. New IoT devices will be required to install in future and those devices shall be patched properly with the existing scenarios? Who will be assigned the responsibility to ensure complete security of the device and data transactions?
3. These situations will require set standards and laws. Are we prepared?
4. If an application service provider is bankrupt or loses his business, how will the users overcome this situation? How will the data be handled and administrated?
5. Will the data collection be a continuous process or will there be rest time for devices?

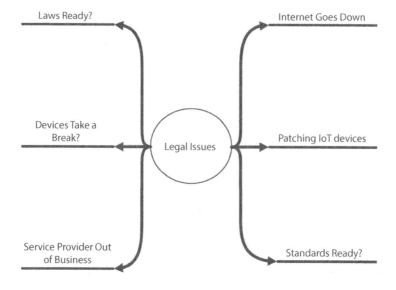

15.3.5   Interoperability Issues

When the computer systems or software can exchange the information and can process the exchanged information, this ability of computer systems is known as interoperability. The proprietary software giants do not want the interoperability ability of their devices just because of a simple reason to get the market edge over the consumers. Therefore, they do not support open APIs of their products [14].

APIs of different IoT devices are very incompatible with each other. To abstract the complexities of IoT devices, a common API management system layer is required. The challenging task to accomplish a common API management system layer will be to simply the common pattern among all IoT devices. Different IoT devices process or sense different types of data. There are varying data representations and to sense heterogeneous data, different APIs will be used in different devices, which further leads to lack of common standards and lack of data semantics to process and analyze data differently. This will be a major obstacle between different IoT devices to communicate i.e. to exchange data [15].

References

1. Bakr, A.A. and Azer, M., IoT ethics challenges and legal issues. In 12th International Conference on Computer Engineering and Systems (ICCES) 233–237, 2017. 10.1109/ICCES.2017.8275309.

2. Osterwalder, A., *Business Model Generation: A handbook for Visionaries, Game Changers, and Challengers.* Wiley, Hoboken, New Jersey, United States.

3. Mukherjee, D., Pal, D., Misra, P., Workflow for the Internet of Things. TCS Innovation Labs, Tata Consultancy Services Limited, New Town, Kolkata, India, 2017.

4. Fleisch, E., Weinberger, M., Wortmann, F., Business Models and the Internet of Things, 9001, pp. 6–10, 2015. Interoperability and Open-Source Solutions for the Internet of Things, Conference paper. https://link.springer.com/chapter/10.1007/978-3-319-16546-2_2.

5. P.V. Dudhe, N.V. Kadam, R. M. Hushangabade, M. S. Deshmukh, Internet of Things (IOT): An overview and its applications, Published in: 2017 International Conference on Energy, Communication, Data Analytics and Soft Computing (ICECDS), Date Added to IEEE Xplore: 21 June 2018.

6. Mark Hung, Gartner Research Vice President, Leading the IoT Gartner Insights on How to Lead in a connected World, Published in 2017 Gartner Inc.

7. https://blog.f-secure.com/attack-landscape-h1-2019-iot-smb-traffic-abound/

8. https://danielelizalde.com/monetize-your-iot-product/
9. https://medium.com/datadriveninvestor/4-stages-of-iot-architecture-explained-in-simple-words-b2ea8b4f777f
10. https://www.industr.com/en/miniaturising-iot-designs-2251501
11. Jindal, F., Jamar, R., Churi, P., Future and Challenges of Internet of Things. *Int. J. Comput. Sci. Inf. Technol.*, 10, 13–25, 2018. 10.5121/ijcsit.2018.10202.
12. Konduru, V. and Bharamagoudra, M., Challenges and solutions of interoperability on IoT: How far have we come in resolving the IoT interoperability issues. 2017 International Conference On Smart Technologies For Smart Nation (SmartTechCon), 572–576, 2017. 10.1109/SmartTechCon.2017.8358436.
13. Sethi, P. and Sarangi, S.R., Internet of Things: Architecture, Protocols & Applications. Hindawi. *J. Electr. Comput. Eng.*, 2017, 2017. Article ID 9324035.
14. Ray, P.P., Internet of Robotic Things: Concept, Technologies, and Challenges. *IEEE Access*, 4, 9489–9500, 2017.
15. Dijkman, R.M., Sprenkels, B., Peeters, T., Janssen, A., Business models for Internet of Things. *Int. J. Inf. Manage.*, 35 (6), 672–678, 2015.

Index

Printed and bound by CPI Group (UK) Ltd, Croydon, CR0 4YY